Aspects of
Central African History

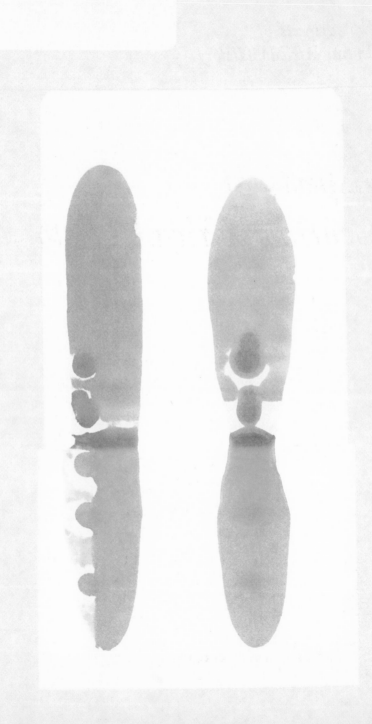

Edited by
T. O. RANGER

Aspects of
Central African History

HEINEMANN
LONDON   IBADAN   NAIROBI

Heinemann Educational Books Ltd
22 Bedford Square, London WC1B 3HH
PMB 5205 Ibadan · P.O. Box 45314 Nairobi

EDINBURGH MELBOURNE AUCKLAND
HONG KONG SINGAPORE KUALA LUMPUR
NEW DELHI KINGSTON PORT OF SPAIN

Heinemann Educational Books Inc.
4 Front Street, Exeter, New Hampshire 03833, USA

ISBN 0 435 94800 8

© Heinemann Educational Books Ltd 1968
First published 1968
Reprinted 1969, 1971, 1973 (twice), 1977, 1980, 1981, 1982

Printed in Great Britain by
Biddles Ltd, Guildford, Surrey

Preface

In 1966 the Ministry of Education in Dar es Salaam asked the History Department of the University College, Dar es Salaam, if they could do anything to help teachers prepare for the central African section of the second paper of the new School Certificate Syllabus in history. The challenge was accepted and in January 1967 a Conference on aspects of the history of central Africa was held at the College under the auspices of the Institute of Education, the Ministry and the Historical Association of Tanzania. This book consists of the papers prepared for the Conference with some revision and addition.

The History Department of U.C.D. found this an interesting and challenging book to write. We hope that others besides teachers may find it interesting to read. We are grateful to Mr Peter Hall, Inspector of History in the Ministry of Education, Dar es Salaam, for suggesting the idea to us. We are grateful also to our students at Dar es Salaam, especially to those who have taken the course on central Africa and who have subjected some of the ideas in this book to searching scrutiny. Without them this book would be much less lucid, even, than it is. Finally we are grateful to the University of Wisconsin Press for permission to summarize and quote from one of the classics of central African historiography, Professor Jan Vansina's *Kingdoms of the Savanna*.

Contents

List of Maps

Pages 273–80

Introduction

Ideally what is needed for the central African region is a comprehensive survey of the whole vast area written by one acute and lucid mind. This book falls short of that ideal. The contributions vary in length and approach. Some of them are summaries of work produced by other scholars; others are summaries of work produced by the authors themselves; others are the first publication of the results of original research. Nevertheless it is hoped that the book may be useful to a wider audience at any rate until the ideal synthesis comes along.

Different though they are, these chapters are animated by a common set of assumptions. It is the assumption of this book that what is most urgently needed is not so much an account of colonial history as conventionally defined but an account of the specifically African side of central African history. It is also the assumption of this book that in dealing with the African history of central Africa it is important to get behind the picture created by the accidents of European exploration and penetration, a picture which emphasizes the importance of African groups which the whites knew well and leaves others out altogether. Because of these assumptions this book concentrates in the nineteenth century on the dilemmas and responses of African societies rather than on the initiatives of white explorers, missionaries, soldiers. It concentrates on the history of indigenous cultivating peoples like the Shona as well as on the history of military intruders like the Ndebele. For the earlier period it reminds us that the fact that the Portuguese were familiar with the Mutapa confederacy does not mean that this was the first or most important of the Shona state systems. In the twentieth century this book deliberately concentrates on the development of African politics, sketching in white policies, actions and ambitions as a necessary setting rather than placing them in the centre of the stage. It is not our intention to claim that this is the only proper and meaningful way to approach central African history. It is rather that there is an existing imbalance which needs to be corrected before central African history can be well taught. This book is not intended to

serve as a self-sufficient account of central Africa; it is a corrective
and supplement to more conventionally planned texts such as
A. J. Wills' and A. J. Hanna's general histories.[1]

Other assumptions are also implied in this book. One is that
it is important in the study of central African history—or of
African history generally—to come as close as possible to the
present day. Thus the chapters of this book attempt to carry the
story, in however sketchy a way, up to and beyond independence
in the Congo, Malawi and Zambia and up to the present violent
situation in Rhodesia. It seems to us essential to do this for a
variety of reasons. One is that only by so doing can the teacher
of history win for his subject its due recognition as a vital and
dynamic study essential to the understanding of contemporary
problems. Another is that one can begin to see flowing in the post-
independence period currents which clearly derive from the pre-
colonial history of the area. The colonial period is of course more
than just an interruption in the flow of specifically African history;
it changes a very great deal. But it does not change everything
and the teacher of history who does not approach the present day
is throwing away the chance of establishing patterns of great
interest. Readers should be alert all the time to establish connections between the earliest and the latest periods. Dr Rodney's
chapter in this book shows one way of doing so. And the alert reader
will be able to establish other connections. The Kongo kingdom
described by Dr Kimambo is the ideal past which animates the
ABAKO movement and the independent churches described by
Mr Masare; and Holden Roberto, leader of one of the Angolan
resistance movements, first emerged into political significance as
the choice of the elders for the revived Kongo paramountcy.

Another assumption of this book is that the specifically African
history of central Africa provides a number of 'unifying themes'
through which it is possible to approach the complex history of this
very large area. In Professor Rotberg's recent general political
history of tropical Africa a note of caution is sounded about the
possibility at present of establishing unifying themes and the lack
of supporting evidence for some of the generalizations hitherto put
forward.[2] It is our assumption that unity of approach can be

[1] A. J. Wills *An Introduction to the History of Central Africa* Oxford University
Press 2nd edition 1967; A. J. Hanna *The Story of the Rhodesias and Nyasaland*
Faber 1960
[2] R. I. Rotberg *A Political History of Tropical Africa* p. viii Harcourt Brace 1965

achieved by asking the same questions rather than by obtaining the same answers. Thus it is clear from this book that its contributors reject the idea that there was an essentially similar type of African kingship operative across the whole central African region from the Kongo to the Mutapa kingdom. The differences between the various state systems described in this book emerge clearly enough even from its brief descriptions. But the theme of state-building is in itself a unifying one. The contributors to this book have asked much the same questions about the origin and organization of states in the areas with which they are concerned; in the variety of the answers lies the richness of central African history. In the same way a whole series of questions are asked again and again in this book: how did various African societies react to missionaries? Why did resistant societies resist and why did co-operating societies co-operate? What is the relationship of nineteenth-century experiences to the rise of twentieth-century nationalism? What is the political significance of the independent church movement? What is the essential character of modern mass nationalism?

The answers to these questions are as richly various as the answers to the questions about African state systems. But in this variety lies not only the richness but also the teachability and value of central African history as an intellectual discipline. Providing the number of examples is limited it can be a fascinating exercise to compare how and why different societies react differently to the same broad set of challenges and stimuli. For this reason the history of one central African people or territory should never be viewed in isolation but always compared and contrasted. We hope that there are such comparisons and contrasts brought out or implied in this book—for instance in its treatment of the African political history of Malawi, Zambia and Rhodesia. All produced recognizably similar mass nationalist movements but we hope this book helps to show how the differences in their preparation and composition partly explain their different developments.

A number of other points may be made about the approach of this book. One concerns the theme of African resistance and response. It may be suggested that this is a fruitful way of pulling this very large area together. Thus it was only in this area that Europeans attempted to establish themselves as political and military masters of extensive territories in the sixteenth and seventeenth centuries. The Portuguese in the Congo and Angola and the Portuguese in the Zambezi valley were attempting what no other Europeans anywhere in Africa were attempting. Obviously, then, one particularly useful comparison to make in teaching the central African region is to compare and contrast the reaction of African societies in the two areas. This is a theme which is stated in the chapters by Dr Alpers, Dr Rodney and Dr Kimambo. And if in this way the theme of African response and resistance can help tie up a large area so in other ways it can help tie together long periods of time. Thus my own two chapters suggest ways in which Shona responses in the nineteenth and twentieth centuries can be seen as following on from their earlier reactions to the Portuguese. Of course it needs to be pointed out that this theme is not restricted to African response to European pressure. This book suggests also the possibility of taking as a valuable theme the topic of the response of settled agricultural political systems to closely knit African military intruders—there are some provocative parallels to be drawn, for instance, between the predicament of the Kongo state when faced by the Jaga and the predicament of the Rozwi state when faced by the Ngoni and the Matabele.

A point which we wish especially to make as historians working in Tanzania is the importance of relating central African history to that of neighbouring areas. There are many senses in which Tanzania belongs logically in the central African region as here defined; its history can hardly be separated from that of the Congo or that of Malawi. It should be very easily possible to make the one flow into the other; to ask of East African history the questions we ask here of central African history and to carry over from East African history all sorts of other questions.

Finally we must return to apology. This book, we are well aware, is nothing more than the rawest of raw material. In particular we have not been able to give due weight to the clement of personality. Yet the African history of central Africa is rich with outsize personalities. Another whole book might have been written around people rather than territories—around Affonso I of the Kongo, Lewanika of the Lozi, Lobengula, John Chilembwe, and so on. Perhaps we may hope that another Conference, perhaps at one of the central African universities, will fill this gap.

Terence Ranger Dar es Salaam March 1967

1. The Mutapa and Malawi political systems to the time of the Ngoni invasions

EDWARD ALPERS

Two extended systems dominated a vast expanse of east and south central Africa for many centuries before the coming of the Ngoni from South Africa in the 1830's marked the beginning of a new historical era. To the north of the Zambezi River there was the little-known Malawi empire, while to the south there was the much more famous empire of Mutapa with its many related kingdoms and principalities. In my discussion of these two political systems I shall point out a number of comparative themes and possible links between them. I shall also raise several questions which arise from this sort of exercise. By so doing, I hope that our more detailed knowledge of the empire of Mutapa may be able to shed some valuable light on that of the Malawi.

MUTAPA

The empire of Mutapa is centred on the magnificent stone buildings of Great Zimbabwe, which lie less than twenty miles southeast of modern Fort Victoria in Rhodesia. At its height, the influence of the empire was bounded on the north by the Zambezi River, on the west by the Kalahari Desert, and on the east by the Mozambique Channel down to the mouth of the Sabi River. To the south it extended across the Limpopo River into the northern Transvaal. That part of Mozambique which lies south of the Sabi and east of the Limpopo seems to have stood outside this area of direct Mutapa influence, although there was naturally a certain amount of spillover. The core of the region is a plateau of rolling plains, ranging between 1,000 and 5,000 feet above sea level and gradually rising from west to east. This area corresponds roughly with modern Rhodesia. Except for the upper reaches of the Zambezi beyond the confluence of the Luangwa River in Zambia, and including Lake Kariba, this plateau is free of tsetse fly and cattle flourish in the predominantly tropical bushland. The eastern half, which corresponds with southern Mozambique, is the most extensive intrusion of the coastal lowlands into the great African plateau, all of it being less than 1,000 feet above sea level. An extensive tsetse belt blankets the northern two-thirds of this eastern region, while the vegetation is mostly of the savannah grasslands type. There are clearly marked seasons, with summer rains from November to March, throughout the entire territory.

Compared to the rest of sub-Saharan Africa, there is an unusual body of archaeological evidence for this region, although much works remains to be done. This provides the foundation of our knowledge for the history of the pre-Mutapa period. There are scattered Arabic records relating to this area from the early tenth to the beginning of the sixteenth century. With the establishment in 1505 of the Portuguese at Sofala, in the same bay as the modern town of Beira, and later at Sena and Tete, a considerable body of documentary evidence becomes available. Finally, we are fortunate in possessing a mass of traditional material which has been collected amongst the peoples living within the former dominion of the empire of Mutapa. Most of this evidence relates to the core of this complex. In particular, virtually no Iron Age archaeological and very little oral historical research has been attempted in the Portuguese dominated sector. But we are still able to construct a remarkably detailed political history for much of this important territorial unit of the African continent.

The Iron Age was introduced into the Rhodesian plateau during the first millennium A.D., by people coming from north of the Zambezi. We do not know exactly who these people were, or what sorts of languages they spoke. They are only known to us through the pottery, iron tools and rubble which archaeologists have discovered in the places which were occupied by these people. Most of these sites have been found in the north-eastern half of Rhodesia, called Mashonaland. There are two very similar early Iron Age cultures in Mashonaland, which take their names, Gokomere and Ziwa, from the places where the most thorough excavations were made. Consequently, we know the carriers of these cultures as the Gokomere and Ziwa peoples. The region inhabited by the Ziwa people stretched from the Inyanga Mountains, on the eastern frontier of Rhodesia, across Mashonaland to well beyond Salisbury. One of the earliest known Iron Age dates in Rhodesia comes from the Ziwa site, where a grave has been radiocarbon dated to about A.D. 300. (For a brief explanation of how this method works, see Appendix A of Roger Summers

Zimbabwe—A Rhodesian Mystery.) The same process of dating has shown that Ziwa pottery was still being made in the eleventh century, so that we know that the Ziwa people were still living there at that time. The Gokomere people were the first Iron Age people to live at Zimbabwe. The era of their occupation of Zimbabwe is known as Period I. We do not know when the Gokomere folk began to inhabit Zimbabwe, but a radiocarbon date of about A.D. 320 has come from the end of Period I. Recently, however, a Gokomere site at Mabveni, near Zimbabwe, has yielded a radiocarbon date of about A.D. 180. Traces of the Gokomere culture have also been found in Matabeleland, in the south-west of Rhodesia, as well as in north-eastern Botswana and the northern Transvaal. So we can see that these Gokomere people, together with the Ziwa people to whom they were apparently closely related, had spread themselves over most of the heart of the future empire of Mutapa.

There were two important successors to the Gokomere people before the arrival of the ancestors of the Mutapa dynasty. One group was the Leopard's Kopje culture people. Like their Gokomere forerunners, these were an Iron Age population who brought new economic and social skills with them into Rhodesia. In fact, it may be more correct to suggest that this new culture resulted from a blending of the earlier Gokomere culture with that which an unknown group of immigrants (who may have had Zambian connections) introduced into Matabeleland, rather than to presume that this was an entirely foreign culture, which owed nothing of its vitality to its predecessor. During the second millennium A.D. this Leopard's Kopje culture spread from Matabeleland into parts of Botswana and the northern Transvaal, although it did not penetrate into Mashonaland. A second culture which entered Rhodesia after the Gokomere people had introduced the knowledge of iron-working is known as Period II at Zimbabwe. As we have seen, the Gokomere people, for reasons unknown to us, stopped living at Zimbabwe during the fourth century. Zimbabwe was uninhabited for an unknown number of years until the arrival of the Period II people. We cannot say where this group came from, but their pottery is quite different from that made by the Gokomere artisans. It also bears only a slight resemblance to that which the Leopard's Kopje potters manufactured, and may well have been the work of immigrants. This earthenware and several other related types of pottery had a wide distribution over central and eastern Rhodesia. While this potting tradition may have continued later in other places, at Zimbabwe itself the end of Period II is dated to about A.D. 1075.

During the first century of the second millennium A.D., then, there were three different groups of people living within the central Rhodesian core area of the later empire of Mutapa. In the north and north-east there were the Ziwa people, who had put down roots and held their own for some eight hundred years. In the south-central area there were the more recently arrived Period II and related peoples, who replaced the earlier Gokomere population, who were related to the Ziwa folk. Finally there were the Leopard's Kopje people, living in the far south and south-west, whose culture seems to have resulted from the integration of the earlier Gokomere inhabitants with another immigrant group. This is the situation as it was found by the next group of immigrants, who were probably the ancestors of the modern Shona-speakers, after whom Mashonaland is named. It appears that the Shona or Karanga, as they are also known, introduced the culture of Period III at Zimbabwe, although this premise is not demonstrable, as we do not know what language was spoken by the carriers of the Period III culture, and Shona is a linguistic term only. Period III has yielded radiocarbon dates which show that it lasted from about A.D. 1075 to 1440. While there is no evidence from which we can determine the origins of the Shona, some scholars think that they may have come from the Congo Basin area and migrated southwards into Rhodesia at the end of the first millennium. Although the culture of Period III shows that great changes had taken place at Zimbabwe, there is still a definite continuity with the culture of the Period II people, who continued to live at Zimbabwe under their new Shona rulers. The Period III culture of the Shona is a more substantial one than that of its predecessors. Huts were larger and better built. But of greater importance is the fact that it is during Period III that we have the beginning of building in stone at Zimbabwe.

The place which we know as Zimbabwe is a large expanse of ground which is dominated by a rocky hill. The stone works, which now lie in ruins, stand on this impressive hill and in the valley below it, to the south. Those on the hill are known, quite inappropriately, as the Acropolis; the main ruin in the valley is called the Temple or, more accurately, the Great Enclosure.

There are other, smaller ruins in the valley. The names Acropolis and Temple, recalling the ancient Greek ruins, were given to the buildings at Zimbabwe by the first Europeans who saw them in the late nineteenth century, but who could not believe that they had been constructed by Africans. Indeed, the myth that the buildings at Zimbabwe were built by non-Africans is still officially propagated by the illegal regime which rules Rhodesia, while a South African has recently gone to great lengths to prove the same point. This prejudiced view is completely inaccurate. The first stone buildings at Zimbabwe were the work of the Shona people themselves. Most of the stone work on the Acropolis was constructed by them in Period III. The Shona also began to build in the valley during the thirteenth or fourteenth century, and the first stones of the Great Enclosure were laid at the very end of Period III.

Although the Shona seem not to have been especially numerous, it is likely that they spread themselves out over a large part of Rhodesia. Traditions indicate that there was much movement of the Shona chiefly families throughout this epoch. Their efforts were apparently centred in the south, for it is there that they established what we may call a provincial capital site. At Mapungubwe, just south of the confluence of the Limpopo and Shashi Rivers, in the Transvaal, the Shona found a place which was extraordinarily like Zimbabwe. On the prominent, steep hill overlooking the valley of the Limpopo they gradually re-created, although on a less grand scale, the pattern of Zimbabwe. By the turn of the fifteenth century the Shona dominated the previous inhabitants of Mapungubwe whose culture was closely related to that of the Leopard's Kopje people. The two populations continued to live side by side, and their cultures naturally became intertwined, but the Shona were the rulers and their way of life inevitably became more prominent as time passed.

What were the Shona doing at Zimbabwe and Mapungubwe? It is quite clear that here we have some sort of state system, in which a small group of chiefly immigrants successfully established their rule over the more numerous Iron Age people who had preceded them into the country. There is no indication that they achieved this dominance by violent means. In fact the archaeological record suggests exactly the opposite, for we have seen that at both places Shona culture coexisted with the earlier cultures and never completely replaced them. Similarly, the key to Shona dominance would seem not to have been superior military power, although this may have been a contributory factor, but rather the possession of superior organizational skills. It is likely also that the Shona commanded new, powerful religious concepts and mystic abilities, for both Zimbabwe and Mapungubwe were ritual centres of outstanding importance. They were especially connected with rain-making and, above all, with *Mwari*, the supreme divine being of the Shona who is worshipped on a tribal level. He can only be approached through tribal spirits called *mhondoro*, who express themselves through mediums called *svikiro*. All evidence at our disposal indicates that the power of the Shona chiefs was based on their control of this religious apparatus, which was the unique way in which the people and the community could communicate with *Mwari*. The Shona chiefs' possession of these intermediary powers was the key to the political and social integration of their state.

There was also a firm economic basis to the Shona states. Arabs coming from the Somali, Kenyan and Tanzanian coasts had been trading to the Sofala coast since late in the first millennium A.D. The staple item of trade was ivory, for which there was and still is a constant and considerable demand in India, as the ivory of the Indian elephant is too brittle to be fashioned into bracelets and trinkets. But the Rhodesian and northern Transvaal area is rich in valuable minerals, especially copper and gold. Armed with their vital metallurgical knowledge, the Iron Age people of this region gradually began to exploit these resources, although on a small scale, well before the arrival of the Shona. Gold and copper artifacts appear during Period II at Zimbabwe, as do occasional imported glass beads from the coast. But it was under the Shona, with their wider hegemony and centralized state systems that trade with the coast became organized on a large scale. Although they did not do the actual mining themselves, the Shona rulers directed the whole economic process of trade. Their rule assured the security of movement which is so necessary to long-distance trading. As contacts with the coast were expanded more attention was undoubtedly paid to elephant hunting and to the production of copper and gold. So it was that the Shona rulers grew more powerful through their control of both the sources of wealth and coastal trade in their kingdom. It must be emphasized, however, that this was not itself the fabled empire of Mutapa. Rather, it was the direct ancestor of that state and the foundation on which it was built. More comprehensively, it is worthwhile here to join with Brian Fagan in stating:

> We cannot emphasize too strongly the profound influence of the earliest Rhodesian Iron Age. people on their descendants. The decorative motifs on their pots, their mining techniques, as well as ritual and economic practices, were inherited, and modified, by their successors. In later centuries, the descendants of the original tribes were dominated by a series of powerful chieftainly families, whose power was based on the mining ability and economic skill of the indigenous pastoral and agricultural peoples of Rhodesia who had arrived from the north many centuries before them.[1]

Up to now, we have been almost exclusively reliant upon archaeology for our knowledge about this area. Indeed, the empire of Mutapa itself is manifested in the archaeological record in Period IV (beginning about 1450) at Zimbabwe, and we have learned much about its material culture through this discipline. But with the coming of the Mutapa dynasty we enter a new phase, in which oral traditions and then written documents give us a much more detailed and personal historical view. According to traditions collected by D. P. Abraham, during the fourteenth century a new group of Bantu-speakers, led by a mythical personality called NeMbire, moved into Rhodesia from the north. Abraham suggests that these people may have crossed the Zambezi in about 1325. Their origins are not known, but they probably came from the Katanga region, for copper artifacts reminiscent of the Congo are found in Period IV levels of occupation. For almost a century the characters who figure in the traditions of the Mbire people, as they are known, are impossible to identify as being real historical personalities. But at the end of the fourteenth century we are suddenly confronted by an individual who, though still in the realm of mythical founders, is on the threshold of historicity. This is Chikura Wadyambeu, genealogically said to be NeMbire's great grandson, whom the traditions identify as the first *mambo* (great chief) of the Rozwi. A generation later he is replaced as *mambo* by a man who may or may not have been his son, but who was the very first individual to bear the praise name of Mwene Mutapa.

What are we to make of this dramatic and rather perplexing state of affairs? Unfortunately, Abraham, the man who has done the most research on the history of the empire of Mutapa, does not satisfactorily answer this question. One interpretation could be that here we have yet another group of chiefly invaders establishing their rule over the earlier population of Zimbabwe. This is one view which has been forwarded by Abraham. To support it there are the Katangese type artifacts associated with Period IV and the tradition itself. There is evidence of a decline at the end of the Shona period of domination at Zimbabwe. On the other hand, none of these lead inevitably to such a conclusion. One can also argue that the new dynasty arose out of the old. The problem centres around the identity of the Rozwi, who dominate the history of this region after 1450. There are numerous conflicting traditions concerning the Rozwi and various scholars have seized on each. But about the only certain thing which emerges from these traditions is that the Rozwi were a very special group. They were not a clan, nor were they a tribe. My own interpretation of the tradition recounted in the previous paragraph is that the Rozwi were a particular Shona group who for some time had held positions of power, most probably ritual, in the Shona kingdom of Period III. They may well have been the original ruling dynasty of the Shona. During the waning, perhaps crisis, years of this kingdom a particular family amongst the Shona rose to prominence, saved the state from total disintegration by virtue of its particular leadership skills, and consequently emerged as the ruling dynasty of a new successor state. This would be the Mbire. I think that it is in this light that one should see Abraham's more recent (1963) hypothesis that the Mutapa dynasty broke away from the reigning Rozwi dynasty, for it is tacitly based on this assumption.

What this interpretation implies is that there was a steady stream of Bantu-speaking peoples of Congolese origin entering Rhodesia from about the end of the first millennium A.D. All of these people are now known to us as Shona; but they did not come as a single tribe. Over a number of centuries there was a continual process of integration of peoples and ideas, beginning with the first encounter of Congolese immigrants with the Ziwa, Leopard's Kopje, and Period II people who inhabited Rhodesia. At a certain point in time, this process gave birth to the predominantly Shona culture of Period III at Zimbabwe. This culture was not static, but like any vital civilization was constantly developing new ideas of its own and absorbing others which were injected into it by more recent arrivals in Rhodesia. The Mbire were just such a group. Whether or not they themselves were Rozwi is immaterial. What matters is that under their leadership Rozwi ascendancy was established or re-established at Zimbabwe. If the Mbire did not necessarily create a new Rhodesian kingdom, they certainly revitalized the old one. With the Mbire *mambo* leading this new Rozwi state we enter the great period of expansion which resulted in the formation of the empire of Mutapa.

The second Rozwi *mambo* of the Mbire line, that is, the successor to Chikura Wadyambeu whom I mentioned previously, was named Nyatsimba Mutota. It was his own peculiar genius which gave rise to the empire of Mutapa. From about 1420 to the middle of the fifteenth century, Mutota embarked on a major military campaign to create a vast personal empire over the entire area with which we are concerned. What were his reasons for doing so? The traditional explanation is that there was considerable overpopulation in the nuclear Rozwi kingdom in the southern part of Rhodesia, as well as a severe shortage of salt supplies. Abraham does not give much credit to these motivations, nor taken alone, do I. They do not seem to be sufficient cause for the sort of empire building in which Mutota got himself involved. Abraham attributes the stimulus to foreign influences. According to an early sixteenth century Portuguese document, it was learned at Sofala from the Africans who came from the interior 'that in the land of Monapotapa (*sic*) there are more than ten thousand Moors'.[2] Although this figure should not be taken literally, there is no doubt that a great many Muslim traders were entrenched throughout the entire area. The importance of their economic stake there is attested to by their extended resistance after 1530 to Portuguese encroachment in the interior. Nevertheless, this evidence is not sufficient to warrant Abraham's conclusion that it was the Muslim traders, seeking a wider protective political umbrella under which they could carry on and extend their trading activities, who 'conceived and implanted in the mind of the Rozwi king a desire for empire'.[3] Certainly this may have been a factor in influencing Mutota's expansionist policy, but there does not appear to be any specific confirmation for this hypothesis. Furthermore, this interpretation leaves an unsatisfactory picture of Mutota as a passive character, who lacked a personal vision and was only stirred to action by the proddings of a group of foreign merchants whose activities depended, in the first place, on his good will as monarch. This is not the sort of man who wages for thirty years a struggle for imperial expansion. Abraham's suggestion seems misdirected on other grounds too. Mutota was already ruling over a considerable kingdom; apparently an ambitious man, it is not too great an assumption to believe that he contemplated extending his territory. Secondly, Mutota was the scion of a dynamic new royal family which had perhaps even usurped power from the previous ruling dynasty of the kingdom. Such a tradition, still fresh and vital, is surely the stuff of which imperial ambitions are made. And finally, turning to the purely economic factor, the advantages of a wider political hegemony must have struck Mutota as forcibly as they struck the Muslim traders operating within the sphere of his patronage. In other words, the influences which led to the formation of the empire of Mutota, like those which had marked the earlier progress of the Shona kingdom centring on Great Zimbabwe, are probably to be found within the internal dynamics of the society itself.

From his centre of power in the south-south-west of Rhodesia, which was known as Guruhuswa, Nyatsimba Mutota directed his attention to the north-east. His exploits earned him the famous title of Mwene Mutapa, or 'Master Pillager', a name which bespeaks the methods of his army. After his death in about 1450 his son Matope upheld the imperial tradition, consolidating his father's conquests and overwhelming new lands beyond them. As Rozwi *mambo*, he clearly merited the praise name which he had inherited from his father. By the time of his death in about 1480, the Mwene Mutapa was recognized as the supreme political authority from the Zambezi to the Limpopo Valley and from the Kalahari to the Indian Ocean. Through direct conquest or voluntary acknowledgement of its suzerainty, the Mutapa dynasty had made itself master of an enormous empire within the space of two generations.

This was by no means a monolithic, completely unified state. Even during Mutota's reign internecine rivalries were rife amongst the junior members of the family whom the *mambo* had placed as subordinate rulers over his new vassals. Lines of communication were badly overextended as the empire expanded. It was impossible for the Mwene Mutapa to be everywhere at once with his army; but the situation demanded it. The maintenance of such a delicate instrument depended largely on the personal qualities of the *mambo*, rather than on any institutional framework, which in any case was probably still in the process of formation.

Both Mutota and Matope possessed these abilities and the empire of Mutapa reached its zenith under their leadership. Matope's son and successor Nyahuma lacked them and the empire collapsed under the strain of conflicting personal ambitions. The raising of such challenges is certainly no surprise when one considers the origins of the Mutapas' rise to pre-eminence. Abraham has published several detailed traditional versions of the rivalries involved. I shall here limit myself to summarizing the main points of the story.

As the boundaries of the new Shona state were extended, it became imperative for the *mambo* to place trusted followers, usually kinsmen, as local governors over the various component regions of the empire. During the great half-century of expansion, Mutota removed the capital from Great Zimbabwe to a new site in the far north of the empire, in Dande country to the south-east of Zumbo. Matope accordingly entrusted the administration of the southern two-thirds of the state to two faithful followers. Changa was appointed governor of Guruhuswa, in the far south where the old capital was. Togwa was made ruler over the central province of Mbire, between Guruhuswa and Dande. To the east, the newly won provinces of Chidima, Manyika, Barwe, Uteve and Madanda were similarly parcelled out among close relatives of the Mwene Mutapa. For the most part, this latter group was too involved in establishing their various rules over the eastern provinces to raise a threat to the paramountcy of the Mwene Mutapa. But both Togwa and Changa, operating as they were from well-established secure bases, and controlling the mineral wealth of the empire, were not limited in this manner. Acting in concert, but with Changa clearly in the lead, they rebelled against the rule of Nyahuma and killed him in battle in about 1490. Changamire, his new name derived from *Amir*, as the Muslim traders called him, ruled the entire empire for the next four years. But in 1494 the first Changamire was himself killed in battle by Nyahuma's son Kakuyo. The revenge of the Mwene Mutapa was not complete, however, for Changamire's son and successor maintained control of Guruhuswa and Mbire. In the following years he even succeeded in winning the support of Uteve and Madanda, through what Abraham calls a 'strenuous diplomatic campaign'; although both the more northerly eastern provinces of Barwe and Manyika remained loyal to the Mutapa dynasty for at least another century.

This was the situation as it was found by the Portuguese. By the beginning of the sixteenth century the empire of Mutapa had already collapsed. In its place there were a number of independent states, of varying size and importance, each ruled by its own Rozwi dynasty. Among these that which was dominated by the Mwene Mutapa was neither the largest nor the most important. The vital Rozwi nerve centre remained in the south at Zimbabwe. The future lay with the Changamire dynasty. Regrettably, we know much less about the Changamires' state than we would like. This is due to two independent factors. In the first place, the Portuguese never reached Guruhuswa. Portuguese penetration of the interior of east central Africa was determined by their desire to control the gold trade coming from the Rhodesia plateau. In this they failed by monopolizing trade at Sofala, of which they had taken possession in 1505. By 1530 the futility of this policy was evident. Muslim traders easily diverted the gold from Sofala by taking it out down the Zambezi, along a well travelled route to the interior. From the Zambezi they sailed to Angoche, south of Mozambique Island, the Portuguese headquarters since 1507, and then on to the north. Consequently the Portuguese sought to cut off this 'illegitimate' trade by establishing their dominance over the Zambezi. In the years after 1530 they occupied Sena and Tete, on the south bank of the Zambezi, both of which previously had been Muslim commercial fairs. In 1544 a military garrison was established at Quelimane to guard the several mouths of the Zambezi estuary. When the Portuguese turned to the business of moving away from the river, they found themselves squarely in the dominion of the Mwene Mutapa, who naturally sought to take advantage of their presence in his struggle against Changamire. Consequently, the Portuguese came to see the history of the region through the very much aggrieved eyes of the once imperial Mutapa dynasty. Fearing that the Portuguese would learn that theirs was not the most important state, they were reluctant to let them wander beyond their own borders, where the Portuguese might come into direct contact with the Changamire. So while we know a great deal about the kingdom of Mutapa in the sixteenth and seventeenth centuries, we know very little about the increasingly important one which was ruled by Changamire. The second reason why we know so little about this state is that, as a result of the Ngoni invasions of the 1830's, the Rozwi ruling dynasty was shattered and its members dispersed to all corners of the country. Thus, it is difficult to recover the oral traditions of this dynasty.

When talking of the empire, or the later kingdom, of Mutapa, we must realize that it was not the only Shona state in this vast region. Its value to the historian is that it stands as one unusually well documented example of a type of state which was common in the area. The details of court ritual, military organization and administrative officialdom we know from Portuguese records; and we have gained knowledge from oral traditions about the operation of the important *Mwari* cult and its relationship to secular power. Both illuminate our ignorance of the other important Shona states. Barwe, Uteve and Madanda, each of which evolved into an autonomous kingdom, are little more than names so far as our knowledge of them is concerned. And the likelihood is that each of these was at least as important as the kingdom of Mutapa during the seventeenth century. As we look at the organization of the kingdom of Mutapa, we must remember that it was not unique, except in its long and intimate contact with the Portuguese. Structurally, it was undoubtedly much like its sister states.

We have previously noted that the key integrative factor in the Shona political system was religion. As *mambo*, the Mwene Mutapa was the ultimate religious authority in his kingdom, for he alone could communicate with the spirits of his ancestors. These ancestor-spirits, or *vadzimu*, were usually consulted at the new moon. Indeed, the Mwene Mutapa is sometimes described as being a divine king, in order to distinguish his functions from that of a purely secular monarch. Furthermore, as the Portuguese chronicler, António Bocarro tells us in 1635, the common folk 'believe their kings go to heaven, and when they are there, call them *muzimos* (from the singular form, *mudzimo*) and ask them for whatever they require. . . .'[4] In other words, each reigning Mwene Mutapa was himself destined, after his death, to become a *mudzimu* and to be worshipped as a national ancestor-spirit. Accordingly, there was a close identification between the well-being of the Mwene Mutapa and the well-being of the state. So long as he flourished, the kingdom would be blessed; his illness was seen to threaten the welfare of the entire state. Another important symbol of the unity of the *mambo* and the kingdom was the royal fire. Located at the court, or *dzimbahwe*, of the Mwene Mutapa, the royal fire burned continually throughout his reign.

From it each vassal chief carried a flame back to his locality and kept it burning as a symbol of national unity. This fire had to be rekindled every year from the royal fire, as recognition of the chief's unabated loyalty to the Mwene Mutapa. At his death all these fires were extinguished. A new royal fire was lighted at the accession of the new *mambo*, and by igniting his own fire from it, each vassal chief affirmed his allegiance to the new Mwene Mutapa.

This was not the only form of control which the Mwene Mutapa exercised over his subjects. Every year his most important subordinate chiefs had to send their own sons to visit him as ambassadors, each carrying appropriate tribute in ivory, gold, slaves and cattle. On arriving at the court of the Mwene Mutapa an ambassador was made to wait for three days before being granted an audience with the *mambo*. At the end of this period the ambassador was received by the Mwene Mutapa in the open courtyard outside the royal enclosure. A vivid description of such an audience was made by Dionísio de Melo de Castro in 1763:

> The Ambassador enters clapping his hands from the moment he passes the doorway of the courtyard right up to the royal presence, who receives him seated on his *Quite*, or chair beneath two sunshades . . . When the Ambassador reaches his determined place he sits on the ground, offers the present which he is bearing from his King, and presents his embassy, not to the Emperor, but to the lowest ranking of his grandees, who then relays the message up through the ranks until it reaches the most important of all the nobility, and it is he who communicates the embassy to the Emperor; and his reply descends to the same junior grandee, who communicates it to the Ambassador. This done the Ambassador withdraws and remains a further three days . . . until the final resolution of the Emperor. Soon after this is received the Ambassador returns to the land of his King. . . .[5]

For his services the ambassador received a portion of the gift, usually high quality cloth, which the Mwene Mutapa sent to his father, the chief.

It is clear from this description that there was an elaborate court ritual and extensive bureaucracy surrounding the Mwene Mutapa. Among the many important figures we may note the Court Steward, the Treasurer and the Commander-in-Chief of the army. The *mbokorume*, usually the senior son-in-law of the *mambo*, was an important political power at court. While a more specialized function was performed by the *nevinga*, the hereditary title of a close relative of the *mambo*, according to the same Melo de Castro, who acted as regent during the interregnum between the death of one and the succession of another Mwene Mutapa. Among the women of the realm the queen-mother of the *mambo* occupied an especially important position.

Returning to the broader political scene, we see that during the seventeenth century the power of successive Changamires, who remain anonymous, grew steadily, while that of the Mwene Mutapas similarly declined. Portuguese meddling in the internal affairs of the Mutapa kingdom aggravated the situation considerably. In May 1629, following a crushing defeat by the Portuguese, Mavura, the newly installed puppet *mambo*, signed a humiliating treaty with them which included this obviously offensive article, which ran directly counter to established court ritual:

> That ambassadors who come to speak to him shall enter his *zimbohe* [*dzimbahwe*] shod and covered, with their arms in their belts, as they speak to the King of Portugal, and he shall give them a chair on which to seat themselves without clapping their hands; and other Portuguese shall speak to him in the manner of ambassadors. . . .[6]

By the end of the century the collapse of the kingdom of Mutapa was virtually complete. First Dombo, the reigning Changamire, deprived the Togwa line of its authority in Mbire; its fate is unknown to us. Following a campaign south across the Limpopo, Dombo took advantage of the weakness in the Mutapa kingdom and a spell of bad relations between the Mwene Mutapas and the Portuguese, to respond to a call from the usurper Nyakambira (about 1692–4) to drive out Portuguese from his country. Dombo waged a ruthlessly effective campaign right up to the Zambezi Valley. Those Portuguese who escaped fled to Tete and Sena. In the process, the Mwene Mutapa's authority, though returned to its legitimate heirs, was reduced to the status of a district chief. The Mwene Mutapa became a puppet of the Portuguese, living close to their valley strongholds. Dombo's military triumph forced the Portuguese to recognize the fact that he was politically dominant in the interior. It is interesting to note here that as a consequence of this situation we have the Changamire emerging from obscurity and being named in contemporary Portuguese accounts. Thereafter, however, he withdrew to Guruhuswa, beyond the ken of the Portuguese, whose African or mulatto trading agents only sporadically reached there from Zumbo, which was founded in the early eighteenth century. Generally, such trade as the Portuguese had with Changamire was conducted by his own people.

So during the seventeenth to early nineteenth centuries we know very little indeed about the politics of this area, except that the Changamire dynasty remained in the ascendant. It seems to have been a prosperous time, for the archaeological record shows that this was a period of great architectural activity in the valley at Zimbabwe. Elsewhere in Guruhuswa, the stone buildings at Dhlo-Dhlo and Khami date from this period. Changamire Dombo's wars had important repercussions across the Limpopo River. Fleeing from his army a people known as the Venda migrated into the northern Transvaal, overran Mapungubwe on the way, and established themselves as rulers over the peoples of the Zoutpansberg between Mapungubwe and the modern town of Louis Trichardt. Not only do the Venda royal clans trace their origin to Zimbabwe and Guruhuswa, but there are numerous stone ruins, called *dzata*, in Vendaland which are similar to the smaller Zimbabwe ruins. Finally, the royal clan of the Lovedu, who live south of Louis Trichardt, derives directly from the Mutapa dynasty and probably crossed the Limpopo some time before the turmoil of the late seventeenth century. Their female chief was reputed the greatest rainmaker in South Africa and tradition says that the charm was stolen from the Mwene Mutapa.

Both the Lovedu and the Venda escaped the fury of the Ngoni. The Shona did not. J. D. Omer-Cooper admirably describes the details of the rise of the Zulu under Shaka and of the *mfecane*, as the consequent dispersal of the various Ngoni peoples is known. All that needs to be said here is that in the early 1830's first Zwangendaba's Ngoni and then Mzilikazi's Ndebele completely destroyed the Rozwi state of Changamire. The ruling house was effectively wiped out and other Rozwi lines were scattered all over the country. But of vital importance for the post-invasion history of this area is the survival and undiminished vitality of the *Mwari* cult, a theme which, though it lies outside our limits, nevertheless should be mentioned here, as it is crucial throughout the history of the Shona-speaking peoples.[7]

In summary, we have noted the continuity in the history of this region as witnessed in both the archaeological evidence and the testimony of oral traditions. We have seen the way in which outside influences were integrated into the pre-existing socio-political structure. We have followed the process of state building and observed the forces which gave unity to these states. And we have mentioned that the most important of these integrative factors, that of religion, survived the Ngoni holocaust. All these ideas should be borne in mind as we turn to the political system of the Malawi.

MALAWI

The territorial limitations of the Malawi political system are considerably more difficult to define than are those of the Mutapa system. The modern distribution of the Malawi is rather different from what it was before the Ngoni invasions. At the height of its influence, the Malawi empire included a great many people who are not themselves Malawi. Nevertheless, we do have a reasonably good idea of these boundaries during the period with which we are concerned. The Malawi proper inhabited the country lying north of the Zambezi, east of the Luangwa River and west of the Shire River, which flows into the Zambezi from Lake Malawi. More precisely, the Malawi inhabited the Shire Valley, so that they were living on both sides of the river. It is extremely difficult to define the northern limitations of Malawi occupation. They certainly were settled on the southern and south-western shores of the lake, perhaps even farther north than the mouth of the Bua River. One could take a straight line running from the most easterly bulge in the middle of the western shore of Lake Malawi to the Luangwa Valley as the northern frontier of Malawi territory. To the north of this imaginary line lived the closely related Tumbuka. To the east of the Shire Valley lived the Lomwe, who share a similar culture with the Malawi but speak a completely different Bantu language. And the Yao lived to the north-east of the valley, in the Mandimba Hills, running from the southern toe of Lake Malawi to Lake Chiuta, approximately along the modern frontier between the state of Malawi and the colony of Mozambique. In using this term Malawi, we must remember that there are no people who presently call themselves Malawi in a tribal context. The people whom the Portuguese knew only by this name in the early seventeenth century are fragmented into various distinct groups who are called Nsenga, Cikunda, Cewa, Zimba, Cipeta, Ntumba, Mbo, Manganja, Nyanja and Nyasa. All of them, except the Nsenga in the extreme south-west, speak a common Bantu language which is called Nyanja, although Malawi would have been an historically more correct blanket term. The Malawi homeland is today crossed by the international boundaries of Zambia, Malawi and Mozambique.

So far scarcely any work in this entire area has been undertaken by a trained Iron Age archaeologist. Thus, in complete contrast to the situation south of the Zambezi, we are totally ignorant of the Iron Age sequence in the country of the Malawi. Furthermore, very little work has been done about the collection of oral traditions among the Malawi. The few traditions which have been published are generally in the nature of official tribal histories and thus each must be approached with a considerable amount of caution.

One such tradition of the Cewa people asserts that their ancestors came from the Congo. But there is another which claims that the Cewa are the original inhabitants of their country. The generally accepted answer to these seemingly contradictory views is that the second tradition represents the voice of a long established local population, while the first version reflects the point of view of an immigrant body of chiefly invaders. The fact that the two main Cewa matriclans have different functions of authority within the society—the Phili holding political power and the Banda carrying out ritual observances concerning the earth—lends support to this interpretation.

This strongly suggests the existence of a situation among the Malawi which parallels that which we observed among the Shona. In other words, the Malawi were not a monolithic population who moved in a block into the country north of the Zambezi. Rather, they were a whole series of different immigrant groups, apparently of Congolese origin, who successively came into the country over a period of many hundreds of years. This hypothesis makes the later diversity among the various Malawi peoples much easier to understand than one which seeks to explain this phenomenon by suggesting that the divisions were caused by later developments which had their foundation in political fragmentation. Here, then, where we are operating in the face of considerable ignorance, the lesson of the Rhodesian Iron Age, with its clear emphasis on the continuity of cultural heritage, serves as a most valuable balance to the otherwise imperfect picture we get of early Malawi society.

Lacking the necessary archaeological evidence, we cannot say definitely when the Malawi invaders, or perhaps simply immigrants, entered the country to the south-west of the lake. They were certainly well established long before the Portuguese moved up the Zambezi. Abraham has recovered traditions which point to a clan relationship between the Mbire (clan *Soko-Chirongo*) and the Malawi migrants (clan *Piri-Chirongo*, that is, Phili). His interpretation of the traditions of the *Piri-Chirongo* Malawi groups, whom he has found living south of the Zambezi, has them entering Rhodesia in the early part of the fourteenth century. Accordingly, we may tentatively date the migration of the Phili Malawi proper to about the same period. Abraham's views on this point have not been thoroughly aired, so that this reasoning is still hypothetical. But here again the possibility for understanding more about the Malawi through comparison with the Mutapa political system is real.

Again in contrast to the Mutapa system, we know little about early Malawi political organization. And what information we do possess is clearly oversimplified. There is general concurrence that the Malawi invaders were led from the Congo into the lake area by a chief whose title was Kalonga, a name which means 'prince', or 'chief'. According to Cewa chiefly tradition, Kalonga sent forth a number of junior matrilineal relatives to settle and to establish their rule over what is now Cewa country. He sent Undi to settle the headwaters of the Kapoche River, and other chiefs like Mkanda, Mwase and Cimwala to various other districts. All of these chiefs (the names being hereditary with the office of chief) are today Cewa. The most prominent among them before the Ngoni invasions, as we shall see, was Undi. Cewa tradition tells us little, however, about the other Malawi chiefs. But we do know that, according to Manganja traditions, before Kalonga sent off Undi and the others, the important Manganja chiefs Kaphwiti and Lundu moved down into the Shire Valley. Kaphwiti, the senior of the two, settled in a western tributary of the Shire, at about the same parallel as the northern part of Lake Chilwa, which lies to the east of the Shire. Lundu located his headquarters farther to the south, below modern Chikwawa, on the right bank of the Shire. Essentially, that is the extent of our knowledge. Like the traditions about the Malawi moving into the country it is clearly not a realistic picture. For example, I have recently been told that Manganja today will tell you that Lundu was originally a Lomwe chief, who only became a Manganja chief later on.

This is about all we can say about the Malawi before the

Portuguese enter the scene. If there was a nuclear 'pure' Malawi kingdom before the establishment of the Malawi empire at the turning of the seventeenth century, we have no further record of it. Things come into rather sharper focus only after the Portuguese begin to penetrate the interior. We have noted that ivory was the staple of trade in east central Africa, but that the Portuguese were lured into the hinterland by the more romantic attraction of gold. It was well known to the Portuguese that the gold in this part of the world came from south of the Zambezi, where there was a mysterious empire ruled over by the fabled Monomotapa. Accordingly, after the Portuguese set themselves up at Sena and Tete, they riveted all their attention on controlling the gold trade and, as we have seen, became intimately engaged with the Mwene Mutapa. Eric Axelson writes of this situation in the following terms: 'It was gold that lured the Portuguese into the interior. It was the absence of gold north of the Zambezi that rendered penetration in that direction unremunerative.'[8] The Portuguese themselves did not explore the northern interior looking for the possibility of trade there, and moreover they appear to have made no effort to deal with the Malawi traders who came down to the river to barter their ivory. Portuguese neglect of this trade, combined with their efforts to evict the Muslim merchants from the Zambezi Valley, appears to have undermined the previously obtaining economic situation. This, in turn, led to a political upheaval of the first order.

There is good reason for believing that the Malawi chiefs depended for much of their power on their control of trade. We know that the Malawi chiefs had a monopoly of the ivory trade and that the ground tusk of every elephant which was killed in a particular chief's territory belonged to him, the hunter keeping the other. We also know from Brian Fagan's work at Ingombe Ilede that ivory was certainly traded down the Zambezi to the coast as early as the last centuries of the first millennium A.D. Ingombe Ilede is located on the north bank of the Zambezi, some thirty miles below the Kariba Gorge, in Zambia. Although it lies beyond Malawi country, it is virtually just around the corner. In the centuries between the radiocarbon dating of Ingombe Ilede and the coming of the Portuguese, there must have been a steady growth in this sort of trade with the peoples living to the north of the river. Malawi country is rich in ivory, and the Muslims were eager to trade for it. Given this situation, it is the Malawi chiefs who would have profited most from this trade with the Muslims.

Admittedly, this is a personal hypothesis.[9] But given the limited sources at our disposal, it seems the most plausible explanation for the violent outburst which shook the Malawi political system in the 1580's. The infamous Zimba migration, which carried devastation from north of the Zambezi to both Kilwa and Mombasa, is one of the most vivid, if incorrectly understood, chapters of East African history. For the Zimba did not just happen, as is the impression given in most elementary, and not a few academic, publications. Their migration was intimately related to the political tensions which were rending the Malawi system asunder. Nor is it merely chance that this upheaval took place when it did. During the first forty years of their involvement in the interior, the Portuguese seem to have done little more than take their bearings. But in the early 1570's they sent two major military expeditions into the lands of the Mwene Mutapa in an effort to eradicate the persistent Muslim presence there. There were also some clashes at this time with some of the Malawi. Although the connection is as yet obscure, there is a strong possibility that the migration of the Zimba is directly related to the intensification of Portuguese intervention in local affairs.

Who exactly were the Zimba? There is little doubt that some of the people whom the Portuguese called Zimba were directly ancestral to the modern population which bears the same name. However, it is even more certain that the migratory Zimba, who swept east and north-eastwards from the Shire, were not. Rather, by comparing contemporary Portuguese accounts with certain oral traditions we can show that these Zimba were actually followers of the important Malawi chief Lundu. That they were called Zimba by the Portuguese is probably due to the fact that Zimba was a general term for any fierce bellicose group. The tradition itself, which was collected near Angoche among the local Makua-Lomwe people, speaks of the *ma-rundu*, or 'people of Rundu', who came into the country 'destroying everything, killing all, and even having cannibalistic habits'. In this and in all its other aspects the tradition corresponds remarkably closely with the main documentary account of the invasion. At the beginning of this century, when this tradition was collected, all the important chiefs in Angoche district traced their descent from the original *ma-rundu* conquerors.

The reason behind this military campaign seems to have been

Lundu's desire to create a larger personal dominion for himself, free from the claims of Kalonga. Lundu's decision to make his move at this particular moment may well have been determined by the economic pressures which were coming to bear on the stability of the Malawi system, as I have already suggested. It was apparently a wise decision, for Kalonga was unable to deal with his formerly subordinate chief for more than two decades. In the meantime, he successfully forged an alliance with the Portuguese, who were finding Lundu as much of a threat to their existence as he was. In 1608 the Kalonga, who is referred to in accounts of the day as Muzura which was either his personal or his praise name, even sent four thousand Malawi warriors to help the Portuguese suppress some rebellious chiefs across the Zambezi who were challenging the authority of the reigning Mwene Mutapa, Gatsi Rusere. The campaign was a success. Making the most of Portuguese gratitude, Kalonga now enlisted their support in his struggle to reaffirm his authority over Lundu. When he did this we do not know, but in 1635 a Portuguese chronicler wrote of the Kalonga Muzura that:

> This King is at peace with the Portuguese, and he used to keep it better than today, before he was so powerful, because since he defeated, with our help, a Kaffir King called Rundo (*sic*), with whom he was fighting, he thinks of making war against us; it is said that some Portuguese have been killed in his lands by his order, and he wrongs us at every occasion.

The most likely dating is between 1608 and 1620. In the latter year we have a letter from Gatsi Rusere proclaiming that Muzura, among other Malawi chiefs, was his ally. Three years later, on the occasion of Gatsi Rusere's death and in direct opposition to Portuguese interests, Muzura attempted to seize the Mwene Mutapa's kingdom for himself. Although he failed, he did manage to seize a considerable amount of booty, including gold. One Portuguese official also noted that his war across the Zambezi had brought trade there to a complete standstill.

I would suggest that the Malawi empire dates from Kalonga Muzura's defeat of Lundu, for with it Kalonga's paramountcy became recognized over just that area which the Portuguese later came to refer to by that name. According to the chronicler of 1635, António Bocarro, Muzura controlled the mainland opposite Mozambique Island, having come 'from the Rivers of Cuama (Zambezi) to conquer the Makua who lived there'. With an army of more than ten thousand at his disposal, he also ruled right up to Quelimane. Bocarro notes further that Muzura no longer wished to be called 'King' by the Portuguese, but demanded that he be addressed as 'Emperor', like the Mwene Mutapa.

A decade later Muzura's relations with the Portuguese were decidedly improved. Portuguese traders who came to his capital praised his hospitality; they reported that he was interested in having the Portuguese send him carpenters' tools so that he could have better boats built for sailing on what appears to be Lake Malawi.

The classic description of the Malawi empire at its height was written by the Jesuit priest Manuel Barreto, who spent four years preaching in the Zambezi Valley during the 1660's. Kalonga, or Caronga as Barreto calls him, was the paramount chief not only of the Malawi, but also of all the people as far as the coast just north of Mozambique Island. The Makua and the Lomwe rendered 'such obedience as they are compelled to by violence' or were 'subjected by force to the Maravi', as the Portuguese spelled the name. Opposite Mozambique the coast was 'infested by the Maravi'. Quelimane was occasionally raided by the local people 'under the name of Maravi'. And as a final tribute to their military dominance of these non-Malawi groups Barreto notes: 'The Maravi are very warlike, and are feared among all the Kaffirs as the (Lomwe) and Makua are despised, so that as any Kaffir is offended at being called a (Lomwe) or Makua, so it is a great honour to be a Maravi.'

Was military hegemony the only factor uniting the Malawi empire? It is doubtful that this was the case, although it is natural for it to appear to be so to an outside observer like Barreto. If we look a bit closer at the Malawi empire we can, in fact, see the same integrative forces at work as with the empire of Mutapa and the Rozwi empire of Changamire. In both cases the military factor certainly played the key role in initially forging the new state; but both these empires were far too extensive to be held together by military strength alone. The disintegration of the empire of Mutapa is a case in point. The unifying factor of trade, controlled from the centre, and that of religious 'hegemony', were the really cohesive forces in the great Rozwi empire. And the religious factor was clearly the most necessary and crucial of these two. Similarly, the unity of the Malawi empire was based to a considerable extent on Malawi dominance of long-distance trade. One of the most important consequences of the creation of the Malawi empire was the opening up of a new overland route from the Zambezi to Mozambique Island. In the 1630's the Captain of Mozambique stated that the origin of this trade was in 'the proximity of the Maravi Kaffirs, who have conquered a great part of the mainland by Mozambique'. The overwhelmingly dominant item of trade from the Malawi side was ivory. There also seems to have been some sort of religious fabric to the Malawi empire. The Manganja rain cult of Mbona was tied to the Lundu chieftainship. Reports of the existence of this cult, as late as in 1960, have come from the district of Maganja da Costa in Mozambique colony.[10] This is especially interesting both because of the name Maganja (Manganja), so far to the east of the Malawi area and where the overwhelming mass of the people are either Makua or Lomwe, and because this district lies directly south of the Angoche region, where we have the traditions of Lundu's invaders. Unfortunately, this is all that we know about this most important topic in Malawi history. Perhaps if we had more information at our disposal we might have a better idea of why the Malawi empire disintegrated as it did.

If one were to believe the few earlier eighteenth-century Portuguese accounts which deal directly with the Malawi empire it would appear to have been flourishing at least as late as 1744. But these reports are quite clearly based on seventeenth-century knowledge. Other more localized notices state plainly that there was no longer any real unity to the Malawi empire. In 1763 one individual observed of the Kalonga that 'It is more than fifty years since this Monarch has been well obeyed and properly respected by all of his Vassals, and today he lives scarcely dominating the districts of his own Court, commanding neither respect nor obedience from the aforementioned Kings, and Chiefs'.

One factor which contributed to the collapse of the Malawi empire was the rise of the Yao as the foremost traders in that part of the continent. The Yao were trading not only to Kilwa but also to Mozambique Island by the end of the seventeenth century at the very latest. By the 1730's they so completedly dominated the ivory trade at Mozambique that the Malawi seem to have ceased trading there. It should be recognized, however, that the success of the Yao may also be a reflection of the Malawi decline, as well as a cause of it. The crux of the matter would seem to lie in the failure of the Mbona cult fully to integrate the non-Malawi folk into a state which was Malawi dominated. There are many possibilities here—linguistic, regional, basic religious differences and the like—but we can do no more than recognize that they do exist. What is certain is that the Malawi empire did not survive the seventeenth century.

During the eighteenth century and on into the nineteenth, Portuguese documents emphasize the petty rivalries and constant internecine clashes among the Malawi. According to one account a certain amount of show was made towards recognizing that Kalonga had a claim to be regarded as the paramount chief of the Malawi proper, but no practical submission was ever made to him. The Portuguese came to regard Undi as the most important Malawi chief, as he was the paramount over the district chiefs with whom they had day-to-day dealings. Not surprisingly, one reads every now and then about Undi's empire in these records. But Undi's chiefdom was not so stable that it could resist the occasional meddling of the puppet Mwene Mutapa in its succession disputes. At the end of the century, when the famous explorer Lacerda e Almeida travelled from Tete to the court of the powerful Eastern Lundu ruler, Mwata Kazembe, on the Luapula River, the Portuguese were still making no distinction between one Malawi group and another, but only distinguishing different chiefdoms. But when A. C. P. Gamitto undertook the same journey in 1831-2, only a few years before the Ngoni crossed the Zambezi, he was able to distinguish some of the modern names by which the several Malawi groups are now known.

It should be clear by now that there is a great deal more that we do not know than that which we do know about the Malawi political system. For example, of the subjects which I have touched upon, we have absolutely no clue as to the fate of Kaphwiti, who is said to have been Lundu's superior. When Livingstone visited the Shire Valley in 1861 he makes only one fleeting reference to the then unimportant chief whom he calls Kapuiti. Similarly, we know very little about the control exercised by the Mbona cult over the imagination of the Manganja themselves. The same is true for the Cewa rain cult which centred around Makewana, under the control of Undi. But if one takes a cue from the situation among the Shona, there are many important and fascinating possibilities which become apparent when they are applied to the Malawi political system. In the same vein one might think about the implications of the term *mambo*, which has its origin among the matrilineal central Bantu-speaking people, within the context of the patrilineal Shona-speakers. Another tantalizing possibility for investigation is that 'From a Princess, the daughter of Monamotapa married to a Marave Chief was born the first Son, who was entitled Emperor Caronga'.[11] Finally, probably the most important question we should ask when comparing the Malawi system with that of the Mutapa is why the Malawi rain cults lost much of their importance after the Ngoni invasions. What were the basic differences in these two African religious systems which caused one to falter and the other to survive intact the exact same catastrophe? Why, during the imposition of colonial rule half a century later, did the one not provide a focus for the opposition of the people and the other play the leading role in uniting all the people? It is by asking questions such as these that we will come to a better understanding of the history of both of these extremely important political systems.

Notes

Only abbreviated references are given for sources cited in the recommended reading list.

1. B. Fagan *Southern Africa* pp. 63–4
2. *Documentos sobre os Portugueses em Moçambique e na Africa Central—Documents on the Portuguese in Mozambique and Central Africa 1497–1840* III Lisbon 1964 p. 17
3. D. P. Abraham 'Maramuca' p. 212
4. Cited in Abraham 'Chaminuka' p. 30
5. In Junta de Investigacões Ultramarinas *Anais* IX 1 Lisbon 1954 pp. 133–4
6. G. M. Theal *Records of South-Eastern Africa* V p. 290
7. See T. O. Ranger's chapter on 'The Nineteenth Century in Southern Rhodesia'
8. E. Axelson 'Portuguese settlement in the interior of south-east Africa in the seventeenth century' Congresso International de Historia dos Descodrimentos *Actas* V 2 Lisbon 1961 p. 3
9. For the sources of the unannotated quotations which occur in the following paragraphs see my 'Malawi Empire and the Yao'
10. T. Price 'Malawi Rain-cults' *Religion in Africa* Edinburgh University Press 1964 p. 120
11. *Anais* p. 139

Recommended Reading

General

Brian Fagan *Southern Africa during the Iron Age* Thames and Hudson 1965. Especially good on Rhodesia

Mutapa

Roger Summers *Zimbabwe, A Rhodesian Mystery* Nelson Cape Town 1964
Eric Axelson *Portuguese in South-East Africa 1600–1700* University of Witwatersrand Press 1960. Contains a great deal of Portuguese-oriented material on the Mwene Mutapa

Anyone who wishes to follow up the oral evidence for the Mwene Mutapas should consult the fascinating but difficult work of D. P. Abraham. The following articles are relevant:

D. P. Abraham 'Maramuca: An Exercise in the Combined Use of Portuguese Records and Oral Tradition' *The Journal of African History* vol. ii no. 2 1961 pp. 211–25
D. P. Abraham 'The early political history of the Kingdom of Mwene Mutapa 850–1589' *Historians in Tropical Africa* Salisbury 1962 pp. 61–91
D. P. Abraham 'The roles of Chaminuka and the *Mhondoro* cults in Shona Political history' (eds.) E. T. Stokes and R. Brown in *The Zambesian Past* Manchester University Press 1966 pp. 28–46

Malawi

M. G. Marwick 'History and Tradition in East Central Africa through the eyes of the Northern Rhodesian Cewa' *The Journal of African History* vol. iv no. 3 1963 pp. 375–90

Thomas Price 'More about the Maravi' *African Studies* vol. xi 1952 pp. 75–9

E. A. Alpers 'North of the Zambezi' in R. Oliver (ed.) *The Middle Age of African History* Oxford University Press 1967

E. A. Alpers 'The Malawi Empire and the Yao: aspects of trade as a factor in the history of East Central Africa' paper presented at the Conference on East Africa and the Orient Nairobi April 1967

Additional Note

Father Schoffeleers is currently engaged in a major study of the Mbona cult and when his results are published they should enable us to answer some of the more important questions which I have raised at the end of my chapter.

2. *The rise of the Congolese state systems*

ISARIA KIMAMBO

In the savanna region of the Congo, south of the equatorial forest, there rose powerful kingdoms and empires whose beginnings can be traced to as far back as the fifteenth century. Long before this time the area must have been inhabited by Bantu-speaking people who by A.D. 800 at least lived in organized agricultural communities and in some places had already made long-distance trade contacts with the east coast. Little was known about the history of these states until Jan Vansina's book, *Kingdoms of the Savanna*, appeared in 1966. The summary which follows comes mainly from this book.

THE KINGDOM OF KONGO

The Kingdom of Kongo was founded, probably in the fourteenth century, by Ntinu (King) Wene (or Nimi a Lukeni), a son of the Chief of the small chiefdom of Bungu, near the present town of Boma. Wene migrated with companions to south of the Congo River and conquered the Abundu and Ambwela people. He married from the Nsaku Vunda clan who held spiritual rights over the land in the area, and whose head, *Mani* Kabunga acted as the earth priest for the whole area. *Mani* Kabunga accepted Wene as his overlord and the latter took the title of *Mani* Kongo. Wene then proceeded to subdue the lands of what later came to be the provinces of Mpemba, Nsundi, Mbamba and Soyo. East of these provinces two small kingdoms already existed: Mpangu and Mbata. Mpangu was incorporated by the governor of Nsundi and Mbata through recognition of the new *Mani* Kongo by the *Mani* Mbata. For this reason the governorship of Mbata remained hereditary. The limits of the kingdom in the north reached the Congo River and also included tracts of land beyond it in the region of Luozi; in the east the border stretched to Stanley Pool and then, following the Nsele River and the watershed between the Kwango and Inkisi, it followed the Loje River in the south

29

to the Atlantic. Besides the six provinces, territories lying beyond the borders in the east, south-east and south recognized the over-lordship of *Mani* Kongo and sent him regular tribute.

The Political Structure. It has sometimes been argued that the kingdom of Kongo was organized by the Portuguese. But our present knowledge about the kingdom indicates that this argument is untrue. In fact, it appears that the Portuguese copied the structure they found in the kingdom of Kongo when they organized the colony of Angola.

The political structure of Kongo is an example of the system which existed on the Atlantic coastal area before the arrival of the Portuguese. It may even be assumed that all the coastal states derived their political institutions from a single original state in the same area before the fourteenth century. This political system had four levels:

1. The basic unit was the *village*, which consisted mainly of a localized matrilineage. The headmanships were hereditary, but no aristocracy existed at this level.

2. The villages were grouped into *districts* headed by officials appointed by the king or his provincial governor. They could all be removed at the king's pleasure. These district chiefs carried out administrative and judicial duties in the districts. Some districts, like Wembo, depended directly on the king, while others were integrated into the six provinces of the kingdom.

3. Each *province* was ruled by a governor appointed by the king and also removable by him. The functions of provincial governors were similar to those of district rulers, although most of them were king's councillors as well.

4. The keystone of the system was the *king*. In the early days every descendant of Wene could claim the position. After 1540 candidacy was limited to the descendants of Affonso I, who by 1700 had become so numerous they formed a class known as *infantes* (aristocrats). There was no royal clan. The actual election of a king was done by an electoral college of nine or twelve members, including *Mani* Kabunga who held a power of veto. Candidates prepared early for election, and when the throne became vacant there were usually two factions at the court, supporting different candidates. The electors then chose the candidate who had the stronger support. Later the Portuguese advisor at the court came to obtain a *de facto* seat (with veto powers) in the electoral council.

There was no standing army; only a royal bodyguard was maintained. The income of the central government consisted of tribute, fines and tolls paid in raffia cloth, ivory, hides and slaves. The royal fishery of Luanda Island yielded *nzimbu* shells for the King and his treasury.

The main strength of this system was the degree of centralization. But it had two main weaknesses: there were no clear rules about the succession, and the strength of the state depended too much on the personality of the King.

There are three important periods in the history of the kingdom of Kongo before 1800. The period of Portuguese contact was followed, after the Jaga invasion in 1568, by a time of recovery and decline which lasted until the mid-seventeenth century; between 1665 and 1710 there was a time of transformation.

1. *The period of Portuguese contact until the Jaga invasion in 1568.*
The first period was dominated by the external contact between the Portuguese and the Kongolese and the effects this contact had on the latter. Diogo Cao had reached the mouth of the Congo in 1482. Three years later he returned with four missionaries and took four Kongolese nobles to Portugal who came back two years later. The King of Kongo was then Nzinga Kuwu. After hearing about Portugal from his nobles, he decided to send an ambassador there to ask for missionaries and technicians. A number of young Kongolese men were also sent to be educated in Portugal. In 1491 the embassy came back with missionaries, artisans and explorers under Rui da Sousa. The chief of Soyo was baptized. Then a church was built at the court, and the king, taking the name of Joao I, followed him as did the royal family and most of the nobility. In 1494 another fleet brought back the Kongolese students from Portugal.

Between 1494 and 1506 no regular contact was maintained, and Nzinga Kuwu and his son Mpanzu a Kitima went back to paganism while the queen mother and another son, Affonso, remained Catholic. This division actually reflected the two factions at the court over the royal succession; Affonso had to leave the capital (probably in 1495) for the province of Nsundi. There he maintained contact with Portugal and in 1504 priests and religious objects were sent to him.

Nzinga died in 1506. Before his death he had advised the electors to choose Affonso as his successor. But Mpanzu a Kitima occupied the court and had the support of *Mani* Kabunga. Although Affonso's army was inferior to that of his brother, he won the battle and contemporary observers believed that his victory was caused by St. James who brought heavenly knights to fight on Affonso's side. His brother was executed, while *Mani* Kabunga was spared, converted to Christianity and transformed his traditional position by becoming the keeper of holy water.

Affonso became a convinced Catholic and pro-European. He spent most of his energy in trying to convert his whole nation. He wrote to King Manuel of Portugal asking for priests and technicians and to Sao Thomé asking for military support. Manuel was interested in seeing a large Christian empire grow up in that area which, he hoped, might eventually link with the yet undiscovered empire of Prester John (Ethiopia). Between 1506 and 1512 Portugal endeavoured to fulfil Affonso's requests.

Yet all this activity seemed to fail. Sao Thomé had obtained the monopoly of trade in this area. Their ship captains tried to make the communication between Affonso and Lisbon as difficult as possible. But worse still, some of the technicians proved to be undesirable. By 1509 some masons refused to work and lived like nobles. Ship captains were rude to Africans, and by 1510 Affonso had to ask Manuel to send a representative who would be responsible for the Portuguese in the Kongo. These appeals led Manuel to codify the programme of 1512 known as the *regimento* (instructions). This document has often been regarded as a master plan from Manuel, but in fact it was a systematic exposition of the demands of Affonso and the means devised to meet them. It proclaimed that Catholic kings were brothers, and that Manuel would help Affonso. Simao de Silva who was sent as ambassador would act as a military adviser and as a judge; he would expel any Portuguese who did not set a good example. Manuel also sent Affonso a copy of the new code of Portuguese law if he wanted to copy it.

Many of the provisions of the *regimento* were never implemented. Affonso declined to take over the Portuguese code; the court was not reorganized with feudal titulature until towards the end of the sixteenth century. The parts dealing with schools, technicians and missionaries were the ones he inspired and so he tried to see that they were implemented. Yet the whole plan was a failure in the long run because of difficulties involved in a planned cultural change on such a scale. The programme itself was ambiguous;

the Portuguese wanted to help the Kongolese as well as exploit them. Their personal greed and ambition directed them into the slave trade at the expense of all other services. The number of missionaries, even if they kept to their missionary work, was very small. The Portuguese came to divide into two factions: the supporters of Sao Thomé, who tried to prevent implementation of the *regimento*, confronted the supporters of the king of Portugal, who were on the side of Affonso. As the slave trade became more profitable most of the Portuguese were drawn into the Sao Thomé camp. The governor of Sao Thomé was able to prevent the creation of a royal monopoly of trade in Kongo by bribing a priest at Affonso's capital. By using the threat of excommunication he made Affonso give up the plan. This was the method used many times by the missionaries in interfering with Kongolese politics.

When Affonso saw that Sao Thomé was ruining his kingdom he asked Manuel (1516) to give him the island but this was not granted. A proposal to buy ships from Portugal so that he could trade directly with Lisbon was also refused. By 1526 the situation had become disastrous. Affonso wrote to Portugal that the traders were bringing ruin; they were even enslaving nobles and members of the royal family. The traders encouraged chiefs to rebel against the King. Affonso decided in 1526 to expel all the whites except the missionaries and teachers, but revoked the order when he discovered that the kidnapping was mostly done by his territorial rulers. He set up a board of inspectors, two of whom were Kongolese and one Portuguese. The board had to be notified before any slave could be bought. If kidnapped, the slave would be freed. For a while it seemed to work. But as the trade expanded it became impossible to control it. By 1530 the Hum around Stanley Pool provided the greatest market, known as *pumbo*. The Portuguese who went there were known as *pombeiros*, although gradually after 1526 this name came to apply to half-caste and African slave-buying caravans as well. By 1530 the annual export of slaves had reached some 4,000 to 5,000.

Affonso died after 1541, and probably in 1545. He must have died a disappointed man, for all his efforts to Christianize and develop his kingdom on the Portuguese model were frustrated by the activities of the Portuguese themselves. His attempt to communicate directly with Lisbon and the Vatican did not work since his communications were often interrupted by the traders of Sao

Thomé. His educational programme only brought the meagre results represented by the class of literate persons at the court. The most encouraging result of the educational and missionary programme probably was to be found in his son, Dom Henrique who successfully completed his studies in Lisbon and was sent to the Vatican to be consecrated bishop. Before 1520 he had returned to Kongo to direct the Church there until his death some time after 1526. Affonso's reign set a pattern in Kongo history for more than a century. Tradition sees him as the greatest King. Later nobody could become a king without proving succession from him.

Diogo I, who succeeded Affonso, proved to be another strong ruler. He tried hard to restrain the activities of the Portuguese in his kingdom. He prevented them from going inland, but the system of caravans led by African or half-caste *pombeiros* continued. In 1556 rivalry between the Portuguese factions brought him into war against the *Ngola* of Ndongo. The partisans of Sao Thomé had opened trade with Ndongo, and those of Portugal persuaded him to go to war against the *Ngola* to punish him. This led to defeat on the side of Kongo, independence for Ndongo and, later, to the establishment of the colony of Angola.

The religious situation had not improved. In 1548 four Jesuits had arrived in the country, but a year later their relations with the king had turned sour. In 1550 all the Jesuits had left Kongo because of the enmity of the king. Two factors were the source of friction in this period and, in fact, throughout the missionary effort: the Catholic Church accepted neither polygamy nor marriage to a close relative.

Diogo has been described as a cruel and lascivious tyrant; others have called him a puppet of European councillors. Neither of these descriptions fit him. Although he was eclipsed by Affonso, he was an able king; firm with the Portuguese but not blinded by hatred.

This first period of Kongolese history ends with the Jaga invasion of 1568. Diogo had died in 1561. Chaos followed during the struggle for succession in which the Portuguese also participated; trade came to a stand-still and the Portuguese concentrated more on Angola. When by 1568 order had been restored at San Salvador the Jaga fell on the kingdom. Erupting from Mbata after crossing the Kwango, the Jaga destroyed the army of Mbata and then invaded San Salvador destroying it completely. The king fled to an island in the lower Congo. The invasion was followed by a general famine caused by the looting of the Jaga. The traders of Sao Thomé benefited by buying the prisoners who included Kongolese nobles. From his refuge, the king appealed to Portugal for help. As a result the governor of Sao Thomé, Francisco de Gouvea, arrived in 1571 with 600 soldiers. After two years he chased the different Jaga groups from the country without succeeding in destroying them. Gouvea remained in the kingdom until 1577 and his presence gave the Portuguese an opportunity to begin the conquest of Angola after 1575 without opposition from King Alvare I.

Who were the Jaga? All authors say they came from the interior, east of Kwango, and that originally they were known as the Imbangala. Some have suggested connection with the Masai or Galla. Yet we know that they were not pastoralists since they killed and ate the cattle they raided and also drank palm wine. They may have had a cultural connection with the Luba-Lunda group. While no reasons for their migration can be given, it must be emphasized that these were not mass migrations. When they arrived in the Kongo region they were on war footing, living in fortified camps. They would kill babies in order to maintain mobility but, when they encountered other groups, they would adopt youngsters of both sexes. By adopting other groups in this way a small band of the Jaga grew into a large army as it moved on. Jaga military superiority was based on discipline, tricks and surprise. Although they are described as cannibals, they were not savages. They may have founded the states of Yaka, Ovimbundu, Humbe and they also participated in building Kasanje.

2. *Recovery and decline from 1568 until the mid-seventeenth century.* The second period begins after the expulsion of the Jaga from the Kongo in 1572. Alvare I tried to rebuild his authority and disengage from the Portuguese after the departure of Gouvea. Between 1584 and 1587 he made new trade regulations aimed at arresting brutality by the traders. A royal committee was to inspect all slaves exported from the kingdom. Both Alvare I and his successor Alvare II tried to rely more on the Vatican than on the Portuguese. Alvare II even allied himself with Ndongo and Matamba against the Portuguese in 1590. In 1595 he had succeeded in having the Bishopric of Kongo created and in 1604 he proposed to become the vassal of the Pope in order to be free from

Portuguese control. This connection with the Vatican did help
Kongo in 1617 and 1623 because the Pope was able to appeal to
the king of Spain to give up an invasion of the Kongolese
kingdom.

During Alvare II's reign the internal situation was getting
worse. Factions were growing in Kongolese politics. Traders were
encouraging local rebellions against the central government.
Alvare II died in 1614, and the Duke of Mbamba made himself a
kingmaker imposing two candidates in succession. In the provinces and districts disorder reigned. This breakdown may have
been caused by excessive taxation, inadequate protection of the
population, kidnapping, devaluation of the *nzimbu* and corruption of the courts. But the main cause was the presence of the
Portuguese, traders and clergy alike. Another important factor
was the rift and rebellion caused by the succession system.

When Alvare III died in 1622, Soyo had been independent.
During the reign of Petro II the Kongolese army was defeated by
the Portuguese from Luanda. Connection with the Vatican and
the Dutch did not improve the position of Kongo. Internally, the
situation grew worse in 1642 when rivalry developed between two
lines descending from Affonso I. Since Affonso the *Kimpanzu* line
had been ruling; now the *Kimlazu* line came to power and as a
result the reigns were short.

By 1665 disorder had spread everywhere. The number of slaves
exported from the kingdom annually had grown to about 15,000.
In that year the Portuguese invaded the Kongo under the pretence
of looking for the gold, silver and copper mines, which never
existed. Many nobles were killed, including the King, Antonio I.
The missionaries were more successful during this period. The
Italian Capuchins had arrived in 1645; they continued with
serious missionary effort until 1700. Missions were opened in the
provinces, but there was no mass conversion. The nobles were
afraid of losing their traditional usages and the Capuchins
infuriated them by their practice of burning fetishes and arresting
traditional ritual leaders and condemning them to death.

3. *The third period of transformation (1665–1710)*, following Antonio
I, was characterized by a wave of hatred of foreigners in the Kongo
—leading to a state of unprecedented chaos. Assassinations of
kings and provincial rulers followed one after another. When the
kingship was reunified in 1710, the king had lost all powers. All

provinces and chiefdoms were autonomous, and the position of the king had become something like that of the Holy Roman Emperor. The strains of the period were reflected among the common people in the Anthonian heresy of 1700. A woman prophet began to claim that she was in contact with St Anthony and that it was her mission to find the man who would end the wars. Her teachings had the air of modern 'Zionist' movements. She claimed that Christ was black and heaven was for Africans and that people should not listen to foreign missionaries. After the prophet was condemned and burned the movement died.

After 1710 the kingdom of Kongo was no longer a unitary kingdom but a series of chiefdoms which still recognized a single king. This change had been brought about by economic conditions. By 1720 there was no longer a single Kongolese kingdom, but three different groups: the Solongo in Soyo, the Mushi Kongo in the central areas and the Soso in Eastern Mbata and part of Nsundi. By 1900 the Ntandu and Zombo (Zumbo) had also emerged as distinct cultural groups. Another change was the decrease in population resulting from the political disruption, perpetual wars, the slave trade, famines and smallpox.

These changes are not simply to be described as decline. They were a result of an extraordinary mutation which took place between 1667 and 1710. The old political structure did not simply collapse, breaking down into small clan or tribal units. Rather it became a new structure with a king and nobles and a huge domestic slave population. The tensions of this new system were no longer chiefly those resulting from the problems of combining in one political unit a number of clans. Lineage became less important and personal initiative and wealth came to play a tremendous role.

THE LUBA KINGDOM

Around 1500 the area between Lake Tanganyika and upper Kasai was organized into a multitude of small chiefdoms. In the western part these were ruled by the Bungo, the ancestors of the Lunda. In the central part lived the ancestors of Luba Katanga and there also existed two bigger kingdoms: the Kaniok and the Bena Kalundwe. Farther east the chiefdoms were small and the inhabitants were called the Kalanga.

About 1500 a great immigrant named Kongolo is said to have appeared in the Kalanga lands. He became the founder of what

has been called the first Luba empire. Traditions do not agree
about the origin of this hero. One version says he came from the
north-east, where the town Kongolo stands today; another says
he came from the Bena Kalundwe in the north-west; and in yet
another version he is said to have been born near Mwibele.

After his arrival he subdued the isolated villages and tiny chiefdoms and built his capital at Mwibele near Lake Boya. Some
time later a hunter called Ilunga Mbili arrived from some place
east of the Lualaba. He was well received by Kongolo and he even
married two of his half-sisters. Ilunga Mbili must have come from
a well organized political system since he is said to have left
Kongolo because he could not stand his behaviour which was not
suitable for a chief. At any rate, in trying to teach Kongolo the
manners of a chief, a quarrel started and Ilunga Mbili returned
to his original home.

The two half-sisters gave birth to two sons after the departure
of their husband: Bulanda bore Kalala Ilunga and Mabela bore
Kisulu Mabele. Kalala proved to be a great warrior and helped
Kongolo to subdue the whole southern part of the kingdom.
Because of suspicion, Kongolo wanted to kill Kalala who escaped
to the country of his father and returned with an army. Kongolo
escaped but was eventually captured and killed. Kalala took over
the kingdom and built his new capital at Munza a few miles from
Mwibele. His reign has been described as the beginning of the
second Luba empire, but in reality it was the same kingdom. The
story of Kongolo and Kalala has become the national Luba epic.
Kalala is said to have conquered more chiefdoms on the western
banks of the Lualaba just north of Lake Kisale and others on the
boundary of the Kalundwe. At his death the kingdom may have
achieved its basic organization.

Although little is known about the Luba political structure, it
appears to have been different from the coastal states. The society
was organized in patrilineages; one or more formed a village,
directed by a headman chosen from the main lineage but officially
appointed by a superior chief who could be the king himself. Like
the coastal states, villages were grouped into chiefdoms and chiefdoms into provinces. But the territorial hierarchy was not
altogether regular, for some villages and chiefdoms depended on
the king directly. A number of chiefdoms were ruled by lineages
known as 'owners of the land'. These were hereditary. Others
were ruled by officials appointed either by a superior chief or by

the king. All the chiefs, except 'owners of the land', were *balopwe*, that is members of the lineage of Kongolo and Kalala Ilunga.

The central government consisted of the king and his title-holders who had to resign at the death of the king. New title-holders had to pay heavily in presents to the new king and in this way titles were bought.

Kingship was based on the concept of *bulopwe*, that is a sacred quality vested in the blood of the male descendants of Kongolo and Kalala Ilunga. Therefore the king had supernatural powers and ruled by divine right. He exercised absolute authority without any superior council to counterbalance his power. In practice, however, his power was limited by the fact that half-brothers could rise against him and would get supporters if he were a tyrant.

Kalala's son Ilunga wa Lwefu is mainly remembered as the brother of Cibinda Ilunga who left the kingdom to found the Lunda empire around 1600. The next period of Luba history was characterized by conquests and fraternal struggles. Besides Kalala's state Luba rulers had established themselves in three other kingdoms: in the Kikonja area, the Kalundwe and the Kaniok.

Around 1700 Mwine Kadilo succeeded on the throne of Kalala Ilunga. With him started the first attempt at expansion. He fought many Songye groups, although he did not incorporate them into his kingdom. His son Kekenya also fought wars, but the actual expansion of the kingdom took place under Kekenya's son, Ilunga Sungu, and his successor Kumwimba Ngombe. Some chiefdoms east of the Lualaba were conquered and annexed to the kingdom. Those in the Lomotwa country were made tributary, and in the Kiambi area on the Luvua, warriors were stationed there to prevent invasion from the 'Bemba' (probably from the Kazembe people). The expansion reached its peak under Kum-wimba Ngombe. After him the succession struggle became greater. Ndai a Mujinga who succeeded him was killed by his brother, Ilunga Kabale who died in 1850. After his death five of his sons were fighting for succession.

Two main tendencies stand out in this period of Luba history: expansion and civil wars. Military conquests were often not followed up by organized assimilation. The main weakness existed in the nucleus itself. Localized patrilineal groups retained too many political functions; they were only nominally integrated.

Two points remain mysterious; why did expansion begin after 1700? Secondly, why did the struggle for succession after Ilunga Sungu involve only half-brothers rather than father and sons as in the previous period? Probably a structural change may have taken place; the explanation offered in traditional interpretation on the grounds of accident and demography is not satisfactory.

THE LUNDA EMPIRE

Lunda myths of origin indicate that the first man was created in the northern part of their country which may mean that this part has been inhabited for a long time. From this area groups may, from time to time, have broken off and settled in the plains on the west under 'chiefs of the land'. Another myth says that the country was governed by Mwaakw, a male twin born from a long line of twins descending from the first man. Mwaakw's son, Nkond had two sons, Kinguri and Cinyama. They were lazy and cruel. One day they beat their father almost to death. Their sister Rweej saved him, so he decided that she should be his successor. This mythical theme thus explains the origin of matrilineal succession.

Rweej succeeded her father and, some time later, Cibinda Ilunga came from the Luba capital and married Rweej and became king. This myth means that Luba *balopwe* conquered the area—many Lunda titles are derived from the Luba. Another tradition says that some of Cibinda's followers left the country to found the Bemba kingdom. The twin brothers of the Queen Kinguri and Cinyama, did not accept the new ruler; they emigrated, one to found the Kasanje kingdom on the Kwango in Angola, and the other to bring Lunda rule to the Lwena.

Rweej had no children and Cibinda Ilunga married Kamonga Lwaza whose son *mwaant* Luseeng succeeded to the throne. He was a good organizer, instituting most of the Lunda territorial and court titles. His successor, *mwaant* Yaav Naweej gave the generic title for the Lunda kingship (*yaav*).

During the first three reigns the kingdom expanded from the valley of the Nkalaamy to the whole area between that river and the Kasai and to the springs of the Lulua in the south.

Lunda political system around 1700. The basic unit was also the village ruled by a council of elders and a matrilineally hereditary headman, responsible for supernatural well-being of the villagers. He could be deposed only by the king. Villages were grouped together, according to the perpetual ties of kinship between their headmen, into districts under appointees who collected tribute or tax and transmitted it to the king through their representative at the court. If the king could not trust the district ruler (*cilool*) he appointed a supervisor (*yikeezy*) to oversee his activities.

The central government consisted of the king, the *mwaant yaav* and his titleholders. There was no standing army, although there were 'travelling chiefs with militarized retinue' used in collecting tribute and carrying out orders outside the Lunda homeland. At the capital there was a small police force.

The whole political structure rested on a twin mechanism of positional succession and perpetual kingship. These meant that the successor acquired not only the material goods or political office of his predecessor, but also the latter's social identity. He literally became his predecessor, taking his name and his social connection. Kinship was therefore perpetual in the sense that two men would become brothers even if they were distant relatives. In this system new titles would be created only after all the old 'positions' in the system had been filled. This was useful because it divorced the political system from the real descent structure and made it not bound to any descent system. This explains why so many central African cultures could take over the Lunda system so easily.

Another aspect of the system making it easy to be adopted elsewhere was the 'indirect rule' feature. Local chieftains could be assimilated into Lunda titles; a Lunda colony could be formed in a non-Lunda area forming a neutral place for arbitration, but a place where one was ultimately subjected without the use of force.

Lunda Expansion in Angola. Kinguri migrated from the Lunda homeland after the arrival of Cibinda. He first settled on the plateau between the Kwango and Kasai. Later, disturbed by the arrival of another Lunda group, he moved towards Bola Casache and arrived at the court of chief Sungwe a Mboluma. His followers plotted with Sungwe and Kinguri was killed. But his nephew, Kasanje ka Imba succeeded him. He migrated towards the Europeans in Angola and settled near Ambaca at Lukamba. He had to move again because of famine, probably in 1613, and with the help of his wife's group in Cassache he was able to subdue the Pende chief, Kilamba.

The conquered kingdom was henceforward called Kasanji. It was ruled in turn by kings from the matrilineages of Kasanji ka Imba, the Kalunga line and Ngonga line. The people were called the Imbangala. Although their history belongs to the history of Angola, their position as middlemen in the long-distance trade was to reach the whole interior to their original homeland.

Lunda expansion is also said to have proceeded farther east, beyond the Bemba into the Bisa country, then to the Nyika and as far east as the Ngonde on Lake Nyasa. These migrations were not mass migrations but small group movements mainly involving the ruling family. There is a possibility that this picture of Lunda expansion may be incorrect. It may be that Lunda reputation had become so great that all the surrounding chiefs would claim Lunda origin. But even this would go far in showing how wide-spread Lunda influence had been.

Lunda Homeland (1700–1850). Naweej's death was followed by a short civil war, after which Muteba became king. He conducted wars against Sala Mpasu to avenge Naweej's death and also fought the Kaniok. His reign is more remembered for the Lunda expansion to the south under two Lunda chiefs (Musonkantanda and Kanongesha) who pushed the boundary of the kingdom to the headwaters of the Zambezi. The period is also remembered for the campaigns of Kazembe who brought the eastern boundary first to the Lualaba and then between the Lualaba and the Luapula.

Muteba was succeeded in turn by his three brothers. Mukanza, the last brother, made two important changes. He gave all the region east of the Lualaba to Kazembe Kaniembo and made him his near equal. Secondly in his own territory he appointed a governor of the whole southern region as a result of the expansion which had taken place.

Three other rulers followed Mukanza, the last one being Naweej II who was ruling in 1852.

The Kingdom of Kazembe. Just after his accession around 1690, Muteba sent chief Mutanda Yembeyembe to fight a faction of the Kosa who lived west of the Lubudi and who had refused to accept Lunda rule. Cinyanta, the chief, capitulated, was well received by the *mwaant yaav* and remained at his court. Later a Lunda blacksmith, Lubunda, was accused of starting a fire which had broken out at the capital. He fled eastwards, and when news came later that he was a ruler of a small chiefdom in the Luapula region, Mutanda Yembeyembe and Cinyanta fitted out an expedition to go to look for him.

On the Lualaba they defeated Mwine Mpanda who became a Lunda ally and led them to the salt pans of Kecila. The chief was defeated and the whole population west of the Lualaba accepted Lunda rule. Soon rivalry developed between Cinyanta and Mutanda. Cinyanta was drowned in about 1710. His children complained to *mwaant yaav* Muteba who decided to invest Cinyanta's son, Nganda Bilonda with the title of 'Kazembe' and allow him to kill Mutanda. But the latter heard about this and fled south.

Nganda Bilonda organized administration in the conquered territories and subdued many other chiefdoms. He left chief Cisenge on the Lualaba with the title of 'Kazembe of the Lualaba' and he himself proceeded towards the Luapula. He defeated the Lomatwa then Nganda died. There was a succession crisis between his followers. They finally returned to Musumba, and *mwaant vaav* Mukanza chose Kaniembo and invested him with a rank equal to his own. Lunda territories were divided between the *mwaant yaav* and Kazembe II. Kazembe Kaniembo subjugated the whole area between the Lualaba and the Luapula.

Before his death, his son (Mukenji) had revolted and made himself 'Kazembe of the Lualaba'. His relationship with Cisenge who had been appointed earlier is not yet clarified. However, the 'Kazembe of the Lualaba' remained an enemy of both the Kazembe of Luapula and the *mwaant yaav*.

Kazembe III Ilunga (or Lukwesa) succeeded to the throne around 1760. He continued his conquests among the Mabwe, the Ngonde, the Tabwa, the Shila and the Bisa. All the Lunda chiefs organized the sending of tribute to Kazembe's court and he in turn sent gifts to *mwaant yaav*. It is likely that the latter still considered Kazembe as his tributary ruler.

The kingdom of Kazembe was probably the greatest in size and the strongest of all Luba-Lunda states. Between 1750 and 1850 it was paramount in southern Katanga and parts of the northern Rhodesian plateau. It was visited by Portuguese expeditions and frequented by traders from different directions.

THE STATES ON THE FRINGE OF THE SAVANNA

In the northern part of the savanna and in the forests of Lake
Leopold II, a number of kingdoms and chiefdoms existed. They
were not created by the Lunda nor did they belong to the coastal
type. Culturally these states can be divided into two

The Bolia group, clustering around Lake Leopold II, belong
to the great Mongo culture cluster occupying the whole central
Congolese depression.

The Tyo (Teke) cluster of the plateau north of Brazzaville and
east along both sides of lower Kasai consists of four sub-groups:
the Tyo (Teke), the Yans-Ding, the Boma-Sakata and the Kuba-
Lele group.

1. *The Bolia Group* arrived from the heart of the forest probably
in the fifteenth century. Their political organization rested on the
principles of *bokopo*. Since the Mongo culture did not have a
political organization, it is possible that the Bolia invented and
elaborated their political organization after they migrated to this
area, unless the group of people from whom they got the system
has disappeared.

In their migration the Bolia are said to have brought sacred
objects of kingship: a lump of kaolin and a piece of ant-hill. Like
all the Mongo, the Bolia were patrilineal but, under the influence
of their neighbours, they changed to dual descent system.

The *bokopo* simply means an 'office'. It is derived from the word
ekopo (leopard skin) which is an emblem of chieftainship. As an
institution, however, *bokopo* is closely linked to the possession of
certain bits of kaolin and ant-hill. The *bokopo* can be acquired
through the mechanism of partitioning the original lump of
kaolin. In this way the Bolia are much more connected with the
divine kingship than any central African group. After the possession of *bokopo*, the king or chief is believed to possess an ability
to help or harm others without outward sign. Before succession
the candidate must therefore undergo a series of tests after the
ancestor had appeared to him and told him that he had been
chosen. It was then his duty to convince the council that he was
the chosen one.

The territorial structure was quite simple. The village consisted of persons patrilineally related, and their headman was
genealogically the oldest member of the community. The villages
were grouped into districts under chiefs stemming from a single

patrilineage. The chiefs were the oldest members. At the court there were limited title officials who were hereditary. No political official could be deposed.

This looks very much like the segmentary system of the Mongo culture. Yet this is not a segmentary lineage organization since the district chief did not only rule his own lineage. This is a system which seems to have derived from a patrilineal lineage organization with the addition of few invertions of a sacralized kingship.

2. *The Tyo (Teke) Group* consists of four sub-groups.

The Tyo (Teke). Their origin is unknown. They say they have always been there, probably pointing to a remote period. We know that in 1491 they were at war with the Kongo. By 1660 they were trading in slaves and tobacco with the Vili of Loango. Their trade with the middle Congo was also well developed.

In the eighteenth and early nineteenth centuries, Tyo culture underwent fundamental changes. Manioc (cassava) replaced maize; several crafts were lost such as melting iron, carving canoes and making fine pottery, as was hunting with bow and arrow; raffia weaving went into decline and cloth began to replace raffia skirts: copper rings replaced raffia squares in trade and payment of bride wealth. Salt making was abandoned. All this happened because the Tyo had become dependent on the slave trade.

In political structure major changes also took place between 1775 and 1830. A group around Abala invented a new political instrument the *nkobi*; this diffused south to cover the whole Tyo area. The organization around 1850 centred on the chiefdom as the basic unit, consisting of a main village (domain) led by a chief and other villages led by local leaders. Headmanship rotated to the other villages. Chiefship was hereditary and the candidate had to belong to a class of aristocrats. The chief's position was based on his relation to the spirit (*nkira*) of his domain who was supposed to take care of the wellbeing of all the members of the chiefdom. It would lead the chief in his settlement of disputes and it would fight witches and distribute fertility.

A hierarchy of chieftainship within the kingdom was linked to the instutition of *nkobi*, which was a basket kept in a special house and which functioned as the shrine of a major *nkira* or spirit. The 'owner' bore a special title but could neither sacrifice nor pray to the *nkira* himself. This had to be done by special families of priests.

The *nkobi* was the justification for the chief's authority. If lost, the authority was lost too.

Above the chiefs was the king who was the symbol of the kingdom. His authority was derived from a possession of a number of sacred objects connected with the spirit of the most important *nkira* (Mkwe Mbali) dwelling in the waterfalls of the Lefini. Before accession, the king underwent a nine-day secret initiation during which he came into contact with this spirit. His main duty was to keep the kingdom prosperous by performing appropriate rituals. His real political power was limited. He had no army and no supreme judicial institution; his village was scarcely bigger than that of the other chiefs; and tribute came to him quite irregularly. In theory he could depose titled chiefs; in practice he could do so only if supported by enough of the titled chiefs.

There was no royal dynasty. Any aristocrat who claimed that his ancestor came from any of the three specified domains could be elected. The electors were the titled chiefs who had no domain or *nkobi* of their own, together with nine of the most important chiefs. This was the main weakness of the system. The king was left at the mercy of the chiefs he was supposed to control. Moreover the system was over decentralized.

The Yans-Ding may have migrated from the west coast, settling west of the lower Kwango. They arrived in the Kwango area only after 1700. Their political structure is based on small settlements of matrilineal clan sections, which are grouped together into chiefdoms under chiefly clans. The chief is assisted by a council of elders with authority over justice. The authority of the chief derives from his position as the head of the oldest clan in the area, which resembles that of founding clan in the Kuba group. The Ding resemble the Yans except their villages are larger and consist of several matrilineage ruled by elected headman. They also give greater role to age grades than the Yans. In this they resemble the Lele.

The Boma and Sakata. No Sakata tradition is known. The Boma claim to have come from the east. The great Boma kingdom was formed before 1641 and possibly as early as the late fifteenth or early sixteenth century. The political village and chiefdom organization was similar to that of the Ding except that the villages tended to become larger.

The Lele-Kuba Group are put together because of common origin and similar language and culture; but their political organizations are different. Both claim to descend from an ancestor, Woot, who came from the Congo River and ascended the Kasai and then the Sankuru.

When the Kuba settled in the country around 1600, they already had a centralized political system. Leaders of migration had become chiefs on two levels: villages of one matrilineage and others of several existed. Then there were chiefs of one or more villages who held sacred regalia but were themselves not sacred. The chief was chosen from members of a royal clan by councils of nine or multiples of nine. The electors were also elected by other councillors from specific founding clans. Chiefs could be deposed, and the council of founding clans wielded most authority.

Immediately after the arrival of the central Kuba, war broke out between the Bieng and the Bushoong with the object of gaining paramountcy over the other chiefdoms. The Bushoong gained ascendancy and the Bieng migrated away, first to the Lele, then southwards where they met the Lunda and the Pend around 1650. The Lunda ousted them and they retreated to found a small but independent chiefdom near Charlesville.

The Bushoong changed their political structure slightly—they granted the king rights over life and death by proclaiming that he could not be removed and by excluding the junior branch of the royal clan from the succession. They thus diminished the power of the council of founding clans. By 1630 the chiefdom was attacked and almost destroyed by the Pyaang (another Kuba group). A new king (Shyaam) from the Ding and Mbuun, but said to be a descendant of a Kuba slave, restored the kingdom and it began to grow slowly. In another century it had reunified all the Kuba chiefdoms.

In its later history, the Kuba kingdom showed two remarkable features: the proliferation of titles and the increase of councils and courts to limit royal power. Yet the system still remained weak because of almost complete autonomy in the districts. Of the central institutions only the kingship and presence of envoys from the chiefdoms at the royal capital could be found.

The Kuba system was also different in certain aspects. The throne was not reserved for persons directly chosen by spirits. No ancestor worship existed. The chiefs derived power not from acceptance by ancestors and nature spirits but from the creator god, who was supposed to put the right candidate on the throne.

The Lele may have had society similar to the Ding and the

early Kuba society. But from 1600 onwards it evolved in a radically different manner. By 1900, the Lele political unit was the village of clan sections with members of founding clans holding special position. But the people were grouped according to age sets. Younger set could not marry but could share a communal village wife in polyandrous marriage. There was one founding clan for the whole Lele, the Bashi Tundu and they claimed to be over-lords. They had a king and several chiefs, but neither the king nor the chief had any say in village politics. The changes in the Lele society were concomitant with a shift in their value system, so that the two highest values, authority and old age, fused.

CONCLUSION

This survey of the rise of the Congolese political systems indicates that too much emphasis has been put on the role of diffusion of African states from one original centre. As Professor Vansina concludes: 'It is unlikely that there will ultimately prove to have been but a single centre of origin for all the central African kingdoms. A hypothesis involving multiple invention, stimulated by contact diffusions and internal evolutions, seems to be more appropriate.'

3. European activity and African reaction in Angola

WALTER RODNEY

There has been significant European activity in Angola ever since the latter part of the fifteenth century. As for African reaction, that continues up to this very minute in the form of the heroic liberation struggle of the Angolan people. During this lengthy period of nearly five centuries, it is the Portuguese who have been the most prominent Europeans in Angola. They established political rule over Angola, they seized the land and exploited the minerals, they tried to capture Angolan minds for Portuguese culture and Angolan souls for Catholicism. But, above all, they wanted bodies; that is to say, human beings to work, firstly, as slaves across the Atlantic and, secondly, as labourers within Africa, producing wealth for Portugal.

In practice, Portuguese exploitation of Angolan labour represented the impact on Angola of European capitalism in its various stages of development. From the fifteenth to the eighteenth century, pre-capitalist Europe moved into the stage of commercial capitalism, building up its wealth by trade. The Atlantic slave-trade was one of the most important means by which Europe increased its financial resources. Later, Europe entered the phase of industrial capitalism, during which Africa became a field for investment and a source of raw materials to be used in European industries. This process got under way during the nineteenth century and, by the end of that century, Africa was divided up amongst several European nation states. Finally, in more recent years, groups of capitalists drawn from various nations (Europeans and Americans) have combined to form international monopolies, which exploit the resources and the people of Africa. Consequently, it can be said that we are now living under the shadow of international monopoly capitalism. This third stage can be seen to overlap the second, and in fact it grew out of the second stage. Similarly, the second had emerged from the first stage and the first had developed from pre-capitalist conditions.

What needs to be examined, as a single theme running through the centuries under discussion, is the reaction of Angolans to these three successive and inter-related forms of capitalism. One basic fact to be borne in mind is that, at the moment of their first meeting with Europeans, the peoples of Angola were living in various types of pre-capitalist society at a subsistence level. That is to say, the people consumed most of the food they grew, rather than producing a surplus for sale. Some goods were exchanged; for instance, salt and fish from the coast were exchanged for iron from the interior, but this was a simple barter process which did not permit the accumulation of profits as in a capitalist system. Such differences as did exist between Angolan peoples were often related to differences in environment. The ways of earning a living and organizing the community among the Bakongo in the tropical forests of northern Angola were rather different from the Herero manner of maintaining life in the dry semi-desert regions of the extreme south of Angola; and contrasts would also be found if one looked at the low-lying coast and the high plateaux of the interior. The operative factor determining Angolan-European relations was the contradiction between the pre-capitalist societies of Angola on the one hand and the European capitalist societies on the other hand; but it is important to notice how differences between various Angolan societies sometimes accounted for their dissimilar reactions to Europeans. Equally, the fact that all the European nations were not exactly alike in their social and economic patterns did affect the manner in which they conducted themselves in Africa.

Of the three stages mentioned above, the first was that of commercial capitalism, often referred to as 'mercantilism'. The period of the world-wide development of European commerce, which began in the fifteenth century with the voyages of Portuguese and Spanish sailors to Africa, Asia and the New World, meant for Africa the beginning of the terrible experience of the Atlantic slave-trade. Considering European slave-trading activities in Angola as part of the broader theme of slave-trading in central Africa, one finds that Angola occupies a special but unfortunate position. Angola and the Congo must be bracketed together as the principal slave-exporting sections of central Africa, both of them having made a tremendous contribution to the Atlantic slave-trade. The area where we now find Mozambique, Malawi, Rhodesia and Zambia sent slaves to places in and around the

Indian Ocean where the demand for slave-labour was not as great as it was in the Americas. Brazil, for instance, could comfortably absorb 10,000 slaves a year, and most Angolan slaves were destined for Brazil. In fact, during the early seventeenth century, Angola was known to supply annually well over 10,000 slaves and the figure increased as time went on. This question of the extent of the slave-trade is the first one which makes Angola stand out from the remainder of central Africa during the sixteenth, seventeenth and eighteenth centuries. Indeed, even when measured alongside other notorious slave-trading regions in West Africa, Angola remains one of the foremost suppliers of slaves to the New World.

Furthermore, it was in Angola that the slave-trade was conducted with the greatest violence. In most other parts of Africa, Europeans bought their slaves from African chiefs. This was despicable but it was the genuine trade of the exchange of European manufactures for African captives. Because of the uneven development of capitalism in Western Europe, Portugal was not able to offer trade goods to the African in competition with other Europeans. On the one hand, the Portuguese tried to use international law and their own naval strength to keep other Europeans from dealing with the Angolans while, on the other hand, within Angola itself they encouraged wars among the African population, as well as sending armies inland to raid for slaves. Such raiding expeditions became notorious in Angola under the name of '*Kuata! Kuata!*' This is another reason why Angola can be seen as a special area within central Africa. Because European activity was intense, African reaction and involvement was equally great.

The first Angolan people to face up to the Portuguese were the inhabitants of the empire of Kongo, who came into contact with the Portuguese in the 1480's. Because of the later partitioning of Africa among European nations, the Bakongo today live in the Congo, in Angola and in the region of Cabinda, which is a Portuguese enclave within the Congo. It has been considered convenient to deal with Portuguese relations with the Kongo empire in Isaria Kimambo's chapter on the Congo in this book; but it is well to bear in mind that European activity within the boundaries of the great Kongo empire is as much part of the history of Angola as it is part of the history of the modern state of Congo-Kinshasa. The Kongo empire was a relatively highly developed political structure, with a strong ruling class and the basic elements of a monetary system. Yet, it was totally destroyed by forces let loose by Portuguese slave-traders. This is an extreme example of what could happen when a pre-capitalist African economy was confronted by a capitalist European economy, even in its early commercial stage.

To the south of the Kongo empire, on the coast between the rivers Dande and Kuanza, lived the Mbundu or Kimbundu people. They were organized within a kingdom known as Ndongo, the ruler having the title *Ngola*, from which the word 'Angola' derives. Apparently, the kingdom of Ndongo had some relationships with the empire of Kongo to the north, for the *Mani* or Emperor of Kongo actually claimed to be the overlord of the *Ngola*, and fought a war in 1556 to try and subdue Ndongo. In any case, the activities of the Portuguese in Kongo and Ndongo were closely linked. Throughout the sixteenth century, the Portuguese slave-traders from Sao Thomé and the Congo preyed upon the peoples of Ndongo, utilizing Congolese intermediaries. At the same time, the king of Ndongo and his nobles were active participants in the slave-trade with the independent Portuguese traders settled at Luanda, just north of the estuary of the River Kuanza. Luanda later became the capital of the Portuguese colony of Angola. This is somewhat ironic because, at first, Luanda was considered as an illegal settlement. The Portuguese king disliked the trade carried on by the 'outlaws' at Luanda, because it lay outside his control and brought him no profit, unlike the slave-trade in the Congo. However, in 1569, the Portuguese were temporarily driven out of the Congo, and the Portuguese king, supported by his nobles and the Catholic church, turned to Ndongo as an alternative centre of Portuguese influence in that part of Africa.

In 1571, the king of Portugal 'gave' Angola to one of his nobles, Paulo Dias de Novais and, four years later, a military expedition was sent to help him conquer Angola and make it his private property. Putting aside what had already occurred in the Kongo, the military expedition of 1575 gave rise to the first of the many episodes of resistance to European domination in the history of Angola. The Portuguese were opposed not only by the Mbundu, but also by two closely related peoples, the Bangalas and the Jagas, who were recent immigrants who had come into Angola from the Congo. Old and new African inhabitants of Angola

fought determinedly for their freedom, and for several years after
the first expedition of 1575 the Portuguese made little progress.
They did win a victory over the *Ngola* of Ndongo in 1580, and
were then able to set up a fort; but they also suffered certain
reverses, such as the crushing defeat of Ngoleme-Akitambo in
1590, which is still cherished by Angolans as part of their
revolutionary tradition.

Nevertheless, the tide of events eventually went in favour of the
Portuguese. They were encouraged not only by the desire for
slaves, but also by the belief that there were rich silver mines at a
place called Kambambe on the River Kuanza, in Mbundu
territory. The resistance of the Angolans kept the Portuguese
from reaching Kambambe until 1605. They found no silver
mines, but they were then in a strategic position to impose their
domination on the Mbundu and to pursue the *Kuata! Kuata!*
slave raids with little restriction.

Those Mbundu chiefs who were conquered were forced to pay
the Portuguese tribute in slaves. Others who resisted were attacked
time and time again by the Portuguese. This meant heavy
mortality as well as leading to the export of large numbers. The
Portuguese strengthened their position by building another fort in
the heart of Ndongo, and in 1624 they were able to appoint their
own puppet ruler.

Meanwhile, Portuguese activity had not been restricted to
Ndongo. Novais had also invaded the territory of Kissama, south
of the Kuanza, and had been successful in his wars against the
disunited and petty chiefs of the area. Farther south along the
coast, the settlement of Benguela was founded, and attacks were
made from there against the Ovimbundu, who were too poorly
organized to resist effectively. The small size of political units and
the lack of unity among the Angolans—these were the two factors
which accounted for the success of the Portuguese in the sixteenth
century and subsequently. Of course, it is important to remember
that European activity within Angola was largely a reflection of
developments within Europe itself. Until recently, the numbers
of Europeans actually settled in Angola were small, but their
influence has always been extremely great, because they had
behind them the economy and culture of capitalist Europe. Even
though Portugal was one of the most backward of the capitalist
economies of Western Europe throughout the period under discussion, it had clear advantages over all of the Angolan peoples,

living at the pre-capitalist stage. Not only in Angola, but in most parts of this continent, Africans existed in small competing groups at little above subsistence level when they were thrown into a relationship with the commercial world of Europe. The sort of reaction which one would expect is more clearly seen in Angolan history than in the history of other areas in central Africa and Africa as a whole—because the clash took place at an early date in Angola and the degree of conflict also was great.

In Angola, the local economy was placed in danger from the outset. When the Portuguese gained control of the coast and near-by islands, they automatically had possession of the areas where salt was manufactured and where, most notably at Luanda, cowrie shells (*nzimbu*) were collected. Both of these items were used as money within parts of Angola and Congo and the Portuguese arranged supplies to their own advantage. However, the most fundamental and revolutionary factor was the introduction of European manufactures. Throughout Africa, European goods started off as luxuries, but rapidly came to be regarded as necessities. Africans were prepared to go to great lengths to obtain European goods, and this proved detrimental to their society and to their economic and political independence.

Although the Portuguese used a great deal of force in Angola and although they had limited supplies of trade goods, it was nevertheless possible to encourage large sections of the Angolan population to engage in slaving in order to procure goods from Portuguese traders. The Portuguese made it clear that they were interested in human beings to be used as slaves and that nothing else which the Angolans had really mattered at that stage in the development of European commercial capitalism. Angolans, who wanted European goods badly, had to submit to this economic blackmail.

It has often been claimed that slaves formed part of African society and that, consequently, it was easy for African chiefs to begin by selling their own slaves. No convincing evidence has been brought forward to support this view; on the contrary, it appears that the sale of human beings was a new feature in most African societies, which came about as a direct reaction to the presence and activities of Europeans.

Yet it is true that the Atlantic slave-trade was only possible because of certain features of African society, most notably the division into small groups and the hostility existing between those groups. Angola was especially unfortunate. Each of the numerous small Angolan political units fought its own independent struggle against the Portuguese. This is not surprising because, before the Portuguese arrived, the Bangalas, Jagas and Sossos were both aggressors against the Mbundu and fighting among themselves. The Jagas and Bangalas were at that time particularly war-like and restless. Their whole life was organized for fighting and raiding under the leadership of a warrior chief or *soba*. Many migrations had not yet settled down and, particularly in eastern and southern Angola, tribes were still in the process of formation when the Portuguese arrived. That is to say, out of an intermixture of peoples of different tribes and clans, new tribes were being formed. Not even the Mbundu kingdom of Ndongo was a united whole, nor were the Ovimbundu to the south. In the nineteenth century, there were supposedly twenty-two Ovimbundu chief-doms, about half of which paid tribute to one or other of the larger groups. Under these circumstances, it proved easy for the Portuguese to exploit existing enmities and gain allies and puppets.

An African nationalist might be tempted to look back at the history of this continent and those individuals who fought along-side the Europeans against other Africans. Anyone who fought alongside the Portuguese in Angola, Mozambique or Guinea today would certainly deserve being branded as a traitor, but the use of such terms about the early Angolan reaction to the Portuguese would be misleading. To say, for instance, that a Bailundo who sided with the Portuguese in 1624 was a 'traitor' to Angola is to imply that the Angolan nation already existed. This was not so. What existed was a number of separate peoples within the geographical area which later became the political unit of Angola. An Ilundo at that time could be loyal only to his own small community, and he regarded the interests of his community as being in conflict with those of other peoples in the region. Therefore, when an Ilundo chief joined the Portuguese against the Mbundu, for example, from his viewpoint he was simply employing the Portuguese as allies against his enemies, and in the process he was benefiting by obtaining a new range of items brought from Europe.

The Jagas and Bangalas provide excellent examples of how differences in the pre-capitalist societies of Africa had made it easy for capitalist Europe to exploit the continent ever since the fifteenth century. Before the Portuguese arrived, a typical Jaga or Bangala *soba* maintained his position and his prestige among his followers by his success in attacking his more peaceful agricultural neighbours so as to obtain the necessities for survival. This meant that here one is faced with two different social systems: one is organized in such a way that the people sow and reap crops and tend cattle and other domestic animals; the other is organized in such a way that food is made available by methods of force. If a *soba* thought that the Portuguese newcomers would capture his war camp or threaten the way of life of his people, he would fight bitterly; but if instead the Portuguese offered him further profitable reasons to go on raiding his neighbours, then he would do so, with the additional factor now that his warriors would seize individuals from the raided villages to sell to the European slave-ships. Some reports tell of the feelings of guilt among those Africans who captured and sold their fellow men, but this was a deeper moral issue not a political one. It must be stressed that the small African political units were being loyal to their own petty interests and in most cases considered that they were employing the Portuguese rather than the other way around.

Those Africans in Angola who thought that they were using Portuguese help for their own purposes were proved wrong. They were also mistaken in their belief that many of their fellow Africans were a greater danger than the Portuguese. As has already been suggested, they should not be branded as 'traitors'. Nevertheless, we need to give full credit to those individuals who rose above the ordinary; there were those Africans who recognized the full significance of the threat posed by the presence of the economically and technologically more advanced Europeans, and who realized that as an answer to this threat it was necessary to work for a greater unity among the peoples of Angola. The involvement of the African and European economies inevitably brought about major changes leading to the disappearance of the small political units, to the creation of a wider unity and to considerable modifications in the system of production. Those who noticed this trend at an earlier date than most of their fellows and those who sought the means of ensuring the welfare of the greatest number of Angolans are to be placed among the heroes of Angola and Africa.

One such outstanding individual was Nzinga Nbandi, a Queen of Mbundu origin and a heroine of Angola. Since Nzinga was born the daughter of the *Ngola* of Ndongo in 1581, six years after the Portuguese invasion of Ndongo, she grew up in the atmosphere of the struggle against the Portuguese. Unfortunately, another of her father's sons was more interested in personal power than in the danger from the Portuguese who were claiming Ndongo as their own. It was this son who seized the throne in 1624, after the death of the father. He was supported by the Portuguese and became in practice a tool of the Portuguese. His attempts to kill off all other persons with claims to the throne caused Nzinga to flee eastwards to Matamba, taking with her many of the Mbundu who regarded her as the real Queen of Ndongo and who were willing to resist the Portuguese.

Nzinga proved her worth by founding, in about the year 1630, an independent state in Matamba, where she had settled. She received the support of the Jaga inhabitants of the area, and although she was herself an Mbundu she organized the kingdom according to the pattern of the Jaga *sobas*. Matamba was thus a military state, created in answer to the Portuguese, who by then had complete control of Ndongo. Queen Nzinga's most striking achievement was her creation of broad alliances which drew together in a common cause several of the peoples of Angola. In 1635 she was at the head of an alliance involving the Mbundu and Jagas of Ndongo and Matamba, Jagas of Dembos, Bangala of Kasanje, the peoples of Kissama and the Ovimbundu of the plateau region to the south. This impressive grouping was maintained for nearly twenty years. During this time, defeats were inflicted on the Portuguese, and they were forced to negotiate with Queen Nzinga. Her pride, courage and resourcefulness both in military matters and in negotiations impressed even the Portuguese.

However, no single individual can change the direction of history. Because she had great foresight, Queen Nzinga could point the way to the future when Angola would achieve unity in the face of the enemy, but the rate of change was determined by the impact of the European capitalist economy on the Angolan situation. From the sixteenth to the seventeenth century, unity among the Angolan peoples was hard to achieve and harder still to maintain. Even before Queen Nzinga's time there had been attempts at alignments which were temporarily successful. For instance, the victory of Ngoleme Akitambo in 1590 was possible because of a recently concluded agreement between the Mbundu

and a number of Jaga chiefs from Matamba in the east and
Dembos to the north. The reigning *Mani* Kongo also gave his
support. This combined force held off the Portuguese for ten
years, but the strain of the war was great and by 1605, when the
Portuguese took Kambambe, not only had the Jagas abandoned
the alliance, but many of them had joined the Portuguese.
Similarly, Nzinga's great achievements ended when some of her
partners switched their support to the Portuguese.

At this point, it is necessary to stress once more that the import
of European manufactured goods into Angola was a powerful
factor determining the way that the Angolans reacted to the
Europeans. This was what drove them to take part in the slave-
trade. As a general rule, groups were prepared to sell captives to
the Europeans so long as they did not lose their political independence and provided that they did not themselves suffer from the
worst effects of slave-raiding. Thus it was that the Jagas of
Matamba who deserted the first coalition of 1590–1600 because
they were many miles removed from the scene of Portuguese
oppression in Ndongo, and had much to gain economically by
opening trade with the Portuguese at Benguela. Naturally, those
Africans who were made slaves were not the ones who welcomed
the European merchants. The residents of areas from which
captives were taken in great numbers resisted by fighting or by
escaping. Strangely enough, however, when those same individuals were a safe distance from the Portuguese they often turned
to slave-raiding. This was true in the case of Kasanje and to some
extent of Matamba.

Like Matamba, Kasanje was founded as an expression of
resistance to Portuguese slave-traders. The rulers in Kasanje were
Bangalas some of whom had moved inland from the coast to the
River Kwango to avoid the Portuguese, and in 1635 they joined
Queen Nzinga's alliance. In the 1640's, the Dutch were making a
strong bid to take over from the Portuguese in Angola and therefore provided the Africans with a European ally against the
Portuguese. However, the Portuguese brought up reinforcements
of soldiers and arms from Brazil, and the Dutch were defeated in
1648. This meant that once more the Portuguese were the only
source of imported goods, and the rulers of Kasanje started to
supply slaves to the Portuguese on a large scale. Queen Nzinga
was more courageous and determined. When her military alliance
broke down she could no longer wage war, but she withdrew

inland and did not set up commercial relations with the Portuguese until 1656. She was then baptized, taking the name Ana de
Sousa, and even though this was not a genuine conversion to
Catholicism, it did signify that even Queen Nzinga had to come
to some understanding with Portuguese commerce.

By the time that Queen Nzinga's long life had come to an end
in 1633, Matamba was on its way to becoming the leading slave-
trading state in Angola, alongside its neighbour, Kasanje.

The majority of the slaves handled by Matamba and Kasanje
in the late seventeenth century came from outside their eastern
borders. During the eighteenth and the first half of the nineteenth
century, the Atlantic slave-trade grew to great heights, becoming
more intensive as well as being carried on over a wider area. A
number of related Lunda peoples such as the Chokwe Sosso and
Luenas, came to dominate the region between Angola and
Mozambique, and made it a vast hunting ground for slaves. The
Lunda kingdom of Mwata Yamvo in eastern Angola was the
most powerful state in central Africa at that time, and provided
the bulk of the victims who were taken by the Europeans from
Angola and the Congo. (The chapters by Edward Alpers,
Andrew Roberts and Terence Ranger deal with Portuguese
activity in Mozambique.)

A marked increase in slave-trading activities also took place in
southern Angola, where Benguela was the point of shipment. The
main suppliers were the Ovimbundu on the plateau, especially
the Bailundo group, who made captives among the peoples to
their east and south-east. Bailundo traders crossed the continent
of Africa and did business at Zanzibar. At the same time, Zanzi-
baris were known to make visits to Benguela. These facts demonstrate the tremendous increase in the central African slave-trade,
which was simultaneously serving both the eastern and the
western coasts of Africa. Sometimes, as in the case of the powerful
Lunda state of Mwata Kazembe on the Luapula, an African ruler
was approached by two sets of traders, one coming from Angola
and the other from Mozambique or Zanzibar.

Competition was fierce during this period. Cutting across the
differences between Africans and Europeans, there were conflicts
between Portugal and other European powers as well as clashes
between African states.

Commercial capitalism or mercantilism always meant that
several European states were conducting bitter competition. Often

it was direct competition between governments but, where private merchants were involved, they were also assured of the support of their own governments. Each state tried to set up monopolies in certain parts of the world, and each state guarded its profits by force. The Portuguese attempted to set up a monopoly over the whole of Africa after their voyages of exploration in the fifteenth century. This was over-ambitious; as time went by, it became obvious that their navy was far below the standard which would have been required to keep away other European competitors. During the seventeenth century, the Portuguese were pushed into the background in most parts of Africa but, with the help of the Brazilians, they had managed to maintain a dominant position in Angola. By the late eighteenth century even their hold on Angola was being loosened because the British and the French were taking a keen interest in the Angolan slave-trade, obtaining their purchases through the port of Loango in the Congo.

In order to trade with the British and the French, Mwata Yamvo used a long overland route to the Congo, via Matamba, Kasanje, Dembos and Loango. More captives went in this direction than to Luanda, whose trade fell to about 6,000 a year. The result was that the Lunda had a struggle with the Portuguese who wanted to cut off this route; while there was also fighting among the African states over the division of profits when a route passed through several political units. States such as Matamba and Kasanje were the middlemen who controlled the routes between the Europeans on the coast and the sources of captives in the interior and, as such, they did have a clash of interests with the Portuguese buyers as well as with the Lunda sellers. However the differences were not fundamental. In 1683, there was an important treaty between the Portuguese and Matamba, which put an end to their trade wars and guaranteed peaceful relations in order to conduct the slave-trade. Much later, the Mwata Yamvo attacked and defeated Matamba and Kasanje; but he could not destroy their power so that they continued to take a share of the profits of the slave-trade.

The events of the eighteenth and nineteenth century demonstrated that the Angolan economy had to a great degree become an extension of the European system of production and distribution, supplying the extraordinarily valuable labour of the Americas. Africans were in no position to avoid this development, and all Angolan reactions after the initial struggles can be regarded as various forms of compromise with and adaptation to the dominant capitalist system.

One of the characteristics of this adaptation to European commerce was the rise of a local class which specialized in procuring goods for export. A large proportion of them were mulattoes, their fathers being Portuguese and their mothers Angolans. They were called *pombeiros*, and it was their function to penetrate far inland in search of captives for sale, and often to carry out raids of their own as has been seen in the previous chapter. They were the counterparts of the Arabs and Afro-Arabs in eastern Africa. Some of the *pombeiros* grew quite wealthy and were the forerunners of a commercial middle class within Angolan society. Others were simple peddlers, known as the 'barefoot *pombeiros*'. These were to join wage labourers as the early proletariat of Angolan towns. The Ovimbundu have a word 'Ovimbali', which they applied to those of their fellows who imitated Europeans and went to live in the towns. These *Ovimbali* were all part of the process of commercialization.

Out of the pre-capitalist Angolan societies, therefore, new groups and classes of people were emerging, earning their livelihood on the basis of the presence of European capitalism within Angola. During the period of commercial capitalism, their numbers remained small, but the main impact of industrial capitalism on Africa was, firstly, to bring large sections of the population within the limits of the European money economy. More and more people would earn money from commerce, by working for wages and by selling crops; while they would use this money in making purchases and paying taxes. In the second place, industrial capitalism led to imperialism, one of whose features was the political domination of Africa by several European states.

The above changes within Angola and Africa were dependent upon far greater changes which had been taking place within Europe for a considerable period, and whose effects became obvious in the nineteenth century. The merchant class in Western European countries accumulated capital through the world-wide exchange of a variety of natural products, such as grain, timber, fish, spices, pepper and slaves. They handled these along with a number of other items which required only a small degree or refinement or manufacture, gold, silver, salt, ivory, wool, dyes and sugar were among the most important. The technological advances in Europe meant that the emphasis was shifted to large-scale manufacturing. Hand-processes were replaced by machinery, as in the case of the cloth industry; primitive machinery using water-mills or wind-mills was replaced by steam-driven machinery, as in the case of the sugar industry. However, Portugal was out of step with these developments which were transforming Western Europe into the young giant of industrial capitalism, and this historical backwardness of Portugal was to have a serious effect on those parts of Africa where the Portuguese were most active, Angola being the chief of them.

By the beginning of the nineteenth century, Britain led the world in the establishment of new steam-driven machinery. Britain was the first to break out of the mercantilist system of monopoly from which it had already derived sufficient profit, and turn instead to free trade, because expanding British industry regarded the whole world as its source of raw materials and as a market for its factory goods. Consequently, Britain could afford to prevent its citizens from partaking in the Atlantic slave-trade (1807) and from keeping slave-plantations (1832). France was not far behind Britain. In Africa, these two industrial nations started to seek new possibilities for profit by penetrating into the interior, especially along the course of the River Niger. Their machinery and railroads required lubricating, while the soap industry required certain vegetable oils, so a market was made available for African products such as palm oil and groundnut oil, which replaced the export of slaves in parts of West Africa.

Meanwhile, Portugal was clinging to the Atlantic slave-trade and to the institution of slavery in Brazil. The Brazilians, supposedly colonial subjects of Portugal until 1822, were the main force behind the Angolan slave-trade and their economy continued to be based on slavery until about 1880. In fact, the Portuguese and Brazilians were responsible for the establishment of slavery on Angolan soil. White traders and wealthy *pombeiros* kept slaves in Angola to carry on their businesses, while there were many Angolans used as slave labour in agricultural schemes run by the Portuguese around Luanda, Benguela and other forts and settlements. In Luanda, in particular, the Angolans who were held as slaves were hardly any better off than those who went to Brazil and the West Indies, for they were engaged in the production of sugar and coffee under similar harsh conditions. In the second half of the nineteenth century, laws were passed to abolish these practices but, like the Portuguese and Brazilian laws against the slave-trade, they were hardly worth the paper on which they were written.

Nevertheless, Portugal could not entirely avoid the new forces of industrial capitalism which were growing in Europe, Africa and America. Since these forces caused a greater scientific interest to be taken in the African hinterland, Portugal also sent out its explorers to probe into the continent of Africa, starting some-times from the Angolan coast and sometimes from the coast of Mozambique. (See Chapters 1, 4 and 9.) This sort of activity was stimulated by the general 'scramble for Africa' and the com-petition of other European powers. Although coastal Angolans were long familiar with the Portuguese, and although there were Portuguese forts and settlements in some up-country areas, the Portuguese had by no means surveyed the whole of Angola by the time of the 'scramble for Africa'. Portugal hastened to push inland so as to be able to claim large chunks of central Africa on the basis of being the first Europeans to arrive there. The more extreme claims were rejected by the influential European nations, but Portugal was given authority over Angola and Mozambique at the Berlin Conference in 1844–5. She was thus faced with the same sorts of problems as the other Europeans in central Africa, namely, the establishment of political control over the areas which they claimed and the production of local commodities for export to Europe.

The imperialism of the period after the scramble required a greater degree of control and oppression by the Portuguese in Angola. The extent of the opposition put up by the Angolan peoples is admitted by the Portuguese themselves, when they speak of the endless wars of 'pacification' which they were forced to wage. There are in Angolan history many excellent examples of what has been called 'primary resistance'—that is to say, the very earliest struggles against the imposition of colonial rule. These primary resistance struggles were especially pronounced in the extreme south and the extreme north of Angola, where they lasted until the First World War.

Pacification of an area meant that the inhabitants had to work for the Portuguese in one way or another, mainly on construction projects, in obtaining rubber for export and in growing cash crops. Portuguese attempts to use the labour of Angola during this epoch of industrial capitalism were moulded by their own economic backwardness and by the historical traditions of slavery and brutality which had been established in that part of Africa. With insufficient capital to allow for the payment of wages in a free capitalist labour market, the Portuguese favoured the continuation of forms of slave labour. In the face of world opinion and of liberal elements in Portugal, the powerful slave-owning whites and mulattoes in Angola simply changed the designation from 'slavery' to 'corrective labour', which was punishment for so-called 'vagrancy'. Later, it became 'contract labour', which was rewarded with a small payment, but which was nearly as inhuman as slavery and in some respects worse because the slave-owner had some respect for the life of his property which did not apply to the contractor or to the Portuguese *chefe de posto*, the administrator who rounded up Africans for labour service.

Angolans found contract labour hateful, so that primary resistance overlapped with and merged into the revolts against this crude exploitation of labour. In the south-east, for example, the Portuguese set up their rule over the Ambos during the First World War after considerable fighting; immediately they had a new battle on their hands over the expropriated lands and the coercion of labour. Meanwhile, in those areas which had come under effective Portuguese administration at a previous date, the inhabitants were already rebelling because the old trade processes had been reversed, and they were being called upon to provide contract labour. The first great revolt of the modern era took place on the Bie plateau in 1902, and mainly involved the Ilundo people. They were losing their lands to the Portuguese, and they were unable to carry on with their own agriculture, because the men who traditionally worked in the fields doing the heavy labour, were conscripted to work for the Portuguese. The Bailundo revolt, under the leadership of Matu ya Kevela, lasted for eighteen months. It was put down at the cost of thousands of African lives but, while it was in progress, it put a stop to all commerce and had the Portuguese in a panic because it spread far into the interior.

Contract labour, which was at the root of the Bailundo revolt, appeared in an even more vicious form in Sao Thomé. Angolan workers were transported there to grow cocoa and coffee, and it was common knowledge that of the tens of thousands who went there supposedly on five-year contracts none were allowed to return. That the Sao Thomé contract labour was nothing but slavery in new clothes was a fact widely recognized internationally. It brought protests from Britain, Germany and the United States, which influenced the Portuguese to terminate this neo-slavery in 1917. More important than the international protests, however, was the determined resistance of Angolan peoples to this system, especially in the Congo province of Angola, where most of the Sao Thomé workers were recruited by force. As early as 1913, fighting broke out in this region because of the export of labour and the armed protest continued until 1917. This confrontation is known, after the name of the leader, as the revolt of Tulante Bula.

It would be impossible to enumerate here the various popular uprisings—small and large—which took place in Angola in the twentieth century. They were unceasing, breaking out in one place and then another. What is equally significant is the persistence of these incidents long after the Second World War. The peoples of Kasanje, who had started growing cotton under duress in 1915, went on strike at the end of 1960 against the conditions imposed by the monopolist company, Cotonang. The answer of the Portuguese was to use napalm bombs, which destroyed seventeen villages and probably killed 20,000 Angolans. As a culminating point, it is not surprising that shortly afterwards the armed national liberation struggle got under way in March 1961 among contract labourers working on coffee plantations in the north.

Nowhere in Africa was European colonial administration accepted without struggle, so in this respect Angola was no exception. The seizure of lands and the imposition of forced labour, along with heavy taxes and corporal punishment, were also common features of European activity in central Africa. In Tanzania, the Maji Maji revolt was deeply rooted in the opposition to forced labour on cotton fields at unremunerative rates. Where Angola went off on a different path was in the intensity of the exploitation and the fact that it never abated right up to the most recent period. As indicated above, this is to be explained by Portugal's own economic weakness and its archaic system of production. Portugal could make little or no economic investment in Angola and could only engage in the primitive and absolute exploitation of labour and muscle-power. This was the same weakness displayed by King Leopold in the Congo, and his rule was correspondingly brutal. To make matters worse in her African colonies, the Portuguese Fascist dictator, Salazar, made it clear that he would build Portugal on the labour of the 'inferior peoples' of Africa. Consequently, Angola and the other Portuguese territories were denied the benefits of gaining strength and becoming free under a liberal capitalism.

Modern imperialism created modern African nationalism. With their roots deep in the past, the nationalist movements took their specific form and dimensions from the conditions created by imperialism. The projection of industrial capitalism on to Africa produced well-defined urban classes—people with technical skills and with a knowledge of the liberal ideology which the Europeans espoused in Europe but failed to apply to Africa. In the rural areas, there was a profound disturbance of the subsistence pre-capitalist economies and the creation of a large money sector, involving cash-crop growers and rural wage-earners. For the vast majority of the Africans, independence did not simply mean the independence which existed before the Europeans took their land. They wanted to lift themselves into the twentieth-century world, modestly symbolized by radios and bicycles, and to enjoy freedom based on knowledge and a more advanced mode of production. Their quarrel against the imperialists was that they could not, or would not, fulfill aspirations for political, social and economic advance. That this charge holds good against the Portuguese in Angola can be seen at a glance.

Portuguese weakness has kept the modern sector of the Angolan economy small, and their policy has been to keep this as the preserve of Portuguese and other white settlers in Angola. Even the simple jobs such as messengers, which would be considered menial in a more developed settler economy like Kenya's were in Angola handed over to poor whites from Portugal. The more responsible jobs were closely guarded against African penetration by the failure to provide Angolans with educational facilities, and by the policy of 'assimilation', by which an African, in order to rise within the ranks of the administration or his profession had to alienate himself from his people and aspire to be Portuguese in every way. This policy has now been ostensibly discontinued, but the underlying philosophy remains the same, namely, that an African within his own cultural setting is inferior and fit to perform only manual labour.

Just as Portugal denied the economic and social advance of Africans within Angola, so they denied the possibility of peaceful advance towards independence. Colonialism elsewhere was defeated by a combination of political argument and the use of force at critical junctures. The political argument rested on the assumption that one could remind the imperialists that colonialism flouted the very basis upon which modern European states are constructed. When to this was added the armed action of the people in Malaya, Kenya and Algeria (to name only the most outstanding), then it became clear that it was not economically feasible to maintain the old-fashioned colonial rule. The developed capitalist countries then conceded freedom to their colonies and embarked upon the more sophisticated devices of neo-colonialism. Here again, Portugal's economic retardation had a profound impact on Angola.

Angola in the 1940's and 1950's had its political and cultural organizations, which could have provided the basis for a peaceful movement of protest against Portuguese colonialism. But, existing as it did directly off the profits made from its colonies, Portugal could not conceive of tolerating any movement leading ultimately to complete independence. To counter the nationalist viewpoint, they put forward the barren argument that Angola, Mozambique and Guinea were 'provinces' of Portugal rather than colonies. They then proceeded to meet nationalist political activity with harsh oppression. Of course, one must remember that the Portuguese themselves suffer under a Fascist dictatorship, so that the policy of the Portuguese Government in Africa since the 1930's has been an extension of Fascism. Whether in Nazi Germany, in Portugal, in South Africa or in Portuguese Africa, Fascism is never amenable to peaceful confrontation. The inescapable logic of the Angolan situation led to the outbreak of an armed national liberation struggle.

When the Angolan revolution broke out in 1961, the Western world pretended to be shocked at the so-called 'atrocities on both sides'. This was the attitude adopted towards revolutionary Congolese fighting against the Belgians and foreign mercenaries. In both cases, the charges overlook the fact that only a handful of whites were killed in comparison with the thousands of Africans who were butchered. Furthermore, it is ridiculous to judge by the same yardstick the violence used by a slave-master to oppress a slave and that used by a slave to break his chains. Five centuries have elapsed since Angola was 'donated' to Paulo Dias de Novais by the Portuguese king. Since then, violence has stamped itself upon the face of Angolan society—the violence of the *pombeiro*, the *chefe de posto* and the Portuguese soldier.

Angolans grew to realize that force was the only answer which could be made to Portuguese domination. In 1957, a rumour spread through Bailundo that guns were found by the Portuguese police in a village of one of their sub-tribes, the Bimbe. Angolans recalled the resistance of the Bimbe in the revolt of 1902, and whispered to one another, 'The Bimbe people will rise again. They were the last ones to surrender.' This tradition of struggle is an important matter. It has now reached a high point in its development because, for the first time, conditions in Angola permit its various groups to react as a single people to the Portuguese. Angola today is a single political and administrative unit, resting on the economic integration of its several parts. Obviously, this was not so in 1500 or even in 1914. Northern Angola for a long time retained its historical links with the Congo, while the extreme south of Angola was an isolated region. One is justified in speaking of the peoples of the geographical area of Angola as if they formed a unit, because the net effect of European activity and African reaction in that region was constantly to bring those peoples closer together. The process is not yet completed. The Portuguese still sow divisions among tribal groups, but the scope for that is lessening rapidly.

Not only is there greater unity, but the fight against the Portuguese has far less of that one-sidedness which one can perceive in the clashes between the Angolans and Portuguese in the earlier period when the technological superiority of Europe was decisive. The very nature of the military engagements shows that Angola is an integral part of a global community. Its techniques of guerrilla warfare can and have benefited from the experience of other peoples in this era of national liberation wars against imperialism. A guerrilla war is primarily a political and ideological operation. Its principal function is to bring the great masses of Angolans on to the stage of history as a conscious and determined force.

The context in which one must conduct a discussion of European activity and African reaction in Angola today is considerably wider than the context in the fifteenth century. Not only have Angolan reactions been conditioned by international developments, but Portuguese activity has really given place to European activity in a broader sense. New problems have been posed by the growth of investments by international monopolies in central Africa. This is a relatively recent phenomenon arising out of industrial capitalism and having as its distinguishing characteristic the fact that the investors have broken with the nationalism which was a feature of mercantilism and the imperialism of the period of the scramble and the First World War. The directors of these companies feel no loyalty to any particular state or government and in turn they do not require the support of any one national government in order to survive. Instead, they are answerable only to their shareholders in several countries, and they co-operate with each other through the machinery of interlocking directorates.

In Angola, the greatest monopoly concern is the diamond company, Diamang, whose exports account in value for half of the total exports of Angola. It is jointly owned by the Anglo-American Corporation of de Beers and by Union Minière. Union Minière is, of course, the Belgian power in Katanga and has American, British and French shareholders; de Beers is primarily a South African investor. The Benguela railway which transports Katangan ore through Angola, is owned by the British Tanganyika Concessions, which in turn is one of the Union Minière shareholders. Besides, the British and Belgians hold large agricultural concessions, and companies registered in the U.S.A. have a monopoly of oil exploration.

It was partly Portugal's weakness which has allowed the penetration of foreign capital into its colonial domains since the late nineteenth century, because the more vigorous capitalist societies treat Portugal itself as an economic colony and field of investment. In addition, it appears that foreign companies have recently been deliberately encouraged in an endeavour to enlist foreign aid against the forces of nationalism. These companies can make super-profits by maintaining the *status quo*. One finds, therefore, that the most mature capitalist form (international monopoly) co-exists with the most backward relations of production (slavery and feudalism). Diamang, which began mining in its giant concessions in the Lunda country of eastern Anglo in 1920, maintains a semi-feudal state which controls both public and private life. There are restrictions on the movement of labour out of that area, and the entire adult male population is virtually the property of Diamang.

The great companies of central Africa help to hold together the Fascist regimes of Africa, South Africa, Rhodesia and Portugal, as well as to intimidate Zambia and the Congo. Co-operation between these countries exists at all levels and they can call upon the help of the other imperialist powers of Europe and America.

Portugal, for example, is better able to carry on its war of oppression in Africa because it is a member of N.A.T.O. The economic, political and military relations between the reactionary states obviously transcends units like Angola and Rhodesia. As a consequence, central Africans are being forced to combine in various ways and to move closer to other African states as far away as Algeria and the United Arab Republic. Angolan revolutionaries and many Africans elsewhere are fully conscious of this supra-national dimension of their struggle.

Undeniably, there has been a constant enlargement of the scale of human activity in central Africa, beginning with pre-capitalist formations, which were small and fragmented. Each rebellion, whether it was that of the Matabele in Rhodesia in 1896, that of Bushiri in Tanganyika in 1889 or that of the Bailundo in Angola in 1902, contributed to greater unity and ultimate freedom. At the moment, all that is clearly discernible is the rise of countries such as Zambia, Malawi, Mozambique and Angola as a consequence of interaction with forces originating in Europe. Perhaps in twenty-five years' time, historians will be concerned with the making of Africa—with the way in which various parts of the continent come together in the face of international capitalism and imperialism.

Recommended Reading

J. Duffy *Portugal in Africa* Penguin 1962. This is a brief but extremely clear analysis of the history and contemporary development of the Portuguese territories in Africa. The same ideas are put forward at greater length in the author's *Portuguese Africa* Harvard University Press

C. R. Boxer *Salvador da Sa and the Struggle for Brazil and Angola* Oxford University Press 1952. A detailed study of Dutch and Portuguese activities in Brazil and Angola in the 1640's

D. Birmingham *Trade and Conflict in Angola, the Mbundu and their Neighbours under the influence of the Portuguese 1483–1790* Clarendon Press Oxford 1966. This is a fully documented and important study. However, students should be recommended to read his earlier and shorter paperback, *The Portuguese Conquest of Angola* Oxford University Press

B. Davidson *The African Awakening* London 1955. Contains a full account of the contract labour system

K. M. Panikkar *Angola in Flames* Delhi 1962. The most thorough analysis of Portuguese colonialism within the context of capitalism and imperialism

A. Ehrmark and P. Wastberg *Angola and Moçambique, the case against Portugal* London 1963. This is concerned mainly with the outbreak of the armed struggle. It shows considerable insight into the problems and personalities of the Angolan revolutionary movements

4. The nineteenth century in Zambia

ANDREW ROBERTS

Zambia lies in the middle of Africa, far from the east and west coasts. Before the nineteenth century it had very few contacts with Europeans, and none directly with Arabs and the world of Islam. The important influences were African and came mostly from the Congo area, to the west and north-west. These influences were partly demographic—the migration of peoples; partly political and cultural—the spread of chieftainship; and partly economic—the development of east-west trade links across the continent. In the nineteenth century this pattern changed. East-west trade continued, but on a new basis, while there were important new lines of contact running north and south. From the north, in East Africa, came Arabs, Swahili and Nyamwezi. From South Africa came African tribes—the Kololo and Ngoni—and Europeans. All introduced major economic and political changes. Some Zambian peoples were conquered by the African invaders, most became involved in the export of ivory and slaves, and all, at the very end of the century, came under British rule.

The background. The history and culture of Zambia has to a large extent been shaped by geography. To the south, it is bounded by the Zambezi River, which runs for much of its course through deep rifts and gorges; below the Victoria Falls, there are few crossing-places. To the east, Zambia's border runs along the highlands west of Lake Malawi, while to the north it runs along the continuation of these highlands between Lake Malawi and Lake Tanganyika. For much of Zambia's past, these features have been partial barriers to the movement of peoples and traders. To the west, however, there are no such barriers. Most of Zambia is part of a great savanna region which reaches west across the Congo basin and covers much of what is now Angola and Congo-Kinshasa.

Zambia displays great cultural uniformity. All its peoples speak

71

Bantu languages, they all know the use of iron, and they all practise some form of agriculture. We know that Bushman-type hunters once occupied the country, but none survive. It is possible, without too much distortion, to group the peoples of Zambia according to their way of life in the nineteenth century:

1. Matrilineal (tracing descent mainly through women); cattle-keepers.
   South: ILA, TONGA
2. Matrilineal; not cattle-keepers.
   East: CHEWA, NSENGA
   North-east: BEMBA, BISA, USHI, TABWA
   Central: LALA, LAMBA
   North-west: KAONDE, S. LUNDA, LUVALE
3. Patrilineal (tracing descent through men); cattle-keepers.
   North-east: MAMBWE, IWA, NAMWANGA
   East: NGONI
4. No special emphasis on any one line of descent; cattle-keepers.
   West: LOZI

The history of these peoples before the nineteenth century is mainly to be studied through their own oral traditions and through archaeology. Excavations over the past fifteen years have shown that iron-working and agriculture were practised in Zambia by about A.D. 100. They have also produced evidence of mining and trading in and around southern Zambia by about A.D. 900. But, so far at least, there is little sign of direct contacts with the east coast; from the fifteenth to the seventeenth centuries, the big attraction in central Africa for foreign traders, such as the Arabs and Portuguese, was the kingdom of Mwene Mutapa, south of the Zambezi.

Oral traditions in Zambia cover a rather later period; the fullest do not seem to go back earlier than the seventeenth century. Some peoples, indeed, remember very little of their past history. One such tribe is the Tonga, in the south, though there is archaeological evidence which suggests that the ancestors of the Tonga had settled in their present country by about A.D. 1100. The peoples of the far north-east trace their origins to East Africa, and this is supported by the general similarity of their cultures to peoples in south-western Tanzania. But the traditions of their chiefs, and of most chiefs in Zambia, point to origins in Congo.

We know that in the sixteenth and seventeenth centuries a number of chieftainships split off from the Lunda state of Mwata Yamvo, in what is now south-western Katanga. Some of these were established in Angola; others were set up in western Zambia, whence they sent tribute to Mwata Yamvo. There was also a dispersal from the Luba states of eastern Katanga; this process is less clear, but it seems to account for most of the chieftainships in northern, eastern and central Zambia. As to the origins of the peoples under these Congolese chieftainships, these are hard to determine because the people tend to relate the history of their chiefs and forget their own, which may be rather different. But it is clear that these peoples are, like their chiefs, culturally similar to societies in the southern Congo. We may suppose that over a period of several hundred years until the eighteenth century, Zambia was settled by various groups of migrants from the southern Congo, some of which established chieftainships. The resulting patterns of cultural differences and similarities, and of political organization, led to groups identifying themselves as 'tribes'.

The political organization of Zambia's tribes varied greatly. Some indeed had no chiefs at all, like the Tonga in the far south, who lay beyond the main area of settlement and influence from the Congo. 'Congolese' chieftainships themselves varied greatly in scale and importance. Some chiefs were respected primarily as leaders in ritual, and had little real political or military power. In some tribes, the chiefs belonged to different clans, and even where they belonged to the same one, as among the Bisa, they were often independent of one another. At the beginning of the nineteenth century there were only three large-scale political units in Zambia, and they were located in three types of geographical environment. There was the Bemba system of chieftainships, on the broad plateau in the north-east between the Luapula and Luangwa valleys. There was the Lunda kingdom of Kazembe, in the Luapula valley itself. And there was the kingdom of the Lozi, based on a flood plain on the upper Zambezi, in the far west. The histories of these kingdoms provide the main threads for studying Zambian history in the eighteenth and nineteenth centuries.

THE BEMBA

In the late eighteenth century, the Bemba political system consisted of a number of territorial chieftainships held by different

lineages of a single royal clan. The exception was the paramountcy, whose holder was called Chitimukulu. This had its own
territory, in the heart of Bemba country, but all the main royal
lineages competed for succession to the paramountcy. In the early
nineteenth century, however, one royal lineage managed to retain
the paramountcy and extended its power by creating new chieftainships for its own members. This process was furthered by
numerous conquests throughout the century; in this way, by contributing to the power of the lineage which held the paramountcy,
Bemba expansion led also to a greater measure of centralization
than their neighbours achieved.

In the first part of the nineteenth century, at least, this expansion was perhaps due mainly to two factors. The Bemba had a
tradition of raiding their neighbours, for the plateau itself yielded
few natural resources and tsetse fly prevented cattle-breeding.
But the central position of the Bemba on the plateau was in fact
an economic and strategic advantage. They had easy access to
the varied resources of surrounding areas: in the north-west
among the Tabwa to ivory and salt; in the north among the
Lungu and Mambwe to locally made cloth and ironwork, and
also cattle; in the east and south-east to ivory; in the south and
south-west among the Bisa to salt and fish. And the Bemba had
plenty of room to expand while other tribes were driven back into
areas such as the swamps of Lake Bangweulu, the Luangwa
valley, or the hills to the north, where it was hard to organize
effective resistance.

THE LUNDA OF KAZEMBE

The Bemba make an interesting contrast with the kingdom of
Kazembe. Bemba chiefs were culturally similar to their people,
even those who belonged to conquered tribes. In any case, the
large unbroken area of the plateau encouraged a continual movement of people, as they moved from one village to another or set
up new ones. The Bemba intermarried with those they conquered
and together with the constant mingling over the plateau this
meant that the Bemba gradually assimilated people without distinction into their own culture and political system. The Lunda,
on the other hand, formed a conquest state with clear divisions
between rulers and ruled. Kazembe (the hereditary title of the
Lunda king) had been the leader of a planned migration from
the Lunda state of Mwata Yamvo, in the early eighteenth century.

He and his Lunda companions subdued the peoples of the lower Luapula valley and formed a governing class. The Lunda adopted their subjects' language, a form of Bemba, but otherwise remained culturally and socially distinct; for example they remained patrilineal, though their subjects are all matrilineal. Over the years, other people came to the Luapula, attracted by its strong government and by its prosperity. The Lunda had introduced cassava from the west and this, together with the fish of the river, supported a fairly dense population within the enclosed area of the valley. Thus a good deal of importance was attached to claims to occupy parts of the valley; there was a strong sense of group loyalty, and people remained conscious of their own clan or tribe as against the dominant Lunda.

Kazembe maintained contact with Mwata Yamvo; he not only sent tribute but traded through him with the Portuguese in Angola, and in this way obtained a few guns. By 1800 Kazembe had extended this trans-African trade route so that it linked up with Portuguese and Arabs on the east coast. Kazembe gained control of copper mines in Katanga; he also subdued several Bisa chiefs to the east, and he employed Bisa as agents for exporting copper and ivory. The Bisa dealt mostly with the Yao, around the south end of Lake Malawi, and they brought back Indian cloth and other manufactures, including beads (which along with cowrie shells were used as currency in the interior).

THE LOZI

The kingdom of the Lozi, which is known as Barotseland, resembled that of Kazembe in certain important respects. It had a special economic base; its fertile plain, about a hundred miles long, is flooded every year by the Zambezi River. It was also a multi-tribal kingdom, in that there was a clear distinction between the 'true Lozi', who occupied the flood plain and the various peoples who lived in the surrounding woodland. On the other hand, the 'true Lozi' were not an exclusive governing class, and there was a gradual assimilation of all subjects of the Lozi king (the Litunga) into a larger Lozi culture.

The Lozi kingdom was founded in the late seventeenth century, by a group which probably came from Lunda country to the north, though this is still vague. The new dynasty introduced for the first time the intensive cultivation of the flood plain, from villages on mounds above the plain. By about 1800 various peoples to the west had been brought under Lozi rule; others to the east and south were laid under tribute, part of which took the form of labour on public works, such as fish-dams, on the flood plain. There was a considerable exchange of local produce between plain and woodland: fish, grain and basketwork for iron-work, woodwork and barkcloth. This made Barotseland fairly self-sufficient. The Lozi were great cattle raiders and, especially among the Ila and Tonga, they also raided for slaves; but they had no wish to sell them when they could be usefully employed in communal labour at home.

The political organization of the Lozi took an unusual form. It reflected the contrast in Barotseland between flood plain and woodland, and the economic interdependence of these two areas. In order to integrate the whole Lozi people, no matter where or how they lived, the government used as units of administration not territorial areas but groupings which brought peoples from different parts of the country under common leadership. One type of grouping, the sector, was for purposes of administration and justice; the other type, the storehouse, organized the collection of tribute and recruitment for communal labour. A system of councils, convened periodically and varying in membership, gave Lozi from all parts some say in the affairs of the kingdom. More-over kinship was a relatively unimportant factor in political and social organization. The kingship, indeed, was hereditary (patri-lineal). But, as at Kazembe's court, princes were excluded from political office. There was no dominant clan and the 'true Lozi' at least had no clans at all, but distinguished themselves by their attachment to historic villages on the flood plain. Thus in some respects the Lozi kingdom was more highly developed than many in Africa and its complexity and efficiency later impressed many Europeans.

These three kingdoms of the Bemba, the Lunda and the Lozi, provide the main threads for the history of Zambia in the nineteenth century. This is partly because we know more about them than about other peoples and chiefdoms, and because through their large size, they were best able to respond to new contacts and influences. All the same they were all relatively fragile. At the key central point—the kingship—they were all based, like the smaller and less successful chiefdoms, on kinship, and they were all prone to being weakened by dynastic rivalry and succession disputes.

Such internal tensions played a large part in shaping their reactions to the new pressures of the nineteenth century, and above all, to the intrusion of Europeans bent on occupying and ruling Zambia.

THE PORTUGUESE

The first Europeans to take an interest in the country north of the Zambezi were Portuguese. In 1714 the governor of Mozambique had set up an outpost at Zumbo, where the Luangwa River joins the Zambezi. Both at Zumbo and at Tete, lower down the Zambezi, there was occasional contact with Bisa traders, but the Portguese were interested in gold and slaves, and by the 1790's the Bisa took their ivory mostly to the Yao farther north. Then Portugal began to think about linking up her African territories. The British took Cape Town from the Dutch in 1795 and it seemed unwise to neglect the interior indefinitely. So in 1798 an expedition was sent up from Mozambique to visit Kazembe, of whom the Bisa had made reports. Its aim was to open up trade with Kazembe and to tap his trade route westward to Mwata Yamvo and Angola. The leader was a gifted Brazilian, de Lacerda, but he died soon after reaching Kazembe's. In any case, Kazembe saw no advantage in letting these white men gain a share in his trade, their arrogant behaviour did not commend them to him; and so they had to return without achieving either of their objects. More news of Kazembe reached the Portuguese from some half-Portuguese traders (*pombeiros*) who set out from Angola in 1806 and reached Mozambique after being held by Kazembe for four years. In 1827 a half-hearted attempt was made to establish a Portuguese colony half-way up the Luangwa valley, on the route to Kazembe's; but this came to nothing. In 1831 a second expedition was sent to Kazembe's from Mozambique but, like Lacerda's, it was really more concerned with the prospects for linking Angola and Mozambique than with developing a mutually profitable trade with Kazembe. Again, the Portuguese had nothing of value to offer Kazembe beyond the usual presents and he doubtless suspected their political motives. Unlike the Arabs a few years later the Portuguese, who were army officers, had no knack of making themselves at home in the African interior. Again, they had to withdraw and their hostile account of Kazembe, together with the appalling hardships they suffered on the journey, discouraged any further ventures of this kind.

The only real gain from the expedition was the journal of the second-in-command, Antonio Gamitto; this has some detailed descriptions of the country and peoples along the route and is a most important source for the history of north-eastern Zambia in the early nineteenth century.

AFRICAN INVASIONS FROM THE SOUTH: THE NGONI AND KOLOLO

Far more important for the future was the impact on Zambia of the *mfecane*, the series of migrations set in motion by Shaka's Zulu empire in South Africa. Zulu raids and conquests forced some peoples to move further and further away in search of security, while the empire itself was torn by dissension and some groups broke away from it. One such group, the Ngoni, took their herds of cattle far away to the north. They crossed the Zambezi in 1835 and finally settled in Ufipa, at the south end of Lake Tanganyika. About 1845 their leader, Zwangendaba, died and there was a general dispersal of Ngoni groups in different directions. Some went south-east and settled in what is now Malawi. Others roamed the plateau of north-eastern Zambia for a time. The Bemba, however, prevented their settling down there and around 1870 Mpeseni, the most important of these wanderers, settled among the Cewa people in eastern Zambia. Here there was a long-established chieftainship, Mkanda, derived from an early stage in the migrations from the Congo. But Mkanda's state seems to have been loosely organized and it offered no real resistance to the Ngoni warriors, whose Zulu military discipline made them far more effective fighters than almost any other people in Zambia. The Ngoni adopted the local language, Nyanja, but they profoundly disturbed the earlier political organization, about which we now know little. The Ngoni retained their accustomed way oi life. They raided for cattle to increase their herds and for captives to increase their armies. They had little use for trade. Like the Lozi, they put prisoners to work rather than sell them to slave-traders, while their assegais were deadlier weapons than any for sale on the plateau until the end of the century.

Another group of South African warrior herdsmen, the Ndebele, established themselves around 1840 at Bulawayo, now in Rhodesia. From here they raided across the Zambezi, among the chiefless Tonga. They did not settle north of the Zambezi but they forced another group from the south, the Kololo, to move farther up the

Zambezi. Here, around 1840, the Kololo leader Sebitwane found the Lozi kingdom split by a succession war and his warriors soon overran it. The contrast between the Lozi and their conquerors could hardly have been more extreme. A people with one of the most complex and intensive systems of agriculture in Africa had been overrun by a small group of nomad warriors whose wanderings had turned them into herdsmen rather than cultivators. The impact of the Kololo, unlike that of the Ndebele farther south, was by no means destructive. They imposed their language with amazing speed upon the various dialect-groups of Barotseland, and this was an important unifying influence. Kololo kingship was far more popular in style than that of the Lozi; the Kololo king remained essentially a war-captain, freely accessible to his fellow-warriors, whereas the Lozi kings, like the Kazembes or Chitimukulus, were hedged about by rituals and taboos and were kept somewhat secluded from the people. There is no doubt that the Kololo kings were well liked by most of their Lozi subjects. But the Kololo never came to terms with the very special circumstances of Barotseland. The Kololo kings made their capitals well to the south of the central plain, among marshes secure from Ndebele raiders. It is not yet clear how far the complex economy and administration of Barotseland was disrupted by the Kololo conquest. There was no destruction of the mounds and canals of the flood plain, which continued to be cultivated by a number of Lozi. But the Kololo political system was very different from that of the Lozi. Men of the same age grade as the king were made territorial governors. For a time, this served to bring tribute into the court, but it was hardly a basis for operating the economy of the flood plain. The Kololo's most serious handicap, however, was their lack of immunity to malaria, which was rife in Barotseland, especially in the central plain. This more than anything else undermined their ability to resist the Lozi when the latter rose against their conquerors.

Various Lozi princes had fled from the Kololo and taken refuge to the north. One of these, Sepopa, raised a Lozi army which defeated the Kololo in 1864. The Lozi killed as many Kololo men as they could, and married their women. But, though Lozi institutions were revived, the problem of royal succession continued to be a source of weakness. Sepopa was overthrown in 1876, and in 1878 Lewanika succeeded but had great difficulty in retaining his position. He partly compensated for this by extending raids farther afield. But Lewanika was himself troubled by Ndebele raids, and his general sense of insecurity was an important factor in shaping his attitude to European visitors.

TRADERS FROM ANGOLA AND MOZAMBIQUE: 'MAMBARI' AND 'CHIKUNDA'

The Portuguese government had failed in its attempts to make a link between its main African colonies. Nonetheless, individual Portuguese, African and coloured traders pushed inland from both Angola and Mozambique during the nineteenth century. Their expeditions in search of slaves and ivory were an important influence among the peoples of southern and western Zambia, just as those of the Arabs and Swahili were in the north-east. By 1797 at least the Luvale, on the present Zambia-Angola border, were in touch with the important kingdom of Cassanje in Angola; and by the 1840's the Luvale were busy exchanging slaves for guns from the Mbundu of Bihe. The Lozi, as we have seen, had no use for the slave-trade and in the early nineteenth century they turned away a party of slave traders from Angola. In 1835, however, the scope of the Angolan trade was greatly extended by the abolition of the Portuguese royal monopoly of ivory. Trade with the west had been one reason why the Kololo leader Sebitwane had settled on the upper Zambezi. In 1848, just after the Kololo conquest of Barotseland, Silva Porto, a Portuguese trader from Bihe, reached the headwaters of the Zambezi. He finally got to Barotseland in 1853, and some of his agents continued eastwards to Mozambique. Over the next twenty years or so, traders from Angola, loosely called 'Mambari', continued to visit Barotseland, selling guns and cloth for ivory and, from the Kololo at least, a few slaves.

Meanwhile, the slave-trade flourished to the north, where Mbundu caravans pushed on east of the Luvale, to trade with chiefs of the Ndembu and southern Lunda, with the Kaonde and with the Lamba. The Ndembu gained little from the trade, for they raided each other and were themselves raided by the Luvale. In the later nineteenth century, competition for slaves in this area was intense, for the growing European demand for cocoa led to the Mbundu supplying slaves for the cocoa plantations on Sao Thomé island. The more skilful chiefs, however, were able to turn the trade to their advantage, especially after the decline of Mwata Yamvo in the 1880's. Chiefs such as Kasempa of the Kaonde threw off Lunda overlordship with the aid of guns from Bihe and even challenged the Lozi king.

Among the Lamba, by 1850, the Mbundu traders met up with Bisa ivory traders, whose old route from Kazembe's to the east had been disrupted around 1830 by Bemba expansion. Bisa traders had never been controlled by their own chiefs and they seem for a time to have moved their trade route farther south. In the 1850's and 1860's, traders from Kazembe's continued to take copper and ivory round the south end of Lake Malawi. The Bisa also engaged in trade on the middle Zambezi, buying ivory from the local people and selling English cotton goods obtained from the Portuguese in Mozambique. But by 1870 or so, Bisa trade seems to have gone into a sharp decline, as a result of Ngoni raids and the development of Swahili and Arab trade in the far north. Kazembe's trade to the south-east ceased; instead, parties from Mozambique had begun once more to revisit the middle Zambezi, partly to get ivory, but also to obtain slaves for the Portuguese estates on the lower Zambezi. In 1861 the Portuguese reoccupied Zumbo, after some Portuguese traders had killed the Lala chief Mbuluma, not far to the north, at the invitation of a rival claimant. Until the end of the century, the lower Luangwa valley was a favourite hunting-ground of slavers known as 'Chikunda', many of whom, like the Mambari, were part African and part Portguese.

THE TRADERS FROM THE NORTH:
NYAMWEZI, ARABS, SWAHILI

Since the early migrations southwards from east Africa, there had been little contact between what are now Zambia and Tanzania. But in the nineteenth century Zambia was drawn into the trading systems of the Nyamwezi, from western Tanzania, and of traders from Zanzibar and the coast. By the 1830's, Nyamwezi traders were skirting Lake Tanganyika in order to obtain copper from the mines of Katanga. In about 1855 one Nyamwezi caravan came to Kazembe's and was allowed by him to continue to the west. The Yeke, as these Nyamwezi came to be called, settled in Katanga and replaced a local chief. Msiri, the caravan leader, made contacts with the Portuguese to the west; he obtained guns and he built up a formidable 'empire' based on trade and raiding. This cut into Kazembe's trade with Mwata Yamvo, and Msiri also levied tribute from people formerly subject to Kazembe. Yeke traders were active among the Bemba, selling copper in exchange for ivory, and a few even settled down as resident craftsmen at the capitals of Bemba chiefs.

The Nyamwezi created a new focus in the heart of Africa for long-distance trade. Meanwhile, a new trade route from Katanga and Kazembe's to the east coast was opened up by the caravans of Arabs and Swahili-speaking Africans. Swahili seem to have visited Kazembe by 1830, and there were certainly Arabs in his kingdom by about 1840. At this stage, their expeditions were relatively weak. One was beaten up by the Tabwa chief Nsama, north-east of Kazembe. In 1853 one Arab trader went through Katanga to Barotseland, but the rising power of Msiri prevented the Arabs from developing regular trade so far west. However, the Bemba chiefs gave the Arabs a ready welcome, and in the 1860's provided them with large quantities of ivory in exchange for cloth, beads and shells. Thus the Arabs found it worthwhile to establish settlements in the area; not in Bemba country itself, for the Bemba were strong enough to keep them out, but among the Lungu at the south end of Lake Tanganyika. In 1867 these settlements combined under the leading Arab trader, Tippu Tip, to defeat the Tabwa. Tippu Tip himself went on to carve out a rich new market for himself in the eastern Congo, but other Arabs settled among the Tabwa, while there were others farther west, at the north end of Lake Mweru.

Thus Kazembe found himself largely encircled, by Arab traders in the north and east, and by Yeke in the west and south. As a result, it became difficult for him to enforce his monopoly of ivory or to dictate the terms of trade. But the impact of the Arabs was political as well as economic. In 1872 a Lunda prince who sought to displace the then Kazembe went to the Arabs for help and thereby fought his way into the kingship. This was, in effect, a revolution. Hitherto Lunda princes had been closely guarded at the capital and denied political office, and this was the first time that a disappointed rival had been able to seize power. The Kazembes had never been popular rulers, and increasing setbacks seem to have made them harsh and oppressive towards their subjects. Now, in the late nineteenth century, the kingdom was also weakened by splits within the Lunda minority as rival groups sought Arab or Yeke support and ralled behind different candidates for the throne.

Thus Kazembe's kingdom, once the chief power in north-eastern Zambia, suffered gravely from the new trade to the north which, unlike the earlier trade to the south-east, lay largely outside his control. By comparison, the Bemba did very well. For all their guns, the Arabs needed local allies, and the Bemba chiefs were strong enough to be effective partners in the business of hunting and collecting ivory, and raiding other tribes for slaves to carry it to the coast. Trade with the Arabs increased the wealth of Bemba chiefs and thus their ability to attract support for new raids and conquests. In the 1870's and 1880's the Bemba took over much new territory to the south and west. The new chieftainships were assigned to junior relatives of the paramount, Chitimukulu. For the time being, Bemba country was knit closer together, while Kazembe's kingdom fell victim to internal disputes.

THE CULTURAL IMPACT OF THE AFRICAN INTRUDERS

In many ways the Ngoni, Swahili, Mbundu and Yeke intruders had an unsettling and destructive impact on the peoples of Zambia. Yet while they undoubtedly brought about an increase in warfare and devastation, they also extended the range of cultural contacts. Guns and cloth, as stimulants to raids and conquests, may have been mixed blessings, but the introduction of new food crops was clear gain for peoples living close to the margin of subsistence. Until the nineteenth century, the only food crops known to most peoples in Zambia were varieties of millet, supplemented by pulses and cucurbits. The new contacts with the west spread the use of cassava, which had been introduced to Angola from South America by the Portuguese. Cassava, a root crop, was especially valuable since it could be left in the ground to alleviate the annual shortage before the harvest of grain crops. The Lunda had already taken cassava to the Luapula; it then spread slowly eastwards among the Bisa. Yeke traders brought it to the Bemba; they also introduced sweet potatoes. By 1850 the Lamba, farther south, had acquired cassava from Bihe traders. Another American crop, maize, also reached Zambia through contacts with Portuguese Africa. Maize was grown north of Lake Bangweulu by 1810 and among the Bemba by 1830; it had probably been transmitted from the Katanga region, but it was also spread by the Ngoni, who had adopted it in the 1830's from the Portuguese on the lower Zambezi.

These innovations were the most important cultural changes

affecting Zambia as a whole in the nineteenth century. Language, for example, was much less affected; the Lozi adoption of Kololo was not paralleled elsewhere, though a few Swahili and Portuguese words came into common usage. Religion was hardly affected before the arrival of the Christian missionaries; Islam made very little impact on Zambia, for the Muslim visitors were traders who had no special ambition to impose their religion, although they might well have done so had they set up states of their own. In certain other respects, however, the intruders' influence was important, if only indirectly. By provoking the movement of peoples and the growth of larger political units, they served to bring Zambian peoples into closer contact with each other. As a result, there was a growing exchange in artistic and ceremonial practices: in music and dancing, for example, and among more utilitarian techniques Bemba immigrants introduced to the Luapula the craft of building huts in mud rather than reeds.

MISSIONARIES

Much of our knowledge of all these new African contacts and pressures on Zambia comes from the writings of David Livingstone, whose travels north of the Zambezi led to the arrival of European Christian missions. Livingstone himself had worked as a pioneer missionary in South Africa. His real ambition, however, was not so much to make conversions himself as to 'open up' central Africa for conversion by others. In 1850 Europe knew little more about central Africa than it had in 1550. The Portuguese had produced some interesting reports, but the basic geographical facts, such as the great lakes and river systems of the interior, were still obscure. Livingstone felt that his first task was to make maps and describe the peoples and countries. Only then would it be possible to make plans for effective missionary work, or to develop new forms of trade which could replace that in slaves.

In 1851, while based in Bechuanaland, Livingstone visited Barotseland. In 1853 he returned and this time he continued his journey to the headwaters of the Zambezi and so through Angola to Luanda, on the Atlantic coast. He then decided to cross Africa. He came back to Barotseland and went on down the Zambezi valley to Mozambique, whence he proceeded to London. His explorations caused a sensation and he raised funds for another expedition. This lasted from 1858 to 1863 and was intended to establish a mission on Lake Malawi. The enterprise was undermined by bad luck, bad judgement and by quarrels among the various Europeans; it ended in failure although important survey work was done. In 1866 Livingstone returned alone to central Africa. He came up the Rovuma from the east coast and travelled through Bemba and Tabwa country to Kazembe's and Lake Bangweulu. From 1869 to 1871 he was in the eastern Congo; in 1871 he met Stanley at Ujiji, on Lake Tanganyika. He then went south, recrossing the route of his outward journey. But he had been far too long without proper medical care. His travel in the swamps around Lake Bangweulu proved too much for him and he died in Lala country early in 1873.

Livingstone had been driven on by an urge to find the sources of the Nile for, like several others, he was not convinced that Lake Victoria really was the main source. But in the course of his vain search he had greatly extended Europe's knowledge of the upper Congo basin. He had also exposed the damage done by the trade in slaves and ivory as Arabs and Africans carried their search for them into the heart of Africa. In a way, European horror at the slave trade was hypocritical, or at least naïve. Europe, with its need for piano keys and billiard balls, was by the later nineteenth century the world's chief buyer of African ivory. In east Africa, as in the southern Sudan, the trade in ivory fostered that in slaves. We have already seen that the European taste for cocoa helped to encourage the slave-trade in western Zambia. But whoever was to blame for the slave-trade, it obviously could not continue unchecked if Europeans, or indeed anyone else, were to do business in central Africa. It presented a direct moral challenge to Christians. Inspired by Livingstone's example, missionaries from England and Scotland set out for Zambia within a few years of his death.

There is a deep irony about the missionary penetration of central Africa; not only was it provoked by the slave-trade, but it was largely made possible by the slave-traders. Missionaries used their trade routes and depended on their good will and even protection. The slave-traders, for their part, saw no threat in these lightly armed eccentrics as long as they kept to their mission work. It was partly on this sort of basis that members of the London Missionary Society (LMS) came inland across Tanganyika and established themselves among the Lungu at the south end of the Lake in the 1880's. There was an especially curious development on Lake Malawi where a Scottish mission began work in 1875.

In 1883 it had an out-station close to Bemba country and a trading company was formed to supply this and other missions in the area. In 1884 the company opened a station at Karonga, at the north end of the Lake and the Arabs to the west were quick to take advantage of this. Much of the ivory they obtained from the Bemba was now exported to the south-east on the company's steamship.

The missionaries hoped indeed that there, as elsewhere in Africa, Europeans could develop local industries and 'legitimate' trade which would displace that in slaves. But their resources were limited and even in their main task of spreading the Gospel the missionaries between Lakes Malawi and Tanganyika were able to make little headway. They had settled among people who were harassed by slave-raiders, especially by the Bemba. For this reason they were welcomed as protectors and their stockaded stations became centres of refuge. In a sense, indeed, the missionaries formed governments of their own. This was less a help than a hindrance; they were seen more as chiefs than as men of religion and, in any case, they could not hope to achieve any widespread influence until they left their stockades and penetrated Bemba country. In the end it was the Catholic White Fathers, having opened a station among the Mambwe in 1891, who first gained a firm foothold in Bembaland, and by that time British officials were ready to take over the area.

The other main area of early missionary activity in Zambia was Barotseland. Here the story was different, though again there were important connections between missions, trade and local politics. Encouraged by Livingstone, the London Missionary Society sent out a party to Barotseland by way of the Cape in 1860. This first attempt ended disastrously; the missionaries reached the court of Sekeletu, the Kololo king, but all but one died of malaria. In any case, Sekeletu was not much interested in visitors from the south since he had begun to do business with traders from Angola. During the next few years a few European hunters from South Africa reached the Zambezi, but Barotseland continued to look west, even after the Kololo were overthrown in 1864.

In 1871, however, a white hunter and trader, George Westbeech, reached Barotseland. The Lozi found his guns superior to those traded by the Mambari. He used ox-wagons, not slaves, to carry away his ivory and, compared with other traders in central Africa, he was unusually honest. Westbeech was allowed to do business from a permanent camp at Pandamatenka, a little way south of the Victoria Falls. He became a respected adviser to the Lozi court, which now began to take more interest in contacts to the south. In 1878 Lewanika, who had just gained the Lozi throne after a bitter struggle, was visited by Coillard, a French missionary with a British wife who had worked in Basutoland and spoke Sotho, which was very similar to the Kololo language spoken by the Lozi.

Lewanika encouraged Coillard to return. Meanwhile, in 1881, some Jesuit missionaries visited Lewanika. They had however annoyed him by trying, in 1879, to set up a mission among the Ila; this had been cut short by disease but in any case Lewanika regarded the Ila as his subjects and resented any intrusion which ignored him. So the Jesuits were sent away. But in 1882 another missionary, Arnot, came up from the Cape, and with Westbeech's help gained Lewanika's favour. Arnot encouraged him to ally not with the Ndebele but with Khama, the leading chief in Bechuanaland, who by this time was a keen Protestant Christian.

Arnot left in 1884, but at the end of the year Coillard returned. A civil war was in progress; Lewanika regained his throne but only with the aid of some Angolan traders. Meanwhile, however, his ally Khama had come under British protection. For Khama this meant security from the Boers of South Africa and from the Ndebele. Lewanika was well aware that the quickening advance of Europeans from South Africa could not be ignored; some alliance with white men, either those in the south or those in the west, was essential to his survival. He decided to follow Khama's example and in 1886 allowed Coillard to found a mission station. Lewanika realized that this would mean a valuable new kind of education for his people, or at least for his sons and those of other Lozi chiefs. If he could keep this education under his control, it could greatly strengthen his own position as ruler, which was still by no means secure.

THE BRITISH SOUTH AFRICA COMPANY

Through their accounts of their travels, Livingstone and other missionaries made Zambia known to the world at large. Yet despite the interest of British missions in the area, the British Government had no ambitions there. Zambia came under British rule as a result of the initiative of one man, the South African millionaire Cecil Rhodes. By 1880 Rhodes had made a fortune on the diamond mines at Kimberley. He was eager to test rumours of rich gold deposits in what is now Rhodesia; those on the Rand had not yet been properly exploited. But his motive for amassing wealth was mainly political; Rhodes wanted to ensure British supremacy in South Africa and in Africa as a whole. This meant extending British power northwards from the Cape and either outflanking or defeating three main obstacles: the Boer republics of the Transvaal and Orange Free State, the Ndebele and the Portuguese who in the 1880's were once more attempting to link up Angola and Mozambique. In pursuit of his ends, Rhodes went into politics and in 1889 induced Britain to grant a royal charter to his newly formed British South Africa Company. This gave the Company powers of government. It meant that Rhodes could use his personal fortune to extend the British Empire in Africa, even though the British Government could not find the money to do so itself. Rhodes had already, in 1888, made agreements with the Ndebele. He now had to establish himself north of the Zambezi and his first goal there was Barotseland.

Barotseland. Encouraged more by Khama's example than by Coillard, Lewanika was eager to seek British protection. He was opposed by a group of Lozi chiefs who guarded the south-eastern approaches to Barotseland and feared that any alliance between Lewanika and the Europeans would be used against them. There was also the fact that Rhodes' Company was not, of course, the British Government and had no real obligations to anyone except its shareholders. However, Rhodes' representative, Lochner, who arrived in 1890, placated the hostile chiefs with large presents and made out that he was really an ambassador from Queen Victoria. So Lewanika signed a concession which gave the Company mining rights throughout Barotseland, while the Company promised to defend Lewanika from outside attacks, to pay him £2,000 per year, to develop trade and to build schools and telegraphs. Almost at once, Lewanika had doubts about the concession, and they were reinforced by George Middleton, a trader who had originally come out with Coillard. On Lewanika's behalf, Middleton wrote a letter to the British Government repudiating the concession, and Coillard later wrote asking Queen Victoria to extend her direct protection over Lewanika. But the British Government took little notice, and it recognized the Company's 'protectorate' over Barotseland in 1891.

Frontiers. Lochner's concession was based on a false estimate of the size of Barotseland; it made out that this covered most of what is now north-west Zambia. Vagueness about its borders led to dispute between Britain and Portugal; the two countries made a boundary agreement in 1891, which limited Portuguese advance north of the Zambezi, but the western border remained unclear and had to be redefined by arbitration in 1905. It still remained to define the Company's claims to the north, while Rhodes was also anxious to prevent the copper of Katanga from going to the Congo Free State of the Belgian king Leopold II. In 1889 Harry Johnston, the British consul in Mozambique, made a series of treaties on Rhodes' behalf between Lake Malawi and Lake Tanganyika. These served to define a border with the Germans in East Africa. In 1890, Johnston sent Alfred Sharpe round by this route to Katanga. On the way, Sharpe signed a treaty promising British protection to Kazembe, but he had no success at Msiri's. Rhodes himself sent Joseph Thomson, the explorer of East Africa, to reach Msiri, but Thomson only got as far as Lamba country. Instead, in 1891, two expeditions working for King Leopold penetrated the so-called 'Katanga pedicle', the second one after killing Msiri. Leopold's claims to this pedicle, which almost cuts Zambia in half, were upheld by a treaty between Britain and Belgium in 1894; this confirmed an informal agreement of 1890 that the border of the Congo Free State with the British sphere north of the Zambezi should run along the Congo-Zambezi watershed up to the exit of the Luapula from Lake Bangweulu and then along the Luapula to Lake Mweru.

THE NORTH-EAST, THE BEMBA AND KAZEMBE

By these means, the Company gained recognition from other European powers of its right to occupy a specified area north of the Zambezi. But it was another matter to gain recognition from Africans, or from Arab and Swahili traders. Lewanika had repudiated the Lochner concession, and apart from Sharpe's treaty with Kazembe there was no other agreement with any other important chief. European powers expected each other to make good their claims in Africa by 'effective occupation'; but the Company paid no further attention to Barotseland until 1896 as it had its hands full in southern Rhodesia. As for its 'sphere' in the north-east, the Company handed over responsibility for this in 1891 to the newly declared British Central Africa Protectorate, which was later called Nyasaland. Harry Johnston, the Commissioner, was preoccupied with a long struggle against the Arab slave-traders on Lake Malawi and in the south on the River Shire. His agents established a few stations for the Company in the far north near Lake Mweru, but they were virtually power-less. In 1894 Belgian forces defeated two important Swahili traders north-east of Lake Mweru, but the British were unable to prevent other traders from importing guns and ammunition. They did launch one armed expedition in 1895. This was against Kazembe, who was supposed by treaty to receive the Company's aid and protection, but he repelled it. In this situation, despite pleas from anxious missionaries, there was no question of the British taking on the Bemba, who continued to raid around the edges of the north-eastern plateau.

In 1895, however, the Company took over the north-east from the British Central Africa Protectorate. In December, Johnston removed a major Arab threat when he defeated Mlozi at Karonga; and in 1896 Company officials, from stations between Lakes Malawi and Tanganyika, began to intercept Swahili caravans as they left Bemba country. A ring was thus gradually being drawn around Bemba country. By this time it seemed possible to avoid the head-on collision with the Bemba which had once seemed inevitable. The Bemba, though still the terror of their neighbours, were deeply divided among themselves. This was due partly to their political system, which was largely based on the uncertain ties of kinship, and partly to their trade with the Arabs and Swahili. The paramount, Chitimukulu, had no trading monopoly, and the outlying chiefs had a greater interest in remaining in close touch with the traders than in promotion to the senior chieftain-ships in the middle of Bemba country. Moreover, the second most senior chief, Mwamba, had built up a wide area of influence in the west which rivalled that of Chitimukulu. The two chieftain-ships came into conflict during the reign of Chitimukulu Sampa from 1883 to 1896. Sampa indeed had little of the support from other chiefs which his predecessor had enjoyed. He did business with the Arabs to the east, and he probably realized that this was threatened by the Europeans. But his attempts to keep Europeans out of Bemba country failed. He quarrelled with Makasa, a chief on his northern border, and Makasa decided to strengthen himself by admitting the White Fathers, who had a mission among the neighbouring Mambwe.

Sampa died in 1896. His successor as Chitimukulu was a feeble old man, and the real power was Mwamba. Mwamba was anxious to avoid committing himself irrevocably to dependence on Europeans, let alone subjection to them; equally, he could not risk provoking a European alliance with any lesser chief. So early in 1897 he received Robert Young, a Company official, but did not take him seriously as he brought no presents. However, in September 1897 Young dispersed an Arab stronghold on the upper Luangwa and chased away a minor Bemba chief who had supported them. This much impressed Mwamba. In 1898 he fell ill and, hoping for medical aid and perhaps also for mediation with the Company, he summoned Bishop Dupont of the White Fathers, who had visited Mwamba the previous year. Dupont, like Young, had gained a local reputation through several acts of skill and bravado, and when Mwamba died in October Dupont was able to take control of his village and prevent the rioting which usually followed a chief's death. Dupont claimed that Mwamba had actually left him his country, but whatever the truth in this Dupont had no chance to become a 'white chief' because Young returned to Mwamba's in November and set up a Company post nearby. The only resistance to this rapid occupation of Bembaland came from two border chiefs in the north-west, who were both still involved in the export of slaves and ivory. They were defeated without difficulty in 1898 and 1899.

In 1899 the Company confirmed its control of the north-east by avenging its earlier defeat at Kazembe's. Kazembe seems by this time to have had little support from the Lunda governors; their harsh rule was resented by the various subject tribes and in any case the area under their control was much less than it had been. In the 1880's the Lunda kingdom had been weakened by Yeke attacks; on one occasion, the Yeke had occupied the capital, and Kazembe had only repelled them with the aid of a Bemba force. After Mlozi's defeat in 1895 several Arabs retreated to the Luapula, and Kazembe must have hoped that they would stave off the European advance; but in the event they deserted him and fled south into Lamba country. As for the Swahili in Tabwa country, these had decided by 1895 to co-operate with the British rather than risk defeat and the loss of their still considerable ivory trade. Kazembe had heard of Young's exploits among the Bemba, and was ready to make terms with him; but the Company decided to deal with Kazembe by sending a large force, with a machine gun, against him. Kazembe saw that resistance was useless; but he could not bring himself to surrender, so he fled across the Luapula into what was now the Congo Free State and only gave himself up in 1900. Once the two great powers of the north-east, the Bemba and the Lunda, had submitted, no other Africans in the area were rash enough to challenge the white man's firearms.

THE NGONI

The Company found it rather more difficult to establish control in eastern Zambia. Here the leading power was the Ngoni chief Mpeseni, whose war band had settled among the Cewa by about 1870. Mpeseni's Ngoni formed a small state of its own, organized on the basis of segments within the chiefly family. The state expanded as the segments increased their numbers by recruiting prisoners of war. Such segments were, as earlier Ngoni history showed, likely to break off and become independent, as Mpeseni himself had done. For a period, indeed, the expansion of Mpeseni's Ngoni, like that of the Bemba, had a unifying effect; by giving scope to the ambitions of younger men it relieved tension and rivalry at the centre. In due course, however, as with the Bemba, the various parts of the state developed different interests and the power of the paramount declined. Yet in spite of this the Ngoni reacted very differently from the Bemba to European intrusion. So far from dividing, they united behind their war-leaders and went to war with the Europeans. One reason for this was that the Ngoni, far more than the Bemba, Lunda or Lozi, were a warrior society. The Ngoni political system was in fact a military organization—fighting was thought to be the only proper occupation for men; and they could not see any future for themselves if war was prohibited. The other main reason for the Ngoni war with the Europeans was that the Europeans themselves saw no alternative to fighting. They were determined to take over Ngoniland, which they believed was rich in gold; they also wanted to recruit Ngoni as labourers for Nyasaland. Clearly, neither object could be achieved until the Ngoni war-machine was smashed.

In 1885 Mpeseni allowed a German, Carl Wiese, to trade and hunt in his country and gave him a large mining concession. Wiese, who had a Portuguese-African wife, gained some influence over Mpeseni and hoped to turn it to the advantage of the Portuguese. Mpeseni refused to make treaties with either Thomson or Sharpe in 1890, but the Anglo-Portuguese agreement of 1891 put paid to Wiese's hopes by placing Mpeseni's country within the British sphere. Instead, Wiese spread stories that Mpeseni's country was rich in gold, and he sold his mining concession there to a new London company. This company, which became the North Charterland Company, sent out prospectors in 1896. Mpeseni allowed them to begin work, but he had no intention of ceasing his raids, let alone of submitting to British rule. Mpeseni does not seem to have favoured war with the British but his son Nsingu, who was the Ngoni war-commander, led a large group who were bent on fighting. They soon had their chance. In 1897 reports reached Nyasaland that the Ngoni threatened the lives of Wiese and an official of the British South Africa Company. The Commissioner in Nyasaland gladly gave the Company military support and early in 1898 the British launched a large force against Mpeseni. The Ngoni mobilized a large force, and they might have won had they mounted a night attack. But the Ngoni relied on the tactics with which they had so often broken up lesser tribes, and these were ineffective against artillery and machine guns. Nsingu was captured and shot, Mpeseni surrendered, and the British took over most of the Ngoni's large herds of cattle, which had themselves mostly been taken in battle.

BAROTSELAND AND THE NORTH-WEST

At the same time as the British South Africa Company was gaining control over the Ngoni and Bemba, it was also, at long last, establishing itself in Barotseland. In the early 1890's Lewanika became increasingly alarmed at the advance of Portuguese troops from the west; in 1896 he agreed with a Company representative to confirm the Lochner concession of 1890 provided that his kingdom, as defined in the concession, was greatly extended; for the Company was obliged by the concession to defend the kingdom. In 1897 Robert Coryndon arrived as the Company's Resident in Barotseland, and in 1900 a final treaty was signed; it allowed the Company to exercise limited authority within Barotseland proper, the area under effective Lozi rule, and general administrative powers throughout the rest of north-western Rhodesia as far as the Kafue River. Lewanika's salary, which he had not received at all between 1890 and 1897, was reduced to £850 but it was agreed that the centre of Barotseland would be closed to prospectors.

Lewanika's acceptance of the British presence influenced lesser chiefs in the north-west to follow his example, even the Kaonde chief Kasempa who had defeated a Lozi army in the 1890's. Ila and Tonga country, parts of which had been under Lozi rule, passed under British control; indeed the 1900 agreement allowed the British to make land grants to white settlers in these areas. Part of Luvale country came indirectly under British control, since the Company recognized Lewanika's claims that the Luvale paid him tribute. But this was true only of a minor Luvale chief whom the Lozi had defeated in 1892. The most important Luvale chief, a woman called Nyakatolo, stood aloof, for her power was based on trade with Angola. She strengthened her links with the Portuguese and when the Angola border was settled in 1905 she came under Portuguese rule. The Zambian Luvale never acknowledged Lozi rights over them and in 1941 they were finally allowed to secede from Barotseland.

Recommended Reading

1. *General works on the history of Zambia*
   (All these have lists of books for further reading)
B. M. Fagan (ed.) *A Short History of Zambia* Oxford University Press Nairobi 1966
   This is a collection of essays by different writers; some deal with the archaeology of Zambia and others with the period covered by oral traditions and early European travellers. There are several photographs, maps and diagrams. It is a paperback.
L. H. Gann *A History of Northern Rhodesia: early days to 1953* Chatto and Windus 1964
   This is a large and detailed study. It deals mainly with the colonial period and with the history of European politics, but there is a useful section on nineteenth-century history.
Richard Hall *Zambia* Pall Mall 1965
   This is also valuable mainly for the twentieth century. It adds a good deal to Gann's work because it concentrates on African politics and takes the story up to Independence in 1964. The earlier chapters are also useful, especially for the 1890's.
H. W. Langworthy *Zambia before 1890* Longmans 1972
Andrew Roberts *The Story of Zambia* Fabers, forthcoming

2. *Special studies*
J. A. Barnes *Politics in a changing society: a political history of the Fort Jameson Ngoni* Manchester University Press 1967
   A study by an anthropologist. Chapters 2 and 3 describe the nature of Mpeseni's state and its reaction to European intrusion.
Ian Cunnison *The Luapula Peoples of Northern Rhodesia* Manchester University Press 1959

An anthropological analysis of Kazembe's Kingdom; two chapters deal specially with Lunda history and political structure.

Andrew Roberts 'Pre-colonial Trade in Zambia' *African Social Research* no. 10 (December 1970)

Andrew Roberts *A History of the Bemba: Political growth and Change in north-eastern Zambia before 1900* Longmans 1973

Max Gluckman and E. Colson (eds.) *Seven Tribes of British Africa* Manchester University Press
This includes general anthropological accounts of the Lozi (M. Gluckman), Bemba (A. I. Richards), Tonga (E. Colson) and Ngoni (J. A. Barnes).

R. I. Rotberg *Christian Missionaries and the Creation of Northern Rhodesia 1880–1924* Princeton University Press
This deals all too briefly (in less than 150 small pages) with a large and important subject, but it is still useful.

Andrew Roberts 'The History of the Bemba' in Roland Oliver (ed.) *The Middle Age of African History* Oxford University Press
A short account, based on the author's fieldwork in 1964-65.

Mutumba Mainga Bull *Bulozi under the Luyana Kings: political evolutions and state formation in pre-colonial Zambia* Longmans 1972

3. *Primary sources*
These are extensively listed in the books already mentioned; I give here only four of the most important accounts of travel by visitors to Zambia in the nineteenth century:

A. C. P. Gamitto *King Kazembe* Lisbon 1960
This is a translation (by Ian Cunnison) of the journal kept by the second-in-command of the Portuguese expedition to Kazembe in 1831–2. It has valuable descriptions of the Cewa, Bisa and Lunda.

David Livingstone *Missionary Travels and Researches in South Africa* London 1857
This is the book which made Livingstone famous. It describes his visits to Barotseland in 1851 and 1853, and his journey through Angola and back across Africa to Mozambique.

David Livingstone (ed. by H. Waller) *The last Journals of David Livingstone* London 1874
This describes Livingstone's last journey including his visits to the Bemba and Kazembe in 1867-8, and his return to Zambia just before his death in 1873.

Tippu Tip (Hamed bin Muhammed) *Maisha ya Hamed bin Muhammed yaani Tippu Tip.* Originally published in 1959 as a supplement to the *Journal of the East African Swahili Committee*; it has just been reprinted
This gives the Swahili text, with facing English translation by Prof. W. H. Whiteley, of the autobiography of Tippu Tip, the Arab trader. It describes briefly his visits to Bemba chiefs in the 1860's and his defeat of the Tabwa (also described by Livingstone).

4. *General historical studies of special relevance to Zambia*

B. M. Fagan *Southern Africa* Thames and Hudson 1966
A clear and very well illustrated brief survey of the archaeology and early history of South Africa, Rhodesia and Zambia.

Jan Vansina *Kingdoms of the Savanna* University of Wisconsin Press 1966
  A general survey, based on a thorough study of published sources, of the
  state systems of the Congo, Angola and Zambia.
A. J. Wills *An Introduction to the History of Central Africa* 2nd edition Oxford
  University Press 1967
  A useful and generally reliable outline of the nineteenth- and twentieth-
  century history of Zambia, Malawi and Rhodesia.

5. The nineteenth century in Malawi

JOHN McCRACKEN

THE AGRICULTURAL PEOPLES

At the beginning of the nineteenth century Malawi was essentially a land of Bantu-speaking agriculturalists. Those at the south end of the lake, who stretched in wedge-shaped formation as far as the Luangwa River to the east and the lower Zambezi to the west, were members of the Maravi (or Malawi) group[1] with their traditions of migration from the Luba country of the Congo basin. The Maravi were members at one time of an 'empire' of sorts linked by commercial ties to the east coast ports of Kilwa and Mozambique. By the 1720's they had been squeezed out of the major trade routes by the more dexterous Yao and Bisa. In consequence they were subjected to a process of political fragmentation which led to the emergence of as many as eight separate Maravi groups; the main ones were those of the Manganja and the Nyanja in the Shire valley and highlands, and the Cewa in an arc to the north and west. Within these groupings were independent chiefdoms such as those of Undi, of Mkanda and of Mwase Kasungu among the Cewa, and of Lundu, a leading Manganja chief. Their power, however, was increasingly limited to little more than the exaction of tribute. Gamitto, the Portuguese explorer, who travelled through Undi's territory in 1831, noted the prevalence of small civil wars among Undi's subjects which he seemed incapable of controlling. Thirty years later, Rowley of the pioneer Universities' Mission party could discern few bonds of unity among the Manganja: 'Central authority existed but in name, unity of action was not the result of it, and patriotism did not exist.'[2]

This portrait of political disintegration did not extend to the Maravi's northern neighbours; the Tumbuka and related peoples to the west of the lake, the Tonga in an enclave on the lakeshore itself and the Ngonde in the plain to the north-west and in the hills rising behind it. Both the Tonga and the Tumbuka had

97

originally lacked centralized authorities. In the Nkamanga area, however, a group of non-Arab traders from the east opened up ivory trade contacts with Kilwa in the late eighteenth century and, through the control of this trade and the disposal of presents, succeeded in imposing a patrilineal system of succession on the Tumbuka of that area and in building up a rough federation of clans under a single leader, the Chikuramayembe.

At the same time the Ngonde were also affected, though in a different manner, by contacts with ivory traders who reached them from the east side of the lake. They were related not to the other groups in Malawi but to those patrilineal peoples of western Tanganyika who possessed in common a distinctive form of centralized monarchy, the so-called Ntemi chieftainship. Originally the Kyungu or Ntemi had been a sacred religious figure living like the Lwembe of the culturally similar Nyakyusa northeast of the Songwe River, in strict religious seclusion. But, due to his control of the greater part of ivory in Ngonde country, he was able to exploit his contacts to gain an almost complete monopoly of the trade. He thus emerged as a secular force through a judicious distribution of the cloth paid to him by traders.

Despite the political effects of long-distance trade, its role in the economies of most of the people of Malawi around 1800 was comparatively slight. Cattle were herded in areas free from tsetse fly, iron ore was mined in regions where it was plentiful, and crops were cultivated with a skill which was to impress later European observers. The Ngonde, in particular, with an economy based upon cattle-keeping and the cultivation of the banana, developed a material culture which attracted the admiration of almost every traveller who chanced upon them. 'Food is everywhere abundant,' wrote Kerr Cross in 1890, 'bananas, sweet potatoes, cassava, yams, Indian corn, beans, peas, millet and other seeds, wild fruits, honey, milk, and beef.' The villages he found especially attractive: 'All weeds, grasses, garbage, and things unsightly are swept away by little boys. . . . Each house is built of bamboo, with clay worked by the women into little rounded bricks. . . . The doorposts are often painted with designs in red, yellow and other colours, and altogether there is an air of comfort and plenty.'[3]

THE NEW INTRUDERS

Upon this pattern of predominantly agricultural activity two new features were imposed in the nineteenth century. The first was the extension and enlargement of pre-European trade from the coast. Up to the 1820's the Arabs and Swahili on the east coast of Africa had been largely content to provide markets for caravans from the interior which were generally controlled by African peoples such as the Bisa, the Nyamwezi and the Yao. From this period, however, the demand for slaves led to the first full-scale Arab penetration inland; this was stimulated by the growth of plantations on Zanzibar, Pemba and on the French islands of the Indian Ocean, and by the vogue in Europe for luxury articles made of ivory. The actual numbers involved were small; by 1888 only four so-called 'white' Arabs were working in the vicinity of Lake Malawi and little more than a handful of Swahilis. They were not generally concerned at first with extending their territorial power, though in the 1840's one such trader established himself in the Marimba district as the Jumbe of Kota Kota where he built up a successful commercial staging post and agricultural settlement. Instead they concentrated in the Malawi region on dominating the northern trade routes, dealing principally in ivory; they left the south to their traditional allies, the Yao. Their expansion, however, was not without its political consequences. Firearms were imported on an increasingly large scale from the late 1850's, and possession of them not only intensified inter-tribal disputes, but also permitted those tribes with whom the Arabs were in close trading relations, notably the Bemba to the north-east of Lake Malawi, to build up their military strength at the expense of their neighbours.

The Yao were another tribe to benefit from trading contacts with the Arabs, which went back at least to the seventeenth century. These people scattered from their homeland east of the lake in the 1850's, partly, it would appear, as a result of internal dissensions and partly because of defeat at the hands of the Makua. Four separate groups moved southward into the southern part of Malawi where they came into contact with the Nyanja with whom, after a period of peaceful co-existence, they clashed in violent warfare. Like the Nyanja, the Yao lacked strong central power, their main political unit being that of the village. Their long involvement in the east coast trade, however, not only gave them an advantage in terms of arms, but also provided the opportunity for the rise of military and commercial leaders who became rich through the sale of slaves and ivory, and who could for a time unite a number of villages under them. The Yao were, therefore, generally successful in the fighting and succeeded in either subduing the Nyanja or in driving them down to the Shire valley.

Culturally as well as politically the Yao resembled the Maravi peoples in many ways. Like them they were matrilineal and matrilocal and deeply involved in agriculture. Their contacts with the east coast, however, as the pioneers of the Arab trading frontier, introduced a new factor into political relations south of the lake. By the 1870's Arab influence was apparent among the Yao in the type of houses used and clothing worn and also in the fact that a small proportion of the tribe had been converted to Islam. Moreover, the chieftaincies already formed were based on the prowess of their leaders in the closely allied occupations of trade and war, and in their hold over supplies of ammunition and slaves. It was through their trading links with the coast that these caravan chiefs won supporters; any attempt to destroy that trade would be to hit at the basis of their power.

The second major intrusion into the Malawi regions came originally from the south. In the 1820's the increasing pressure on land in Natal led not only to the rise of the Zulu but also to the splitting away of a number of militarized groups. One of these was the band of refugees under the sub-chief Zwangendaba who became known as Ngoni. After stopping for some years near Delagoa Bay the Ngoni moved northwards through Mashonaland, raiding as they went and incorporating the captives into their state. In 1835 they crossed the Zambezi near Zumbo, halted for a time in Nsenga country, and then continued their northward advance up the Malawi-Luangwa watershed as far as the country between Lakes Malawi and Tanganyika where Zwangendaba died about 1845. Succession disputes followed resulting in widespread fission. One group made its way northwards up the east coast of Lake Tanganyika to Unyamwezi; the remainder stayed together till after the death of the regent Mgayi. Then two comparatively small secessions took place, the one of Zulu Gama, a commander not of royal descent, who went eastwards round the north end of Lake Malawi and eventually to Songea, the second headed by Ciwere Ndhlovu to the hills near Domira Bay. Meanwhile the dispute between the three leading contenders was settled only by Mpezeni moving off south-west into Bemba country, where he was repelled, and finally settling in the modern Fort Jameson district, where his group soon established their dominance over the local Cewa. Mtwalo, a second claimant, placed himself under the third, Mbelwa (Mwambera, Mombera) who in the 1850's advanced up the Henga valley into the land of the Tumbuka, smashing the 'empire' of the Chikuramayembe in the process.

Much earlier, before the Zambezi had been crossed, yet another group, that of the Maseko Ngoni, had broken away from Zwangendaba and moved up the east side of the lake. There they came into contact with Zula Gama's Ngoni coming down from the north. After a period in which the two groups coalesced, the Maseko Ngoni broke away and retraced their steps round the south end of the lake to the hills of the modern Dedza district.

With their unified political system, centred upon a paramount chief, their formidable military machine based on age-set regiments and their Zulu-type tactics and weapons, the Ngoni were capable of mounting attacks upon other African societies which could rarely be resisted. Unlike the Yao, they lacked all but the most minor connection with the east coast trade, their main economic activities being those of pastoralists and cattle-keepers, while their main relations with other tribes was that of war. Constant raids upon their neighbours were made, partly to obtain supplies of food; but more important, they took captives, not for the slave-trade but for incorporation into their state, particularly as the dependents of the chief and his senior lieutenants. Indeed the whole political structure depended on raiding, and thus upon the maintenance of an efficient army. In a society lacking almost entirely the conventional forms of wealth, power lay in the number of dependents a man might control. But whereas among the Yao this could be achieved indirectly through success in trade, the Ngoni relied almost entirely on the direct method of capture in war. Moreover it was through raiding and the organization of the state for war that recent captives were themselves assimilated and provided with the opportunities for advancing their own position.

THE EFFECTS OF INVASION

For Europeans entering the Malawi regions in the 1860's and 1870's the combined effects of Yao and Ngoni raids, and the activities of semi-Portuguese freebooters in the Lower Shire and Luangwa valleys, seemed to make that area what a later writer was to describe as 'one of the dark places of the earth, full of abominations and cruelty'.[4] All were agreed that it was the central slave-producing country for the east coast trade and there can be no doubt as to its considerable extent or to part, at least, of the cruelty involved; though any estimate of the extent of that trade must be taken as provisional, whether it be that of Consul Rigby, quoted by Livingstone, of 19,000 slaves from the Malawi region passing through the customs house of Zanzibar, or that of E. D. Young in 1875, of 20,000 slaves annually crossing the lake. As late as 1876 Robert Laws could write of walking 'over several miles of the ruins of villages, strewn with broken pots, grinding mills whose noise had ceased and here and there a bleaching skeleton'.[5] In the 1890's vivid eye-witness reports were still being given of the devastation resulting from Ngoni raids.

Till the political history of Malawi at this period has been given the detailed attention that it deserves, any overall assessment of the consequences of these forced intrusions must remain largely a matter of speculation. It is difficult, however, to accept fully the picture of widespread chaos and destruction, capable of resolution only through the introduction of European forces, that has been so extensively propagated by recent historians relying heavily on the evidence of early European travellers. These pioneers, Livingstone especially, tended to avoid areas of strong rule and moved by preference among the weaker peoples, the raided rather than the raiders. Even when their accounts were not coloured by the propaganda needs of home missionary societies, they remained selective ones drawn largely from experience of the most unsettled regions. It is this perhaps which led to the obvious discrepancies between the confident, widely repeated claims of extensive de-population in the Malawi regions and the observed fact that of all areas in central Africa, Malawi is the one with the densest population and has been so since the earliest records were kept.

In fact annihilation was by no means the common lot of a conquered people. Ngoni chroniclers looking back in the 1930's on the period of raiding, regarded it in an almost imperial sense as an age in which peace and justice were brought to a divided people by the sword. 'Before the Ngoni came to this country,' wrote Ishmael Mwale of the central kingdom, 'the villages were small and isolated from one another. There was constant pouncing on people to catch them as slaves. When the Ngoni came they had one law for all people and they had courts to hear cases where their law was enforced. There was freedom to travel in the land where the Ngoni ruled because they had peace within their boundaries.'[6]

Mwale's account is no freer from selection and distortion than those of more frequently quoted authors, but it does point to an important and often neglected factor—the security supplied to those who became incorporated within the Ngoni states. Certainly the unheaval resulting from this process cannot easily be under-estimated. Rain shrines were destroyed and their officials scattered, tribal groups were driven to inaccessible lakeside and mountain sanctuaries, thorn stockades and mud fortresses were thrown up as places of refuge. But the nature of this disruption must also be understood. Malawi by the 1870's was less a land of chaos than of fluidity, with confusion resulting not from the absence of political systems but from the presence of too many clashing and competing ones. In this situation the tendency noted by Professor Oliver in East Africa 'for the strong to grow stronger and the weak to be annihilated' hardly appears to apply.[7] One centralized power, that of the Cewa chief Mwase Kasungu, gained strength and prestige from successfully combating the Ngoni; another, that of the Chikuramayembe, collapsed at the first blow. One disorganized tribal group, the Nyanja near the lake, were brought within the confines of an intruding state; another, the Tonga, found unity of a sort and strength in resistance. Geographical accident rather than the political structure of the societies concerned seems to have played the determining role.

Yet one broad distinction can legitimately be drawn. In the southern districts, the Yao and the Maseko Ngoni between them, with some help from Mpezeni's Ngoni to the west, came to politically dominate the Maravi round the lake and in the Shire and Dedza highlands by the 1870's. Only in the Shire valley did the Nyanja succeed in averting the invasion, and there strong and determined military leaders, such as the Portuguese ex-soldier Belchior, the former slave Chibisa and the handful of Kololo refugees introduced by Livingstone from Barotseland, were able to carve chiefdoms for themselves out of the prevailing conditions of uncertainty.

In the north, however, the reluctance of Arab or Swahili merchants to burden themselves with territorial responsibility before the mid-1880's meant that, despite the expansion of the northern Ngoni, at least three pockets of agriculturalists remained politically independent. The Ngonde, though fiercely attacked by the Ngoni at the time of Zwangendaba's march north, were left virtually unmolested by Mbelwa and the Bemba on the far side of the Luangwa valley. Not till 1887 when the first attempts were made by Arab traders headed by Mlozi to establish their suzerainty, did they come under considerable pressure once more. Farther south, Mwase Kasungu, the only Maravi leader to maintain substantial political power, was able to utilize his control over the trade route running inland from Kota Kota to obtain a substantial supply of firearms which he used to defeat an Ngoni *impi* sent against him in the 1860's. Subsequently he was able to make an alliance with Mbelwa who in return for the military aid he supplied, agreed to leave him unscathed. Finally the Tonga, though hard pressed by Mbelwa's Ngoni from the 1850's, still retained their independence. Considerable numbers of Tonga, particularly women and children, were captured by the Ngoni and incorporated into their state. They managed to preserve their tribal identity, however, partly because of their close proximity to Tongaland. In the mid-1870's they revolted and fled down to their brethren at the lake shore. There they settled in four or five fairly large stockaded villages consisting of a number of smaller villages coming together for protection, and there, at the largest of the Tonga settlements, that of Mankhambira, in 1877 an Ngoni *impi* sent in pursuit was defeated.

RESPONSE TO THE MISSIONARIES

The early interest of missionaries in the Malawi regions was aroused in part because of the promising line of communications into the interior offered by the Zambezi-Shire water route, and in part because of David Livingstone's belief in the potentiality for agricultural development on cash-crop lines of the Manganja people. In fact the Yao invasion of the Shire highlands, disrupting agricultural settlements, was already under way by the time that the first Universities' Mission party arrived in the 1860's, and the later permanent settlements of the 1870's were confronted largely by new intruders.

The political pattern thus established explains in part the different ways in which Africans reacted to the missionary presence. To the Amachinga Yao at the south end of the lake, the Livingstonia Mission of the Free Church of Scotland established at Cape Maclear in 1875, had little of value that they could acquire.

Sufficiently secure in their political position not to require the aid of external allies, the Yao possessed in Islam, still a minority faith, an alternative historic religion and an alternative source of modernizing skills to those offered by Livingstonia. More important, they recognized as the greatest barrier to missionary influence the apparently irreconcilable demands of their economic structure—that the maintenance of their own political power depended on the continuance of the slave-trade—and the revolutionary economic demands of the missionaries that they should abandon slave-trading and turn to commerce along the line of the Shire River. It is not surprising that little use was made of the missionaries in their six years' sojourn on the edge of Yaoland, or that tension between individual Yao chieftains and the mission settlement should increase as the latter sought for refugees from the formers' villages to swell the ranks of its dependents.

A different pattern existed in the Shire highlands. The Amangoche Yao there had been driven to the south by their Amachinga cousins and were subjected to raids by the Maseko Ngoni of the Dedza highlands. Consequently they saw some value in an alliance with the Blantyre Mission of the Church of Scotland, established a year later than Livingstonia. Blantyre's successes were not quickly achieved. Between 1879 and 1881 it was involved in a scandal of mismanagement which resulted in the mission being virtually refounded. By the mid-1880's, however, it was beginning to extend its evangelical and educational influence, though in circumstances in which the mission's residential role as a small colony were uppermost. The mission intervened repeatedly in the political and judicial process, judging a wide range of cases not only at its stations but among the surrounding Yao chiefdoms. In Professor Oliver's phrase, it became 'a power in the land, and not a spiritual power only'.[8]

These southern developments were eclipsed by events in the north, to which Livingstonia turned from 1881 following the evacuation of Cape Maclear and the establishment of a station at Bandawe in the heart of Tongaland. The lack of involvement in the slave-trade and the absence of Islamic influence among them were both negative reasons for the desire of the Tonga to ally themselves with the missionaries. More positive reasons were the external political pressures imposed upon them by the Ngoni, who continued to raid towards the lake in the 1880's with the hope of regaining control of their 'children', and the internal competitiveness of their society in which a premium was placed upon individual achievement.

Education, in consequence, was sought for with an enthusiasm equalled only in east or central Africa at this period by the Baganda. By 1890 over two thousand pupils were regularly attending school. They were doing so, moreover, less to strengthen and modernize the existing political structure, as among most of of the other African societies who were quick to encourage education, than to provide individuals with the necessary techniques for grappling with the newly intrusive Western economy. From 1886 Tonga were using their new skills to obtain jobs as clerks, foremen and interpreters in the infant work markets of the Shire highlands where the first settler-based economy of its type north of the Limpopo had been established as a result largely of the efforts of the missionary-inspired African Lakes Company, founded in 1878. Though Europeans were aware only of the extensive dependence of the Tonga upon them, the initiative did not lie entirely on one side. At a time when most of their neighbours were still trying to reach some working relationship with the new intruders, the Tonga were utilizing the new forces for their own benefit. The lead taken in this field by the late 1880's would not easily be surrendered.

Inland, the northern Ngoni, in contrast to most Ngoni military states who tended to be unreceptive to Christian advances, also began to utilize the skills of the new intruders in the years before the imposition of colonial rule. The balance of power in their favour on which depended the continued vitality of the state, was tilting against them in the 1880's as firearms flooded into the interior and into the hands of rivals such as Mwase Kasungu, the Arabs and the Tonga chief, Mankhambira. As early as 1887, N'gonomo, the military commander, informed Mbelwa, according to the missionary Elmslie, that it was only through the aid of the Senga with their guns that the Bemba had been defeated in a recent battle. Without their support he refused to attack the Tonga at Chinteche, Mankhambira's stockade.[9] Pressures to adopt alternate functions to those integral to a raiding society were thus growing with the mounting capabilities of the tribes beyond their frontier to repel attacks. Internal pressures were also apparent in the growing divisions between Ngoni chiefs and their councillors, often captives incorporated into the state, and between Mbelwa and his various sub-chiefs.

Mbelwa, therefore, was in no position to ignore the mission as a political force, even though the military nature of the state offered him few opportunities of utilizing it in the type of constructive role visualized for Church Missionary Society agents by Mutesa of Buganda. Instead he followed two principles: first, he attempted to isolate the mission from any potential rival, whether it be the Tonga or another Ngoni chief; and second when that failed by 1887, he requested that it open stations throughout the tribe, partly to remove a source of internal conflict by making its material assets widely available, and partly, perhaps, to get it to act as an integrating force within a splintering polity.

The effects by the 1890's were impressively clear. Mission centres had been established in all the major divisions of the state, and schools were in operation which drew their pupils from members of the royal Jeri clan as well as from captives and the recently incorporated. At the same time, the attractions of wage labour was beginning to draw increasing numbers of Ngoni to the growing work centres, even before the introduction of hut tax. New ladders for the ambitious were being created. Advancement was no longer to depend entirely on prowess in war.

BRITISH INVASION AND AFRICAN RESISTANCE

Malawi came under British rule between 1889 and 1904. Before 1889 the only Britons strongly interested in imperial expansion in this area were the missionaries and their supporters. From their earliest days in the country they sought government support: first to reinforce the anti-slave trade campaign and reduce the difficulties involved in missionary participation in civil jurisdiction; and latterly to check the advance of the Arabs, whose attempt to establish political control at the north end of the lake from 1887 appeared to threaten their own position; and also keep out the Portuguese who in the 1880's began to advance claims to the Malawi regions. Dr James Stewart, founder of Livingstonia, produced a scheme as early as August 1877 for the appointment of a commissioner with a steamer on the lake and a small armed force; this was followed by frequent appeals to the British Foreign Office to prevent Portuguese and Arab encroachments, growing in desperation as the failure became increasingly plain of all attempts by the African Lakes Company to dislodge the Arabs from their stockades.

At first the British Government refused to act decisively. 'It is not our duty to do it,' declared Lord Salisbury. 'We should be risking tremendous sacrifices for a very doubtful gain.'[10] In 1889, however, Cecil Rhodes offered to pay for the administration of the territories north of the Zambezi as well as those south, in the hope that eventually he would obtain control of both. Freed from the need to finance the extension of British rule, Salisbury accepted the desirability of keeping Scottish missions out of Portuguese hands. In September 1889 a protectorate was declared over the Shire highlands. Two years later the arrival of Harry Johnston in Malawi as the first commissioner and consul-general marked the opening stages in the campaign to transform the paper partition into the reality of formal rule.

African responses to the extension of British rule were largely determined by the essential interests of different societies and the extent to which the colonial government impinged upon them. Most agricultural societies accepted the transition comparatively easily; on a superficial level at least their interests and those of the British did not violently conflict. Ngonde headmen, threatened with political extinction by the attacks of the Arabs, actively supported the Administration's forces in their assault on Mlozi in 1895, and witnessed with good grace the establishment of a government post at Karonga. Tonga chiefs who signed treaties with the African Lakes Company in 1885, repeated the performance for Johnston four years later. Some of them petitioned for the appointment of a magistrate to their district in 1894 and again in 1897.

The later intruders, however, responded in a different way. Just as Arab and Yao leaders had found their religious faith and economic interests to be incompatible with those of the missionaries, so they found that they could not adjust themselves easily to the new challenges of European power. John Moir, manager of the A.L.C., put forward a plan to wean the Yao from the slave-trade to acceptance of the British Protectorate by subsidizing the price paid for their ivory, thus attaching them to the European-dominated line of trade via the Shire River rather than to the old Afro-Arab link with the east coast. Johnston, however, was not prepared to compromise with policies of gradualism. His own methods, in Sir Clement Hill's words were 'simple: treaty or compulsion, your money or your life'.[11] Requested to abandon slave-trading when no economic alternatives existed, the Yao and the Arabs, with the notable exception of the Jumbe of Kota Kota, whose wary alliance with Johnston may be explained by the relatively strong agricultural base that he possessed, gradually and in piecemeal fashion turned to resistance. Between 1891 and 1895 a series of small wars were fought in which the tiny British force employed was by no means always successful; in December 1891, for example, Maguire, the commander of the British troops, was killed in an abortive attack on the most powerful of the Yao chieftains, Makanjira. The defeat of the Arab, Mlozi, in Karonga district in 1895, after a campaign which for the A.L.C. had lasted eight years, signalled the end, although Makanjira succeeded in avoiding capture through an astute use of the artificial boundaries established between Portuguese and British areas of control.

The Ngoni states with their formidable military systems and dependence on raiding were also likely candidates for resistance. None of them deliberately clashed with the British and all were prepared to use diplomacy and make concessions in order to retain their major interests unharmed. For the Maseko Ngoni and Mpezeni's Ngoni, however, such stratagems could delay but not prevent conflict. Both dominated areas in which European economic interests were involved which could not be fully exploited, the British came to feel, without the prior defeat of the existing rulers. In 1896 Gomani, Chief of the Maseko Ngoni, was attacked because of the obstacles he had placed upon labour recruitment from his country to the plantations of the Shire highlands. Two years later, Mpezeni also collided with the new forces following the discovery of gold in his territory and the pressures of white settlement upon it. Only the northern Ngoni, remote from the seats of European administrative and economic power, succeeded in avoiding direct confrontation. During the 1890's their young men were slowly transforming themselves from warriors into migrant labourers. When in 1904 an agreement was finally made with the Protectorate Government it ensured that the one remaining major interest of the Ngoni would be preserved. A special clause declared that no obstacles would be placed against their moving south into fresh land beyond the limit of their now exhausted domain.

In their different ways all societies had worked to accommodate themselves with the British. Though some resisted and others collaborated, the difference was less one of aim than of the means used to achieve that aim.

By 1898 the period of primary resistance was over. For some

societies the long drawn out process involved had permanently weakened their political systems. In certain areas of Africa, notably Northern Nigeria, the speed with which colonial rule was established permitted the continued existence of indigenous systems with much the same vitality as of old. In Malawi, however, the weakness of Johnston's forces made it necessary for a 'spoiling policy of weakening, dividing and wearing down' to be followed which left the Yao states, in particular, shorn of much of their cohesion.[12] Though the common statement that the power of chiefs in southern Malawi was almost completely destroyed by the 1890's is considerably exaggerated, a residue of truth undoubtedly remains. The old systems were to prove themselves generally unsuited for dealing with the new challenges of colonialism.

Notes

1. I use this term to distinguish peoples of the former empire from those of the modern state
2. Henry Rowley *The Story of the Universities' Mission to Central Africa* London 1866
3. D. Kerr Cross 'Geographical Notes of the Country between Lakes Nyassa, Rukwa, and Tanganyika' *Scottish Geographical Magazine* VI (1890) pp. 283–4
4. J. W. Jack *Daybreak in Livingstonia* Edinburgh 1901 p. 18
5. Laws to Duff 26 February 1876 National Library of Scotland mss. 7876
6. Quoted in Margaret Read *The Ngoni of Nyasaland* London 1956 pp. 88–9
7. Roland Oliver and Gervase Mathew (eds.) *History of East Africa* vol. I Clarendon Press Oxford 1963 p. 210
8. Roland Oliver *The Missionary Factor in East Africa* Longmans 1952
9. Elmslie to Laws 10 December 1887 N.L.S. mss. 7890; 13 May 1888 N.L.S. mss. 7891
10. Quoted in Ronald Robinson and John Gallagher with Alice Denny *Africa and the Victorians: The Official Mind of Imperialism* Macmillan 1961 p. 224
11. Quoted by Eric Stokes 'Malawi Political Systems and the Introduction of Colonial Rule 1891–1896' in Eric Stokes and Richard Brown (eds.) *The Zambesian Past: Studies in Central African History* Manchester University Press 1966 p. 371
12. Stokes pp. 354–5 and 360

Recommended Reading

A useful general introduction with whose interpretation of the nineteenth century I do not completely agree is:
A. J. Wills *An Introduction to the History of Central Africa* Oxford University Press 2nd edition 1967

For the Ngoni see:
J. D. Omer-Cooper *The Zulu Aftermath* Longmans London 1966

Missionaries in the pre-colonial period are dealt with by:

Roland Oliver *The Missionary Factor in East Africa* Longmans London 2nd
edition 1965

A detailed study concerned with the formation of the Protectorate is:

A. J. Hanna *The Beginnings of Nyasaland and North-Eastern Rhodesia 1859–95*
Clarendon Press Oxford 1956

And this can be supplemented by a study of the leading British administrator
of this period:

Roland Oliver *Sir Harry Johnston and the Scramble for Africa* Macmillan 1957

For African resistance see the articles by Stoke on 'Malawi Political Systems'
and by Rennie on 'The Ngoni States' in:

Eric Stokes and Richard Brown (eds.) *The Zambesian Past* Manchester
University Press 1966

6. The nineteenth century in Southern Rhodesia

TERENCE RANGER

THE PATTERNS OF SHONA LIFE AND
THE END OF THE ROZWI EMPIRE

Before the nineteenth century the history of the area that was to become Southern Rhodesia was essentially the history of the Shona-speaking peoples, of their making and of their achievements. At the beginning of the nineteenth century there was little to show that this would not continue to be so. In the year 1800 the population of the area overwhelmingly consisted of people who spoke one or other of the dialects of Shona; Shona speakers also dominated large areas of what is now Portuguese East Africa. The Shona dialects were mutually comprehensible and a man could pass through the whole sweep of country from the coast to what is now western Matabeleland without leaving one language and culture area. Bounded by the Zambezi to the north, by the Limpopo to the south and by the coast to the east, the Shona area had a unity of historical experience unusual if not unique in east and central Africa.

In 1800 the patterns of Shona life still persisted. We know little about the political history of the Rozwi empire but archaeological, oral and documentary evidence combines to tell us that the Rozwi dynasty of Changamire and its aristocratic supporters still lived among the great stone enclosures of Zimbabwe and on the stone-supported platforms of Khami and Dhlo-Dhlo; that they continued to control gold production and to enjoy trading contact with the Portuguese towns on the Zambezi; and that their influence still extended over most of what is now Southern Rhodesia. Their 'empire' was not in 1800, and probably never had been, a strongly centralized state system. It took the form, rather, of 'over-rule'; the supremacy of the Rozwi Mambos was recognized by the chiefs who continued to rule the districts; the approval of the Rozwi was required before the installation of a new chief; Rozwi authority was maintained by both spiritual and military sanctions.

Underneath the umbrella of Rozwi influence all sorts of developments took place; the system was never static. In the early years of the nineteenth century, just as in the eighteenth century, new groups were moving into the area, especially into the high plateau country of what became central Mashonaland. Sometimes there were clashes between intruders and those already settled; sometimes there were wars between two rival chiefs. But we should remember three things. One is that these movements were taking place within the Shona world and not from outside it; the peoples who moved into the central Mashonaland plateau came from the old Mutapa area or from western Mashonaland. Another is that these peoples accepted the Rozwi over-rule once they had established themselves. And the third is that the wars which were fought among the various peoples of the Rozwi empire were not at all like the wars of the later nineteenth century. They were limited and conventionalized affairs which did little to destroy or even to modify the patterns of Shona life. These patterns were, in fact, common not only to the peoples of the old Rozwi empire but also to the Shona peoples who lived outside it, in the old heart-land of the Mutapa kingdom, for instance, or in the belt of country between the Rozwi and the Portuguese spheres of influence.

Despite differences in regional environment, the economic activities of Shona-speaking peoples everywhere followed a broadly similar pattern. The Shona were everywhere cultivators rather than pastoralists. And their agriculture was a rich one. Over the centuries the Zambezi valley had received crops from outside Africa and diffused them to other areas. By the nineteenth century the Shona could make use of wide variety of crop types. Thus the first white settlers in Melsetter in 1893 listed 'mealies, poko corn, kafir corn, millet, ground-nuts, beans (five sorts), egg fruit, cabbages, tomatoes, peas, pumpkins of sorts, water-melons, cucumbers, sweet potatoes, chillies, tobacco, bananas and lemons, and all these grown to perfection'. At the same time an early settler in western Mashonaland was describing the successful and varied agriculture of chief Mashiangombi's people. 'The path wound through fields of mealies, kafir corn, rukwaza, sweet potatoes, pumpkins, peanuts, and then across rice-beds in the marshes'; cattle and goats were herded; and game abounded to provide further fresh meat. All Shona were involved in this cultivation except specialists in the arts of government and religion. Then men cleared the ground and together with the women planted, weeded and harvested. The young men also hunted, usually in communal groups. This Shona agriculture proved readily capable of expanding to meet the demands of the new white population after 1890 and for the first ten years at least the whites depended upon it for the greater part of their food supply.

A number of crafts flourished among the Shona—white observers claimed in the 1880's that Shona technical skills were 'really astonishing' and that the Shona stood first 'in the industrial arts of a rudimentary civilization' of all the tribes south of the Zambezi. Cloth was woven from wild cotton or bark fibre; elaborate and highly ornamented pottery was made; at court centres like Zimbabwe and Khami there developed carving in ivory and soapstone and a skilful use of gold for decorative purposes—gold beads, gold wire, paper-thin gold plates to cover models of animals. The Shona were skilled iron workers and produced hoes, hatchets, spears, arrows, and so on.

Internal trade was well developed. Shona groups especially skilful in iron working or close to rich deposits of ore would barter iron goods for cloth or tobacco with other Shona peoples. Tribute to the Rozwi was often paid in the form of these products. In addition there continued the long-established trade in gold and ivory with the agents of the Portuguese traders from the Zambezi towns. The Rozwi court, and to a lesser degree the kraals of the chiefs, were the centres of this trade. The Portuguese brought cloth, beads, flintlock guns and a variety of other goods. This trade was important to Shona political leaders and they understood very well how it worked. There was little question of the Portuguese agents being able to coerce or to swindle the Shona in the territory that became Southern Rhodesia for they were operating in an area under Shona political control and in which chiefs kept a tight control over gold extracting and washing operations and over ivory collection.

The Shona peoples shared certain religious ideas and institutions as well as these economic patterns. Broadly speaking there seem to have been two institutionalized religious systems operating in the Shona area around 1800, both of which made use of a basic pool of religious concepts and which were closely inter-related.

One of these systems was the cult of the high-god Mwari. Mwari was believed to speak in the thunder and to manifest himself in the lightning. His messages could be understood by his servants, among whom were especially the Rozwi, wherever they were given but he manifested himself particularly in certain caves. Around these caves developed cult shrines attended by an elaborate apparatus of priests—one group to act as the eyes of the god, to receive those who came to offer sacrifice or to ask advice; another group to act as the ears of the god and to forward petitions to him; and another group to act as the mouth of the god and to retail and interpret his commands. It seems that there was such a shrine near to the major court-centres of the Rozwi state and Rozwi power depended to some extent upon an alliance with the Mwari priesthood. In many areas of the Rozwi confederation there existed local representatives of the cult whose duty it was to make at least annual visits to the central shrines, to report the major events of the past year, to carry gifts and to return with the commands and advice of the god. In the nineteenth century such an organization seems to have existed throughout what is now Matabeleland and most of western and southern Mashonaland.

In other areas the prestige of the Mwari cult was high but it did not exist in organized form. Here the high-god Mwari was approached rather through the spirits of the dead. In northern, eastern, central and most of western Mashonaland an elaborate system of spirit mediums existed. These mediums were men or women believed to be possessed by the spirits of dead kings, or dead chiefs, or by great personified nature spirits. The Mutapa empire had been supported by the influence of the senior mediums who spoke with the voice of past Mutapas or of the great spirits who had been powerful in the area from before the time of the Mutapas themselves. And when the Mutapa empire passed away the influence of the senior mediums remained great—Dzivaguru in the north-east, Nehanda in central Mashonaland, Chaminuka in western Mashonaland. Their influence extended beyond the boundaries of the basic Shona political units, the paramountcies.

Both systems were complex, subtle and deeply rooted. They commanded the spiritual loyalty of the Shona people. Whites who believed in the 1890's that the Shona had no religious feeling and no concept of the divine could hardly have been further from the mark.

The political patterns of Shona life were formed by the inter-action of the paramountcy units. These were the largest political units below the Rozwi Mambo. Each was made up of a number of wards which in turn were made up of a number of villages. A village was under a village headman who allocated land for the use of all its inhabitants; a ward was under a ward head, who allocated land for the establishment of new villages, heard disputes and ensured the performance of rituals relating to the agricultural year; the paramountcy was under the chief. 'The power of the Shona chiefs was relatively limited,' an anthropologist tells us. 'They did not have centralized and disciplined age regiments whereby they could exercise military control, and though they were at the head of the traditional legal system subjects could and did appeal from them to the ordeal . . . The system of collateral succession found in most tribes limited the power of any one family, tribal advisers exercised constant restraint on the behaviour of chiefs, tribesmen could transfer allegiance, apparently without difficulty, from one chief to another.'[1]

The Shona chief was nevertheless a man of great importance. He stood in a special relationship to the land and was ultimately responsible for its allocation; through the spirits of his dead ancestors and his relations with the mediums who represented them he was also responsible for the fertility of the land. He was given great respect and commanded real loyalty. He was the custodian of tribal property; prisoners of war and cattle taken from those found guilty of witchcraft and other serious offences. He had the right to call on communal labour. He was given a share of all the game taken by the communal hunting groups in his para-mountcy and in particular he had the right to the tusks of all elephants killed in his area. The chief was therefore the wealthiest man in the tribe, drawing upon tribute, fines, gifts and the profits of external trade. He was also supposed to be the most generous and hospitable man in the tribe, drawing people to him by his lavish patronage.

The prestige of the chief was further increased by his position in the whole stream of Shona history. The Shona peoples had a highly developed historical sense and many chiefs stood in a long line of paramounts of the same title who had been associated with the great political systems of the past. A number of rituals clustered round the Shona chief emphasizing relationship with the past, his links with the founding ancestors of the paramountcy, his inherited relationships with the original owners of the land. And just as the Mutapa was partly supported and partly limited by his alliance with the great mediums of the Dzivaguru hierarchy and as the Rozwi Mambo was partly supported and partly limited by his alliance with the priests of the Mwari cult so the Shona paramount had similar relationships with the spirit mediums of the paramountcy.

All this description of the Shona chief does little to bring him to life. To do this we may quote from Herbert Chitepo's remarkable poem, *Soko Risina Musoro*, which draws upon the tradition of the Manyika people and which deals with their paramount chief, the Mutassa. In this poem we can feel something of what it meant to be a paramount in the high days of the Shona world.

'O you people of the citadel,' cries the praise-singer, 'and all you who have come from afar, behold and listen. He who stands here is the Night-walker whom you know, he it was who led us here and gave us the blessing of a country. We knew him while we were yet across the Zambezi, that he had the heart of a lion. All men who saw him were astonished to see him, they turned to look upon him twice, thrice and yet a fourth time. All men feared him and numbered his blessings. They knew that even God had made choice of him.' 'We greet you on bended knee,' says a counsellor, 'you the branch of the tree of our tribe. You are the Lion, you are the foe of the land, you are the bull in this our kraal. You are the one who has power to pray to those who are ahead in the nameless place. We are your children, O King, we are the fruit of the stem of the great tree, the tree of the Lion.'

The chief in Herbert Chitepo's poem rules in the last part of the nineteenth century in a world which is becoming strange but he looks back to the time 'long ago, when I sat upon this throne, governing all the land. I ruled but I ruled with the power which comes from my forefathers, the power without beginning, which I thought was endless. We fought battles and were victorious, and returned home with gold and riches.' Most of our evidence suggests that the beginning of the nineteenth century was indeed a time of relative prosperity. The Rozwi maintained an overall supervision; wars between paramounts were limited in scope and effect; the Portuguese were content to send traders into the area; there were no other intruders. In 1893 the famous hunter, F. C. Selous, drew a picture of Mashonaland as it must have been 'some fifty years ago'. 'The peaceful people inhabiting this part of Africa must then have been at the zenith of their prosperity. Herds of their small but beautiful cattle lowed in every valley and their rich and fertile country doubtless afforded them an abundance of vegetable food.' The paramount chiefs were then 'rulers of large and prosperous tribes . . . whose towns were for the most part surrounded by well built and loop holed stone walls . . . Hundreds of thousands of acres which now lie fallow must then have been under cultivation . . . while the sites of ancient villages are very numerous all over the open downs.'

In the 1830's, however, the whole of Shona society was exposed to new and powerful pressures. A series of invading groups from the south burst in to the Shona area with greatly destructive effect. In the late 1820's a number of fugitives from the fighting which accompanied the rise of Shaka's Zulu empire entered southern Portuguese East Africa. Three groups in particular were of import- ance to the Shona. One of these was commanded by Soshangane, a defeated Nguni general, whose followers came to be known as the Gaza. In 1831 he defeated the forces of the other two leaders, Zwangendaba and Nxaba, driving them into what is now Rhodesia.

Soshangane and his Gaza then set out to create an empire east of the Sabi River and between the Zambezi and the Limpopo, an area occupied by thousands of Shona speakers. They settled among one of these peoples, the Ndau. The Ndau and many other groups were subjected to Gaza rule; raids were made on the Portuguese trading towns of Sofala, Tete and Sena and the Portu- guese were forced to pay tribute. These events shook up the patterns of Shona history in the area. The Ndau people were pro- foundly affected by the arrival of the Gaza in their midst; large numbers of Gaza words passed into their language; many Ndau men were conscripted into the Gaza armies; and there was much inter-marriage. At the same time the long established trading system between the Portuguese towns and the Shona paramounts was badly shaken and the prosperity of both parties to the trade declined.

Meanwhile the other two groups, the Ngoni of Zwangendaba and of Nxaba, were forcing their way into what was to become Southern Rhodesia. Zwangendaba first marched to the Zambezi; then turned into the heartland of the old Mutapa empire. From there he moved south into the eastern section of the Rozwi empire, taking stock and captives as he went. Somewhere in modern

Mashonaland he ran into Nxaba's army and there was a fierce fight between the two sets of raiders. Defeated, Zwangendaba moved westwards. Soon he and his men found themselves in the nuclear territory of the Rozwi Mambo and his aristocratic supporters. They fell upon the complex culture of the Rozwi and did their best to destroy at least its material manifestations. They sacked Zimbabwe, Khami and the other Rozwi centres; archaeologists have found in their excavations vivid evidence of their violence. At Zimbabwe many skeletons were found by those who first dug in the great elliptical building; the remains, so R. Summers believes, of those who died when the building was rushed by the Ngoni. At Khami the passage which ran to the Mambo's hut was stuffed with grass and fired; huts were broken down and pushed down the sides of the granite *kopjes*. And at a Rozwi centre then called Manyanga, but known henceforth as Taba Zi Ka Mambo (the hill of the Mambo), Zwangendaba's Ngoni besieged the last effective ruler of the Rozwi system.

'Of all the countries we passed through,' a survivor of Zwangendaba's forces recalled in 1898, 'there was one which struck us as most desirable. This was the country in which a people called the Abalozwi lived. They built their villages in granite hills which they fortified with stone walls. Their chief, Mambo, put up a stubborn fight and then fled into the very hilly granite country, making it difficult for us to subdue him and his people.' At length he was besieged at Taba Zi Ka Mambo. 'They threw down beads and skins and hoes and offered us cattle and sheep go away and leave them in peace . . . but we were not to be propitiated. . . . Next day they came out again on the rocks and directed us to stand below a certain strange over-hanging rock. It looked like a big balcony giving standing room to about 200 men. Hereon were gathered the Mambo and his counsellors, jabbering and chattering like a lot of monkeys. This rock stands about a hundred feet above where we were standing with a sheer drop, and it is here that Mambo threw himself down in our midst to fall dead and mangled at our feet. . . . The next day we found that these people had deserted that part of the country during the night and as we wished to continue our trek north-ward we packed up and took up the trail leaving Mambo's mangled remains where he had fallen.'[2]

The Ngoni did indeed take up the trail; most of them left Rhodesia and pushed on into what are now Zambia, Malawi and

Tanzania. But their brief incursion had important effects for the Shona. No Shona paramountcy was destroyed by them although it may be that the balance of power between paramountcies was affected. But a considerable number of Shona captives were taken and absorbed into the Ngoni horde. Some of these, especially the diviners and prophets, soon came to play an influential part among the Ngoni. This involuntary migration of Shona, indeed, meant that people of Shona descent played some part in the histories of Malawi and Tanzania. Shona ex-captives were an important element in the politics of the Northern Ngoni of Malawi during the Scramble period; the famous Ngoni leader in southern Tanzania, Songea, was of Shona stock as was the chief religious officer of the Tanzania Ngoni.

The most important effect of the Ngoni raids was that the Rozwi power was broken just at the time when the Ndebele were about to settle in their country. The Ndebele were the last and most important of the intruders from the south. Under their remarkable leader, Mzilikazi, they had broken away from Shaka's army; moved into Sotho country and incorporated many Sotho into their ranks; raided what is now central and northern Transvaal and established a settlement there. In 1837 they were driven out of the Transvaal by Boer commandos and moved in two groups northwards into what is now Rhodesia. The two groups met in what had been the core of the Rozwi kingdom and settled down to build up an Ndebele state. The Rozwi, who had not recovered from the Ngoni attack were unable to offer much resistance to the Ndebele. Some of them were absorbed into the Ndebele state system in which the lowest caste came to be known as Lozwi. Others survived in small groups to the north-east where they bitterly remembered the days of their prosperity. 'How can we pray now that the Ma Tebele have conquered us?', they complained to a missionary in the 1880's. 'We are afraid to go pa dsimbabwe (to the graves) but offer our little offerings in our villages and houses. Our oppressors have taken all we had.' Others, including the family of the Mambo, fled eastwards to take up residence among the Shona of western and central Mashonaland.

In this way the Rozwi empire came to an end. But its memory and its prestige lived on among the Shona in a way that was to be important later. Many Shona chiefs continued to recognize the ritual seniority of Rozwi officers living in their area; the Shona people generally regarded 'the Warosi as God's chosen people and have great respect for them'. Even the memory of Rozwi military power lived on into the 1890's. 'The Barosi's are the big people of the country,' said a Karanga of the Fort Victoria area in 1897. 'We are afraid of the Barosi because they sometimes attack us with an *impi* like the Matabele and kill us.'

Moreover the religious institutions of the Rozwi empire and its tributary paramountcies outlived Rozwi political power. The Mwari priesthood moved from the now desolate court centres of the old Changamire empire into the Matopos hills south of the main area of Ndebele settlement. Messengers continued to go to them from all the areas in which the cult had organized existence. Even the Ndebele, anxious to be on good terms with the God of the land, sent regular tribute to the Mwari shrines though Mzilikazi and Lobengula were careful to restrict the influence of the cult as much as they could. In Mashonaland the senior spirit mediums continued to exercise an influence wider than the boundaries of the individual paramountcies. After the overthrow of the Rozwi kings they became the only focus of a wider Shona loyalty. In western Mashonaland the mediums of the great Chaminuka spirit rallied the Shona in the face of Ndebele raiding. In fact Shona religious institutions showed a remarkable capacity for survival. In Malawi, as Edward Alpers tells us, it seems that the Cewa rain shrines were broken up and their officers scattered during the invasions of the nineteenth century; the traditional religious system there does not seem to have provided the agricultural peoples with stiffening against either African or white intruders. In Rhodesia, however, the Mwari priests and the spirit mediums were still to play an important political role.

THE CHARACTER OF THE
NDEBELE AND GAZA STATES

The intruding groups from the south organized themselves on different principles and had different attitudes to those of the Shona. The Rozwi empire had been a far-flung and not highly centralized affair. It had to be extensive in order to exploit long-distance trade and it could not be highly centralized because it was extensive. The Ndebele and Gaza systems, on the other hand, were highly centralized and strictly limited in area of settlement. All Ndebele settlements fell in a radius of some fifty miles around the king's kraal; where the outlying parts of the Rozwi empire kept in touch by sending delegates annually to the royal court and to the shrine of the high-god Mwari, all the members of the superior Ndebele castes could attend in person the various annual rituals of the Ndebele state. This concentration was possible because it had a different economic basis. The Ndebele were neither primarily interested in trade nor in controlling scattered gold mines or washing pits; they closed down the old mine shafts in their area of influence. Their economy depended partly upon a mixed cattle keeping and cultivating agriculture and partly upon a raiding system which ensured a steady supply of cattle, men and food. Concentrated man-power was their strength. It was because of concentrated and disciplined man-power that the intruding groups were able to overthrow the pre-existing political systems, even though in other ways these systems were more sophisticated and at least as successful in solving political and economic problems.

The ruler of the Ndebele state was primarily the leader of this concentrated man-power, the commander of the armies. His authority was different from that of the Rozwi Mambo or the Shona paramount chief. It depended upon control of cattle and captives rather than on control of land; the basis of Ndebele political organization was military rather than territorial.

The area of Ndebele settlement was divided into four provinces, each under its 'great chief' or senior *induna*. The province was not made up of a number of villages or of territorial wards but of a number of regimental towns. These towns were known only by the name of the regiment which occupied them. Each regiment was commanded by its *induna* and the provincial senior *induna* also commanded his own regiment and regimental town. While the Ndebele were settled in Rhodesia this system had an obvious territorial aspect, but it could operate just as easily when the Ndebele nation was on the march.

The king kept close control over the system. The *indunas* were a powerful group but they owed their power to the king's appointment. Unlike the Shona chiefs, Ndebele *indunas* had no hereditary or ritual claims to office. They could be, and sometimes were, removed and replaced. The king also maintained control over the provinces through the practice of placing his many wives in the regimental *kraals* from which they reported all significant developments. The king, moreover, had his own special regiments. These were the newly formed regiments whose members were drawn partly from the young men of the established regimental *kraals* and partly from captives. They underwent a strict period of training at the royal *kraal* and after being formed into a regiment they were regarded as being on probation until they had proved themselves in war when they were allowed to wear the head-ring and to marry.

Both in theory and in practice the Ndebele king was the fount of all authority. 'All land, cattle and people belonged to him. He was the supreme commander of the army and the supreme judge. All major decisions should be made by him, and only he had the power of life and death over his subjects. He was the centre of the great annual ceremony of the Inxwala, the First Fruits ceremony . . . which was the biggest ceremony of the Ndebele nation and which everyone tried to attend. . . . The king was informed of every detail of what happened in his country; of casualties or births among his herds of cattle, of domestic incidents among his people, of the arrival and movements of Europeans, and so on.' 'This idea,' wrote the missionary Father Hartmann in 1893, 'that every one of the nation is gravitating towards their chief, brings in a forcible way home to them that they are a compact mass, a force of collected strength, and therefore invincible.'[3]

The Ndebele system was remarkably successful in assimilating the large numbers of captives picked up on the march to Matabeleland and the continuing large numbers raided from the Shona and other peoples. The nation was organized on a caste basis rather than on tribal or clan divisions. The original Nguni element were known as the Zansi caste; they monopolized the key positions of command. Those absorbed into the nation during its period amongst the Sotho peoples were known as the Enhla caste; these had become, in effect, a part of the aristocracy. Those captured in Rhodesia became known as the Lozwi or Holi caste. Some of them were drafted into the regiments, where great pains were taken not only to teach them Ndebele military skills but also the Ndebele language.

Both Mzilikazi and his successor Lobengula were men of outstanding ability and under their guidance the Ndebele state showed considerable strength. Its unity survived the disputed succession after Mzilikazi's death in 1868. The missionaries had expected the death of the founder of the system to be followed by its breaking up; by a struggle for power among the *indunas* and by a revolt or flight of the subject caste. But in the event they found that 'the loyalty of these unenlightened heathens was something more than ordinary; nay, it was nothing less than infatuation. I have never heard,' wrote the missionary Sykes, 'of such devotion to a royal family and to the will of a sovereign as the Amandabele were showing.' Until its overthrow in 1893 the Ndebele state was not faced by any serious threat of disunity or revolt.

The Gaza state was organized on less successful lines. 'In building up his kingdom Soshangane employed the age-regiment system and Zulu fighting methods. The chiefs of conquered tribes were treated as vassal sub-chiefs and the young men were taken and trained by military *indunas* in the fighting methods of their conquerors. Members of the Nguni nucleus, however, constituted a distinct class called "ba-Ngoni" in contrast to the newly incorporated peoples who were known as "ba-Tshangane". The new recruits were segregated in regiments of their own under "ba-Ngoni" officers. They were subject to discrimination and on the battlefield these more expendable subjects were put in the front line.' It will be seen that Soshangane did not attempt to assimilate his conquered subjects as thoroughly as Mzilikazi. Mzilikazi did not recognize vassal sub-chiefs within the Ndebele state proper; members of the Holi caste were mixed up with members of other castes in the regiments and were taught Sindebele. The result was, as J. D. Omer-Cooper tells us, that within the Gaza state 'tensions based on cultural differences persisted. As Soshangane grew old he began to believe himself bewitched. Suspicion fell on the newly incorporated peoples and many of the "ba-Tshangane" were killed. A party of Thonga broke away and succeeded in escaping to the Transvaal.' When Soshangane died in the late 1850's it proved that rivalry among the superior Ngoni groups was also a danger to the Gaza state. A struggle for power broke out between two of Soshangane's sons, Mawewe and Mzila; both parties turned to outside powers for aid, Mawewe to the Swazi and Mzila to the Portuguese. Mzila's victory gave the Portuguese some sort of foothold in his kingdom. These weaknesses in the Gaza state remained to trouble Mzila's successor, Gungunyana, who had to face a large-scale revolt of his subject peoples in 1890 as well as the increasing pressure of the whites.

These difficulties of the Gaza state help us to appreciate the remarkable extent of Ndebele success. The Ndebele state was the most formidable and the most stable of all the systems thrown up by the Nguni diaspora.

THE EFFECT OF NDEBELE POWER
UPON THE SHONA

As we have seen the actual area of Ndebele settlement was a compact one. But whites believed that all the Shona peoples of the area which became Southern Rhodesia were affected by destructive Ndebele raids, that their political and economic systems were shattered, and that in many areas the Shona were on the verge of extinction. 'The poor Mashunas,' wrote Selous, 'unskilled in war and living, moreover, in small communities scattered all over the country without any central government, fell an easy prey to the invader, and very soon every stream in their country ran red with their blood, while vultures and hyenas feasted undisturbed amidst the ruins of their devastated homes. Their cattle, sheep and goats were driven off by their conquerors and their children . . . were taken for slaves. In a few years there were no more Mashunas left in the open country, the remnant that had escaped massacre having fled into the mountainous districts to the south and east of their former dwellings, where they still live.' Even this remnant was exposed, so whites believed, to a continued threat of extermination. 'If no stop is put to these raids,' wrote Father Hartmann in 1893, 'it will go on until the Mashonas are exterminated. . . . The Mashonas are a complete wreck physically, intellectually and also morally. In my constant intercourse with them I hear it oftentimes said that if the white men do not protect them they will emigrate from the country.'

These assertions were wildly overstated. It is important to try to establish the real situation. It is certainly true that the Ndebele system depended upon raiding both for its continued supply of cattle and manpower and for the maintenance of the morale of its armies. It is certainly true also that the Ndebele often raided the Shona. On the other hand it is also true that they did not continue raiding communities who were prepared to submit and to offer regular tribute. And it is also true that the Ndebele had many other enemies to fight over and above resistant Shona communities. Full-scale wars were fought between the Ndebele and two neighbouring African rulers, Khama of the Tswana and Lewanika of the Lozi. Bearing these factors in mind we may look more closely at the actual impact on the Shona.

For this purpose we can divide the Shona peoples into five groups. The first group were the Shona who were incorporated into the Ndebele nation as members of the Lozwi or Holi caste.

These were derived partly from Shona living in the area of Ndebele settlement and partly from those captured in raids. J. D. Omer-Cooper describes what happened to many of these captives. 'When first taken they were given to the captors to serve as weapon-bearers and cattle-herders but when they grew older they would go to Mzilikazi and present a petition. "We are men, O King; we are no longer boys; give us cattle to herd and to defend." If the king approved he would entrust a number of cattle to their keeping and appoint an experienced *induna* who would choose a place for a new military settlement and train them as Ndebele soldiers.'[4]

The second group were Shona living near to the area of Ndebele settlement or in pockets within it who were subordinate to the Ndebele but not fully assimilated into the nation. In 1857 Moffat noted that 'many of that people [the Mashonas] live among the Matabele and, besides numbers who are living as servants and youths amalgamated with the Matabele, there are many towns or villages where they are permitted to live in their own way, but muster for public service when called on'. Such Shona groups were 'associated with the Ndebele state rather than fully a part of it', but they also tended to adopt the language and culture of the Ndebele and to take pride in their identification with them.

The third group consisted of a large number of Shona peoples who lived in a great circle around the area of Ndebele settlement, who were neither associated with nor absorbed into the Ndebele state but at first raided by it and then made subject to it. The Kalanga of the south-west, the Karanga of Fort Victoria area, the Zezuru of Hartley and Charter and southern Lomagundi, the Rozwi, Tonga and other groups to the north of Inyati, all fell into this category. What did Ndebele activity entail for all these peoples?

One of the Ndebele raiders himself gives us an idea. 'The next few years,' he remembers of the period after Mzilikazi's arrival in Matabeleland, 'were very exciting, for we were always out raiding and subduing the neighbouring tribes and collecting tribute from their chiefs. If they submitted and acknowledged our King's sovereignty and if they gave cattle freely we left them alone but if they refused we fought them and burnt their kraals and took their young people into slavery. After we had discovered the country of the Maswina and their people our King partitioned it off into districts and each of the chiefs would be allotted his district in which he would collect the King's tribute, and then the raids ceased except when some Maswina chief misbehaved himself or refused to pay tribute.' What is being described here is not merely anarchy but the operation of a system; as Omer-Cooper writes, 'undoubtedly a cruel and sanguinary system but based on principles which were easily understood. It made no demands on the labour of the Shona and Ndebele overlordship generated no deep sense of personal humiliation.'[5]

Once they had submitted and begun to make regular payments of tribute the Shona peoples of this third area were left to get on with their own internal political and religious life. No attempts were made to change the system or to incorporate them into the Ndebele state. By Lobengula's time raiding as such was more or less a thing of the past in this area. In 1904, for example, the Tonga chief, Pashu, refused to pay hut tax to the British South Africa Company administration. He answered their claims to have saved him and his people from Ndebele raids. 'Pashu stated that while under Mzilikazi's rule they were continually carried off, yet after Lobengula's accession he was left unmolested so long as he paid his tribute of skins, feathers, etc., to the King.' Other peoples also found Ndebele rule preferable to that of the whites. In 1854 Moffat found that the Ngwato people tributary to the Ndebele spoke 'favourably of Moselekatse and seem quite shocked at the very idea of his rule being compared to the tyranny of the Dutch Boer'.

By the time the British arrived on the scene, then, Ndebele military action against this third group of Shona and other peoples was limited to punitive expeditions against a chief who 'misbehaved himself or refused to pay tribute'. These punitive expeditions were relatively limited in scope and aimed at the chief and his immediate supporters rather than the whole tribe. Thus when chief Lomagundi was encouraged by the arrival of the British South Africa Company to repudiate his submission to Lobengula and refuse tribute in 1891 a small Ndebele force was sent to the district; its leaders consulted with the senior religious authority of the tribe and obtained her approval to punish the chief; and the chief's village was then attacked and destroyed. This example shows an interesting interplay of Ndebele power and Shona institutions.

The fourth group of Shona consisted of those who lived beyond the tributary circle but who were still exposed to Ndebele raids.

Here we are dealing mostly with the peoples of the plateau of central Mashonaland, the area around modern Salisbury and the areas to the north and east of it. It was in these areas that Ndebele raiding proper was still going on right up to the white occupation in 1890. Raiding was going on because the Shona peoples of this area had not submitted to Ndebele authority and did not pay tribute. It seems clear that the destructive character of these raids has been much over-stated. Each raid was certainly destructive in itself but the Ndebele were operating a good distance from their base in relatively small parties and in country favourable to the defenders. Full-scale war as such involving large Ndebele armies was not waged on the central Shona; in many areas Ndebele raids were few and far between. Even in areas where raiding was more frequent the Ndebele found difficulties. 'These people all cleared into the granite ranges and hills to build their strong-holds,' the Ndebele warrior recalls, 'and kept a keen watch on our movements. They also developed a sort of code of calls and ways of sounding their drums and sent messengers to keep one another informed of our every movement. So it became very difficult to take them by surprise as time went on. In such cases we bided our time and trusted to luck to catch them unawares on some future occasion.' This account is confirmed by Father Hartmann himself, the very man who thought the Shona were in a state of complete mental, physical and moral breakdown. Hartmann witnessed an Ndebele raid on chief Kunzwi-Nyandoro's people in the Salisbury district. As soon as the alarm was given the people herded their animals into a great cave on the side of a steep hill 'in an inconceivably short space of time' and 'without the least sign of any panic or confusion'. Indeed the people were 'all in very good spirits'.

The peoples of the strong chiefs of the plateau area managed to maintain a substantial independence during this period. 'Although there were only loose and shifting alliances among this group,' writes Father Devlin, 'they did form a barrier of strong, independent peoples with good natural defences. It was this that kept them free from the slave traders in Portuguese territory. It procured them also comparative immunity when the terrible invasions from South Africa began. . . . In 1868 Lobengula succeeded Mzilikazi. His warriors finding nothing more to pillage in the south and west advanced against the central peoples. . . . After initial terror the central peoples held firm in their stone forts;

Makoni's men, the Hungwe, even won a pitched battle. . . . The four chiefs meanwhile found time to carry on their traditional feuds, Mangwende against Mtoko and Makoni against Mutasa.' In 1889 the hunter, Selous, entered this upland area in an attempt to obtain concessions from its chiefs. 'The Matabele claim to the country is utterly preposterous,' he wrote, 'and cannot hold water for a moment. Should the latter at some future time be inquired into by a Commission I am and shall be prepared with evidence in the face of which the Matabele claim could never be allowed. . . . It rests entirely on the strength of the raid made in 1868, for the two subsequent raids made respectively in 1880 and 1883 did not touch the country.' In the concessions obtained by Selous and no doubt also worded by him the Shona signatories declared themselves to be 'chiefs of a free and independent nation paying no tribute either to Lobengula, chief of the Amandabele, on the one hand, or to the Portuguese Government on the other. And the said chiefs declare that the Amandabele have made but three raids into their country . . . doing but little damage and suffering some loss themselves and never having made the slightest attempt to conquer and occupy the country, only a very small portion or which has ever been trodden by a subject of Lobengula.'[6]

The fifth group of Shona consisted of people who were not raided at all by the Ndebele and who lay outside their range of activity. When the British South Africa Company officials entered Mashonaland in 1890 their claim to the area depended upon a concession from Lobengula. Nevertheless they soon became convinced that Selous was right to say that the Ndebele had never exercised authority north and east of the Hunyani River, and that Ndebele raiding had never gone further than the 32nd parallel. 'Between the Sabi and Ruzarwe rivers there are chiefs who acknowledge *no-one's authority*. They have certainly *never* been under Matabele authority nor have they ever seen any Matabele.' The Shona who lived in the old nuclear area of the Mutapa kingdom, those who lived east of the Sabi, and so on had faced other pressures, including Gaza raids, but had not felt the impact of the Ndebele.

Thus it can be seen that it is wrong to regard the Shona as a people on the verge of extinction and to write the history of nineteenth-century Rhodesia as though they did not exist except as victims of the Ndebele. This is the way in which the period has too often been presented so that it becomes impossible to understand why or how the Shona rose against the whites in 1896, or why Shona institutions have shown such vitality in the twentieth century. This picture came into existence largely because English writers have drawn only upon sources in English and Englishmen came into contact with the area through Matabeleland. Their imagination was dominated by the powerful Ndebele state; until 1890 few of them had penetrated to Mashonaland. Later it was an article of English belief that they had rescued the Shona from Ndebele oppression and that white settlers in Mashonaland had inherited large depopulated areas as the result of Ndebele raids. The Portuguese, whose approach to the area lay through territories held by 'independent' Shona chiefs, had a very different estimate of the continuing vitality and significance of Shona society.

WHITE PRESSURES
ON THE SHONA AND NDEBELE

The Portuguese had, of course, been in contact with the Shona peoples for a long time. At one time they had established themselves in what became Mashonaland but had been driven out at the end of the seventeenth century by the Rozwi Changamire dynasty. The Changamire power came to an end in the 1830's but the Portuguese were in no condition to take advantage of this. Indeed, Portuguese authority reached its lowest ebb with the rise of the Gaza empire; most of the Portuguese landowners in the Zambezi valley abandoned their estates and the towns of Tete, Sena and Sofala only survived by paying annual tribute to the Gaza. 'The Negro is absolute master here,' wrote one Portuguese official. 'If we cannot dominate the Negro along the coast, how can we dominate him in the interior?'

However Portuguese power and ambitions gradually began to revive from the 1870's onwards. To begin with this was the work of the remarkable Goanese adventurer, Manuel Antonio de Sousa, nicknamed Gouveia. Gouveia built himself a semi-private empire in the Zambezi valley by dint of playing the game of African politics by African rules. He married the daughters of African chiefs, set himself up with all the state of an African paramount and recruited large African armies. With these forces he drove the declining Gaza power away from the Zambezi valley. He then turned his attentions to the Shona paramountcies. In 1873 chief Mutassa of Manyika paid him homage; ten years later he overthrew the ruling dynasty in the great old Shona paramountcy of Barwe and was himself recognized as the paramount chief. In 1889 Gouveia's power had become so considerable that Gungunhana, King of Gaza, removed his capital from Ndau country and marched south with 60,000 followers to a new site near the Limpopo in order to escape it.

Throughout the 1870's, 1880's and early 1890's the Shona chiefs of central and eastern Mashonaland were much involved in the wars sparked off by Gouveia's ambitions. He was much more of a factor in their politics than the Ndebele and very much more of a factor than the English whose arrival in Mashonaland and defeat of Gouveia in 1890 was hardly prepared for at all by previous significant contacts with the Shona. Gouveia exploited the divisions between the Shona paramounts and stimulated a bewildering and shifting pattern of alliances, involving the Makoni of Maungwe, the Mtoko of Budja, chief Kunzwi-Nyandoro, and many others. But it is hard to say who used who in all this. The Shona chiefs got, through their involvement with Gouveia, firearms which enabled them to beat off Ndebele raids more readily and which they were able to use in the 1896 rising. Moreover in the end Gouveia's empire collapsed, though this was admittedly partly due to his arrest by the British in 1890. At any rate in the early 1890's there was a successful revolt against him in Barwe in which he was killed and the Shona territories south of the Zambezi in what was to become Portuguese East Africa 'reverted briefly to their quasi-independent state'. By this time many of the Shona peoples who had been involved with Gouveia were in British South Africa Company territory but this fact made little difference to their preoccupations at first. During the first years of Company rule the Shona chiefs of the central and eastern areas continued to send fighting men across the border to assist the Barwe rebels against Gouveia.

Gouveia was not the only source of Portuguese pressure, however. In the late 1880's the Portuguese Government began to turn its attention to its African possessions. It realized that unless it established effective possession of areas with which Portugal had been so long associated these would fall to other European powers. Therefore, Portuguese expeditions began to be dispatched into places such as Mashonaland and Gazaland in an attempt to secure treaties with the chiefs. Gungunhana of Gaza tried to play off the Portuguese against the British and sent emissaries to

Natal; the Shona chiefs, however, regarded these newcomers as merely another in the long sequence of strangers who had passed through Shona territory in the nineteenth century. They cheerfully accepted gifts and flags but did not regard themselves as in any sense subject to Portugal. The Portuguese expeditions penetrated as far as Lomangundi and began to arouse Lobengula's alarm.

In the end nothing came of these Portuguese pressures because the boundary between Rhodesia and Portuguese East Africa was settled in Europe rather than in Mashonaland. But once again it is important for Shona history to realize that many Shona chiefs were involved in the business of treaty making at the same time as Lobengula was trying to deal with the much better known white pressures in Bulawayo.

Meanwhile the forces which were eventually to occupy Mashonaland were building up. We compared earlier the Ndebele and the Gaza state systems to the Rozwi empire and the Shona paramountcies. A similar comparison might be made between British pressure and Portuguese. Portuguese pressure really fell into a centuries old pattern; its most effective exponent, Gouveia, was effective precisely because he played the Shona game. British pressure, however, represented something new and newly formidable; against the power behind it neither the Portuguese nor the African peoples stood much chance of success. British pressure on central Africa was an overflow of the dynamic economy of South Africa. In the second half of the nineteenth century that economy had been revolutionized; diamonds and gold had sparked off a great surge of capitalist development. British expansion into central Africa was backed up by the growing railway and telegraph systems of South Africa; it could draw upon very considerable local resources of men and capital and was in this respect not only stronger than the Portuguese but stronger than any other colonial thrust in east and central Africa; and it was stimulated by Anglo-Boer rivalry.

English-speaking South Africa wanted to push into central Africa for a variety of reasons; because it was believed to be minerally rich; because it offered good grazing land; in order to outflank the Transvaal. The Boers wanted to push into central Africa to get grazing land and to avoid being outflanked. The Ndebele found themselves the focus of both Boer and British pressures. Matabeleland shared a frontier with the Transvaal and, after a British protectorate was declared over Bechuana-land, English-speaking interests could take this western route to Bulawayo.

The story of the dilemma in which these pressures placed Lobengula is so much better known than other aspects of nine-teenth-century Rhodesian history that I will not go into it at length here. What is most interesting for our purposes is to examine how the Ndebele reacted to these pressures. In some African state systems powerful motives existed for co-operation with one or other of the incoming white forces. Sometimes a ruler wanted protection from external enemies; sometimes a king wanted sup-port against internal rebels; sometimes the prospect of increased trade or of improved agriculture was welcomed; sometimes the prospect of education or technical advance. These factors operated both in Barotseland and in Bechuanaland where Lobengula's enemies, Lewanika and Khama, both sought British protection. None of these factors operated in Matabeleland. The Ndebele state was not strong enough to resist an attack by Europeans but it was certainly strong enough not to fear attacks by its African neighbours; it did not feel the need of protection. Lobengula had been able to overcome opposition to his accession and sub-sequently managed the difficult and turbulent politics of the Ndebele with supreme skill; he did not wish to ask for European aid against internal enemies—though he did use the threat to do so on one occasion—and he knew that any attempt to do so would mean civil war. He was not interested in improved trading opportunities. We shall see later what was his attitude to mission-aries. In short, Lobengula and the Ndebele as a whole felt they had nothing to gain by involvement with whites. Their aim was to live in 'Chinese isolation'; to continue their system without interference. Many whites thought that the Ndebele state was suffering all sorts of internal strains and external pressures and that it was breaking up. The truth seems to be that the Ndebele state was too successful on its own terms to be able to accommodate itself to the new era. As Richard Brown puts it, 'Matabele society was inherently unsuited to adapting easily to the incursion of European power and it neither collapsed nor was transformed but was swept aside'.

This 'sweeping aside' was in the end inevitable. But before it happened Lobengula played his part with much skill and always retained control over his internal situation. One of the reasons whites hated the Ndebele so much, indeed, was that they had to submit to Lobengula's authority inside Matabeleland. In 1887, for instance, young Frank Johnson, leader of a would-be prospecting party into Mashonaland, who was prevented from entering that area by Lobengula, expressed himself as follows: 'Oh ye spirits of departed negrophilists and followers of "Exeter Hall" if only you could feel what is felt by us today, at the knowledge that we white men and *Englishmen* too, are under the thumb and utterly in the power of a lot of black scoundrels there is little doubt that your *"brotherly love"* for niggers would receive a serious check!! Brothers indeed! d... scoundrels!! . . . To feel oneself under the power of a nigger is worse than being in prison and quite enough to bring on fever.'[7]

Lobengula tried to play off British against Boers and sections of British against each other. He tried to concede as little as possible and to delay the implementation of that little. He kept his regiments in check because he knew that war would be fatal to the Ndebele. But he was against too strong and determined a current. Rhodes was able to outwit and outplay him. Rhodes bought out his rivals so that apparent enemies of his were really in his service; and he played what he called the 'Home Rule trick' with great success. Thus the famous Rudd concession on which the British South Africa Company Charter was based and on the strength of which the occupation of Mashonaland was undertaken, was obtained from Lobengula because verbal promises were made that it would in fact protect the Ndebele from further white pressure. It was promised that not more than ten white men should enter Lobengula's country to work mines and that they 'would abide by the laws of his country and in fact be his people'; it was promised that notices would be put in all English and South African papers warning other whites to keep out; it was promised that the rifles of the ten whites should be at Lobengula's command were he to be attacked. As Richard Brown writes, Lobengula 'must have felt that he had gone a long way towards solving both his problems. On the one hand he was to receive a powerful armoury which could be used if the threats of Boer or Portuguese filibusters materialised, on the other, at the price of only ten white men in the country, who were to be under his authority, it was to be sealed against further white penetration. . . . It is not difficult to imagine that Lobengula believed that in signing the concession he had reconciled the irreconcilable and dealt satisfactorily with the external threat without at the same time unduly heightening that from within.'

But of course the verbal agreements were not included in the text of the concession which allowed the concessionaries to work mines and to take all steps necessary to do so throughout Lobengula's dominions. Once the concession had been obtained and then the Charter on the basis of it the pressure intensified. Lobengula, realizing some of the implications of his agreement to the concession, endeavoured to undo the damage; he tried to announce his repudiation of the concession through press statements and delegations; he tried to refuse or delay permission for the actual entry of Company men into his territory. But the stakes were too high for these attempts to frustrate Rhodes. If Lobengula proved difficult he would be swept aside. Early in December 1889 Rhodes signed an agreement with young Frank Johnson, whose hatred of the Ndebele we have seen above. This provided for a sudden attack on Bulawayo by a force of 500 whites and an auxiliary force provided by Khama, to 'so break up the power of the Amandabele as to render their raids on surrounding tribes impossible, to effect the emancipation of all their slaves and further, to reduce the country to such a condition as to enable the prospecting, mining and commercial staff of the British South Africa Company to conduct their operations in Matabeleland in peace and safety'.

At the last moment Lobengula gave way just enough to avoid this confrontation. He gave Jameson definite permission to prospect in the south of the kingdom and indefinite permission to prospect in Mashonaland if gold were not found in the south. This was enough for Rhodes who was already worried by Portuguese activities in Mashonaland. It was decided to abandon the idea of an attack on Bulawayo for the moment and to occupy Mashonaland by taking a column along the eastern borders of the Ndebele area, without bothering about trying to find gold in the south and in defiance of the fact that Lobengula had given no permission for the *occupation* of Mashonaland. 'The consequences of this new and final plan are two in number,' wrote the secretary of the Company. 'Firstly, if Lobengula looks on in silence and does nothing the Charter will occupy Mashonaland. . . . If on the other hand, Lobengula attacks us, then the original plan . . . will be carried out to the very letter . . . he must expect no mercy and none will be given him. . . . If he attacks us, he is doomed, if he does not, his fangs will be drawn, the pressure of civilization on all his borders will press more and more heavily upon him, and the desired result, the disappearance for ever of the Matabele as a power, if delayed is yet the more certain.'[8]

Lobengula chose to allow the pioneer column to enter Mashonaland in 1890 and by so doing bought another three years of Home Rule. The Company was preoccupied with establishing itself in Mashonaland and with driving the Portuguese out of Manicaland and had no desire for a rapid confrontation with the Ndebele. The Shona meanwhile received these new visitors with little surprise expecting them also to move on as all the rest had done. But sooner or later the clash was bound to come. It came in August 1893. An Ndebele raiding party was sent to punish Shona defaulters in the Fort Victoria area with strict instructions not to attack whites. These instructions were observed but Shona servants of white people were killed and mining interrupted. Rhodes at first wished to overlook the incident because he was not ready for a war at that moment and hoped to postpone it to 1894. He argued that the incident really proved Lobengula's wish to avoid any attack on whites. But Jameson, the Administrator of Mashonaland, decided that the moment had come. Settler opinion was aroused; missionaries were prepared to publicly support the need to 'punish' the Ndebele; and as Jameson cabled: 'we have the excuse for a row over murdered women and children now and the getting Matabeleland open would give us a tremendous lift in shares and everything else. The fact of its being shut up gives it an immense value both here and outside.'

Lobengula still desperately tried to avoid war. Although Company propagandists asserted that Ndebele armies were massing for an attack on the whites it is clear that the Ndebele took up purely defensive positions. Lobengula sent messages and delegations south stressing his desire for peace; the delegates were 'accidentally' shot and the messages ignored. A force of Company Volunteers was recruited on the promise of land and cattle; the necessary incident of Ndebele firing on British troops was manufactured; and the invasion of Matabeleland began in October 1893.

Stanlake Samkange describes the last act of the drama. 'When Lobengula heard about the death of his indunas sent to Cape Town with Dawson he was dumbfounded and mad with rage. . . . "The white men," he declared in exasperation, "are the fathers of liars." He ordered his army to "hloma" and appeared before them daubed with paint and carrying an assegai. In front of thousands of his warriors, Lobengula drove the assegai into the earth and the warriors responded with shouts of "Bayete! Bayete! Bayete! Uyi Zulu!!", leaping high and hitting their shields with knobkerries causing such a din as made the whole earth shake in response to the King's order to meet the advancing foe. In the excitement, few noticed that the assegai broke its shaft as it hit the earth—a bad omen.' The omen was justified; at the river crossings of the Shangani and the Bembesi Ndebele attacks were murderously broken up by machine gun fire. Lobengula and his remaining forces fled to the north and Bulawayo was fired, the whites who had been living there left unharmed. 'The campaign is virtually over,' wrote Selous in November, 'and the fair-haired descendants of the northern pirates are in possession of the great King's kraal and the calf of the black cow has fled into the wilderness.' At some time early in 1894 Lobengula died in the wilderness and the Matabele kingdom came to an end.[9]

It will be useful to close this section with an Ndebele view of these events taken from the oration of the *induna* Somubalana in August 1896. 'Excepting for occasional expeditions to hunt or punish all was peace in the land. But still it was not to be. The white man looked north and saw that there was gold upon the plains, which the Matibili had come to with so much blood and so many tears. Well King Lobengula knew the power and strength of the white man, honoured the white queen, and desired no quarrel. So when there came emissaries and ambassadors, begging concessions and presents of land and rights to mine, begging upon their knee, squatting low before the great King, Lobengula met them as a brother; killed beasts for them; extended hospitality; sent young maidens to them, and gave them half his kingdom. So the white men came with their rifles and they sat down in that half of the kingdom which had been given them to mine in, to take away the gold, and when the gold was finished to take themselves away with it. Three short years after the Mashonas gave trouble again. The Mashonas were Lobengula's subjects, and the white men has no business with the Mashonas, to protect them or shield them from the King's justice. So impis had to be sent to punish these Mashonas, and they had collided with the white man. And then the white man had come again with his guns that spat bullets as the heavens sometimes spit hail, and who were the naked Matibili to stand up against these guns and rifles? So the white man took from the Matibili the land as they had taken it from the Maholi and the Mashonas. And their King had been driven into exile. He had sent presents of gold, a peace offering, and the presents were taken and the peace was refused him.'[10]

In other parts of central Africa missionaries helped to prepare African societies for the impact of European rule in various ways. Sometimes they acted as advisers to chiefs—and gave them sensible and disinterested advice. Sometimes they provided education and skills which gave the people among whom they worked a favourable position in the early stages of colonial rule; sometimes they became so committed to 'their' people that they acted as effective spokesmen for them and defended their interests against the new colonial administrations. And very often they prepared African societies for the impact of other Europeans by beginning the process of introducing new ideas and new demands. The missionaries in Barotseland; the missionaries among the Tonga and Northern Ngoni in Nyasaland; the missionary advisers of Khama in Bechuanaland; all these played an important part in lessening the shock of the confrontation of blacks and whites in central Africa.

In the territory which became Southern Rhodesia missionaries did not play any of these roles. This was because they could not achieve a position of influence within Ndebele society even though they were established in Matabeleland and because they failed to establish themselves in Mashonaland at all.

The Ndebele first made contact with missionaries as early as 1829. From 1859 missionaries of the London Missionary Society were permanently established in Matabeleland. These missionaries were made use of by the Ndebele in various ways. They were used to mend guns; to inoculate cattle and give medical treatment to men; to write letters and to interpret; one missionary was even used to transport the keepers of the royal charms to court and back to their homes. But the Ndebele had no intention of allowing the missionaries to achieve influence. Mzilikazi and Lobengula saw clearly that their teaching would undermine the basis of the Ndebele state which depended upon raiding and the caste system; the two kings did not feel the need for literacy since the administration of the concentrated Ndebele state was efficient without it; and they did not feel any desire to become involved with the economic system of southern Africa out of which the missionaries came. In these ways they were different from Lewanika of the Lozi who wanted literacy to improve his elaborate bureaucracy and who wanted to develop trade. Lobengula did not admire the teaching of the missionaries which advocated 'putting everything on Christ that he would bear our sins for us'. Such a doctrine, he thought, was suitable only for white men since he had noticed that 'whenever they did anything wrong they always wanted to throw the blame on to others'. So the missionaries were kept in a sort of quarantine for thirty years. They made no converts and anyone who showed signs of becoming friendly to them was removed to another area.

As for the Shona, missionaries found it difficult to reach them at all. Lobengula refused permission for mission stations to be set up in Mashonaland and approaches to it other than those controlled by the Ndebele king were blocked to missionaries by the hostility of the Boers and the Portuguese. In 1877 Coillard, who later exercised such an influence over Lewanika, tried to set up a station in western Mashonaland at the kraal of chief Mashiangombi. He was removed by a force of Ndebele warriors and taken before Lobengula who warned him not to repeat the attempt. Later on, when it was more possible for missionaries to enter the Shona area, few thought it worth trying to do so. Father Devlin tells us: 'During the years around 1880, when missionaries, traders and political agents waited with varying purposes at Lobengula's kraal, only an occasional hunter had found his way on to the vast healthy plateau of Mashonaland. The London Missionary Society under J. S. Moffat . . . had arrived in 1859 but they remained always in Matabeleland. The Jesuits came in 1879, but they too shared the general illusion that the Mashona were the abject "dogs" of Lobengula and that the only people worth converting were the invaders from the south. Consequently, when Fr. Law . . . with one other priest and two very able Brothers, set out from Bulawayo, their only aim was to reach the kraal of Mzila, Lobengula's ally and counterpart. . . . Selous, the famous hunter, accompanied them as far as the gap in the great watershed; there he turned north to his favourite haunts on the high plateau, but he urged them to come with him and evangelize the Mashona. Instead, they turned south through the tsetse ridden valleys to Mzila's kraal, where the two priests died—heroically, but with nothing accomplished. The only missionary to come specifically for the Mashona was the Anglican Bishop Knight-Bruce on an exploratory tour in 1888; but the gallant bishop was in such a hurry and knew so little of the language that his report is not very enlightening.'

The results of all this were quite important. Missionaries certainly did little to modify the shock of the confrontation for either the Ndebele or the Shona. 'The Bechwana tribes in the Protectorate will bow to our advance and adapt themselves to the inevitable without much difficulty,' wrote Moffat, 'but not so the Matabele . . . It seems hard to understand why the grace of these thirty years missionary effort should have been rejected by the Matabele so utterly. Had they accepted it there might now have been sufficient enlightenment to enable them to meet the white man half-way and to mitigate the severity of the inevitable shock.' Moreover because they were excluded from the Ndebele system the missionaries became hostile to it. They did not give Lobengula disinterested advice; indeed there is reason to suppose that the missionary Helm was a knowing party to deceptions of Lobengula in the interest of Rhodes. Generally the missionaries believed that no progress could be made until the Ndebele system was broken down and they believed that this could only be done by force. Thus they welcomed the arrival of the British South Africa Company forces in Mashonaland in 1890. 'The hateful Matabele rule is doomed,' wrote one of them in that year. 'We as missionaries, with our thirty years history behind us, have little to bind our sympathies to the Matabele people, neither can we pity the fall of their power.' 'The wrath of God,' wrote the same man, was now descending on the Ndebele for their 'constant and persistent refusal' of the Gospel for a whole generation. God, he rejoiced, was about to 'speak in a very different manner' to the Ndebele than that which his missionaries had been forced to adopt.

Missionary support was a major source of strength to Rhodes in his advance into central Africa. And the results of the absence of missionaries in Mashonaland before the arrival of the whites were also important. Elsewhere in central Africa missionaries had success with the old agricultural peoples who now found themselves sandwiched in between aggressive and strong intruding societies. Some people thought that the Shona interest and skill in craftsmanship, their comparatively pacific and settled mode of life, favoured missionary penetration. Even though Shona devotion to their own religion would probably have made difficult any real alliance with the missionaries, it is interesting to speculate on the reaction of Shona chiefs to the prospects of an alliance with a strong missionary presence. It is interesting to speculate also whether, if such alliances had been established, the missionaries themselves would have been so convinced that the Shona interest lay in the occupation of their country by white settlers.

These are mere speculations, however, because in the event the missionaries entered Mashonaland with the white settlers and as their allies. Let us take the example of the Catholic Church. The Jesuits had made many attempts to penetrate central Africa. In the late 1870's they opened stations in Matabeleland but the Bulawayo station was abandoned in 1887 and the Empandeni station in 1889. The Jesuit Fathers swore not to re-enter Matabeleland until the Ndebele kingdom had been overthrown. Instead they entered Mashonaland in the wake of the British South Africa Company. A Jesuit Father accompanied the Pioneer Column as Chaplain; Dominican Sisters were recruited to set up hospitals and mobile ambulances. The missionaries turned to the Shona only after they had established themselves as preachers and nurses and teachers to the white community; to the Shona they were completely identified with the other whites.

There was no chance under these circumstances of a real alliance with Shona chiefs. An attempt to set up a mission station beyond the effective boundaries of Company administration in Mtoko where it would have been dependent on the land grant and protection of the powerful chief was abandoned and the Catholic stations were set up on land granted by the Company without reference to the local Shona authorities. Africans were attracted to these stations as refugees from the authority of the chiefs and headmen. 'Among the numerous kraals of the country,' wrote the founder of Chishawasha mission, 'there will be some who will avail themselves' of the opportunity 'to escape the tyranny of the indunas who are bullies'.

Moreover the Catholic fathers and sisters were emotionally committed to the Company administration. Any criticisms which might be levelled against its treatment of the Shona were balanced by the missionary support of the Company against the Ndebele. In 1893 Father Prestage cabled to Rhodes in support of Jameson's decision to make war on Lobengula after the Fort Victoria incident. 'Dr Jameson has asked my opinion as to the justice of punishing the Amandabeles at once. Without prompt punishment there is every probability of the same atrocities recurring.' The Dominican Sisters, awaiting the call to set up a hospital in the newly conquered Bulawayo, put it more simply: 'Of course *our men* have taken the country and we shall follow them.'[11]

Few converts were made in either Mashonaland or Matabeleland before 1896 and when the Ndebele and the Shona rose in that year mission stations, alien Christian Africans, and indigenous Africans loyal to the missions were made a particular object of attack.

THE ADMINISTRATION IN MATABELELAND AND MASHONALAND: REASONS FOR THE NDEBELE AND SHONA RISINGS

Mashonaland. When the Shona attacked mission stations in 1896 missionaries were taken completely by surprise. They had thought that the Shona were grateful for protection against the Ndebele and they had not learnt enough about the Shona to understand their attachment to their own religion and forms of government. In the same way other whites failed to realize that so far from their arrival in Mashonaland preserving the Shona it greatly disrupted the valued Shona way of life.

Most whites did not realize, for example, that the Shona of central and eastern Mashonaland had been carrying on a trade in gold and ivory with the Portuguese and their agents which was valuable to them in all sorts of ways. It was valuable because it provided guns; it was valuable because it gave the chief the means of wealth and hospitality; and it was valuable because in return for the gold and ivory the Portuguese agents were able to provide a wide range of goods at low prices. The first Administrator of Mashonaland, Colquhoun, did realize the value of this trade to the Shona. In December 1890 he proposed that the Company should buy 'up gold at the same rates Portuguese did. A considerable traffic was carried on by Portuguese bastards for which payment was made to natives by cotton limbo, etc. It will prevent dissatisfaction if we continue this trade.' But the trade was not continued; the Company was interested only in European gold mining and tried to stop the sale of gold dust by Africans to merchants from the Zambezi. It was assumed that the Company had brought many increased opportunities of profitable trade to the Shona. But the Shona did not find it so. The hunter, Selous, tells us that they found the prices of goods brought up from South Africa and sold by the Company much too high: they 'had been accustomed to dealing with the Portuguese traders from the Zambezi; and as these men got their merchandise by water carriage from Europe right up to Tete and then employed slave labour to have it carried up country, they could afford to sell very cheap'.

In this economic field the Shona of the central and eastern districts at first welcomed the Pioneers as an additional source of trade. They then discovered that the Company administration intended to displace the old trade patterns and to replace them by an economy controlled by the whites. The same thing happened in the field of politics. A number of Shona chiefs were quite prepared to welcome the whites in 1890, partly as allies against the Ndebele, but partly also as another force which might be exploited in the game of Shona politics. Early police patrols found that the various Shona chiefs tried to recruit them against their local rivals, and in the same way farmers and prospectors were drawn into local skirmishes and controversies. The administration thought that all this showed an acceptance of white rule; but the facts were different. To the chiefs it was not a matter of whites on one side and blacks on the other; each chief was seeking for temporary white allies to balance the allies his rival might manage to recruit. This was not an unrealistic way to look at the matter since white farmers took opposing sides in local disputes and since the British were balanced by the Portuguese in the minds of the Shona chiefs in eastern and central Mashonaland for months if not years after the arrival of the Pioneer Column. The Shona paramounts played one white interest off against another; chief Makoni signed a treaty with the Company and immediately thereafter signed another with the Portuguese because the Company had gone on to make an alliance with his rival Mutassa; Mangwende and Lomagundi accepted Portuguese flags with no intention whatsoever of accepting Portuguese sovereignty; and in the same spirit they accepted the presence of the Company and the settlers which almost all Shona believed to be temporary.

In the early period, then, relations with individual whites and with the authorities could be cordial enough. The American settler, 'Curio' Brown, tells us of his visits to the kraal of chief Mashiangombi, where Coillard had tried to set up his mission and where the Shona rising broke out in June 1896. There, as he sat down to meals of maize porridge and relish, he was asked: 'What were the whitemen doing at Harare [Salisbury]. . . . What the whiteman intended to do with the gold they were digging and how soon they would have enough of it and then return to Diamond [Kimberley].' Brown replied: 'We are here for all time, and in a very few years thousands of white men will come with their wives and children and build big towns out of burnt red mud —towns larger than all Mashiangombi's villages put together.'

Gradually Mashiangombi's people and others began to realize that Brown and the other whites meant what they said. The whites intended to stay—and they intended to make the chiefs subject to them. There would be no more question of alliances but a demand for submission. This was brought home to the chiefs in a variety of ways. Land began to be alienated in certain areas particularly suitable for farming and white settlers arrived to set up house without any permission having been sought from the chief. The white theory was that the land in Mashonaland could be granted by the Company as concessionaries from Lobengula; the Shona chiefs did not regard themselves as subjects of Lobengula and one of the most cherished rights of the chief was the right to allocate land.

Then the whites began to assume the right to punish the subjects of the chiefs, even though the punishment often seemed more like armed raids than anything else. Chiefs began to adopt a cautious and often hostile attitude to the whites. In Maungwe, for example, paramount chief Makoni refused permission for an Anglican missionary to enter his kraal in 1892. 'White men were his enemies,' he said. 'They had killed some of Mangwende's people and outraged the women. After assuring him again and again that I was his friend,' reported the missionary, 'we were admitted and then he said, "If God sent the white man to teach him and his people why did God send the white man to kill and outrage the native peoples?".'

As far as the chiefs were concerned the last straw came with the demand for the payment of hut tax in 1894. Before that time the implications of what the whites were demanding were not clear to the chiefs; but the demand for hut tax could mean only one thing. They were being asked to submit to the whites when they had not been conquered nor disarmed. In most of the books about Rhodesia one gets the impression that after the arrival of the whites in 1890 the Shona quietly accepted the authority of the Company until they suddenly rebelled in 1896. The reality was different. For two years before the co-ordinated risings of 1896 the Shona chiefs tried individually to defy the demand for tax.

There is much evidence of this resistance in the files of the Southern Rhodesian Native Department which was set up in 1894 to collect tax. Before the creation of the Native Department no attempt had been made to administer the Shona at all; even after 1894 collection of tax was the main interest of the new officials. The new Native Commissioners soon discovered that the Shona were not prepared to welcome or to passively accept white control. 'On many occasions,' Native Commissioner Weale of the Marendellas District records, 'the messenger boys were driven off by the natives, who refused to pay hut tax and in some cases the natives fired on them, telling them they would do the same to the white man too, and it was found necessary to arm a percentage of the messengers with Martini rifles and ball cartridges for self-defence in the future.' Weale was instructed to keep these clashes out of the press and out of public notice. 'One of the effects of this policy was to lead people into the false belief that the natives were too cowardly ever to rise in open rebellion, which was disproved in 1896, causing a feeling of false security and unpreparedness, which was to prove disastrous.'

Some Shona chiefs were able to resist the payment of tax successfully. One of these was chief Kunzwi-Nyandoro, whose men were well-armed with guns from Portuguese East Africa, and who occupied a strong fortified kraal. In October 1895 his men drove off the Native Commissioner's messengers when they came to demand tax. In April 1896, two months before the general rebellion broke out, Kunzwi 'refused to allow the Native Police to collect hut tax in his district and had sent the Police back to Mr. Campbell with a threat that he would kill all Police and white men in his district'.

Chiefs were hostile to the whites because they found they undermined their chiefly prerogatives, such as controlling external trade and granting land use rights, and because the demand for tax payment threatened their political independence in a way that the mere settlement of whites in Mashonaland did not. The mass of the Shona people who lived in areas where there was white settlement or white mining or white administrative officers were also hostile to the new order. They were directly affected by the collection of tax which usually took the form of the seizure of cattle and sheep. 'The kraals are complaining that in some instances they are left without a single beast,' it was reported in 1895 in western Mashonaland. Later that year the Executive Council decided to suspend collection of tax for three months and thereafter not to take it in the form of stock 'in view of the fact that at this rate there would be no cattle left to collect in a year or two'.

The Shona people were also affected by white demands for labour. Before the formation of the Native Department labour was often taken by force by individual settlers backed up by police. 'The Mashonas were in the habit of clearing away from their villages on the approach of any white man,' wrote the new Native Commission in Hartley in 1894. 'The chiefs have appeared to have so little authority over their men that anyone in want of boys . . . have had to press the first that they came across. Hence the reason of boys clearing away from their kraals.' After the formation of the Native Department collection of labour became its responsibility. But there was little improvement. In 1897 the American missionaries in Melsetter described the Native Department procedure as 'sending native constables through the country collecting the natives by armed force, compelling them to labour here and there, wherever their services happen to be required, whether they are willing or not, their wives being seized as hostages, in case they attempt to escape'.

So, as it became clear that the whites intended to stay and clear what their staying meant, the Shona peoples of the western, central and much of the eastern districts were prepared by their chiefs and religious leaders to rise up against the whites. Recently Grey Chivanda has collected some oral evidence in the Mazoe district which helps us to understand how the Shona saw the situation. The Mazoe area was not tributary to Lobengula. 'Politically the Africans of the Mazoe area considered themselves free from the rule of any other people or tribe, though they had continually to watch against the Matabele.' They were in regular trading contact with the Portuguese on the Zambezi.

When the Pioneers arrived at Harare (Salisbury) the spirit mediums of the Mazoe Shona advised them: 'Don't be afraid of them—they are only traders. But take a black cow to them and say, "This is the meat with which we greet you".' The chiefs sent cattle and in return received cloth and blankets. 'The Europeans

. . . said they were looking for gold and asked for help in prospecting as well as peace to enable prospectors to carry on their work. A people who were used to trade . . . readily understood what the newcomers were looking for and even co-operated in the search for gold.' Some of the Mazoe Shona acted as guides to the gold-bearing areas; others volunteered labour in return for cloth; chief Hwata hoped to ally himself with this new power and sent his relatives to serve the whites and to be educated. But none of this meant an acceptance of white rule. 'An exchange of presents didn't mean that the Africans had given up their sovereign or land rights; the Europeans were not there by virtue of conquest either. The chiefs and the people did as they pleased with their lives and wanted to be left alone to plough and hunt.'

But soon the Shona of the Mazoe found that the white settlement was putting intolerable pressure on their way of life. The chiefs found land being alienated to white farmers without reference to them—'They couldn't listen to the talk of Africans as the owners of the land. . . . The whites coveted our land, its resources and riches.' The visits of Portuguese traders came to an end. The chiefs were faced with the tax demand—'Hwata and Chiweshe refused to pay tax to Europeans because they were strangers. For three or four years Europeans were demanding tax and it didn't seem logical that one who wasn't acknowledged as a ruler should demand tribute.' Moreover the chiefs found their authority challenged by the new Native Police. These Police were either recruited outside the district or from among the 'servants or semi-slaves' of the chiefs, the so-called Vanyai. 'These people were quick to switch over to the Europeans either for refuge or because they wanted European goods. They were among the first to join the native police, people who welcomed an opportunity for revenge on their former masters.' The Police 'thought they had a right to everything they came across. They would demand some goats, beautiful girls to cook for them, and then make these girls their mistresses. . . . Their raids caused the Mashona to think of the Europeans as bad as the Matabele.'

Many people were compelled to work for whites and then mocked because they did not understand what was required or beaten. 'Good or bad you were beaten.' Some of the chiefs, even, were beaten. 'Most people, when they saw the behaviour of Europeans change as they struck more roots in the country, said desperately, "We thought they were good people".' Soon the

Mazoe Shona moved out of despair to plans of action and preparations for the rising began.[12]

Matabeleland. The situation in Matabeleland during the first years of Company administration was quite different from that in Mashonaland. The Shona did not regard themselves as conquered; the Ndebele knew that they had been. The Shona were not disarmed; the Ndebele knew that anyone carrying arms ran the risk of being shot on sight. In this way the apparent paradox arose that before the 1896 risings the supposedly cowardly Shona offered scattered but significant armed resistance to the demands of tax collectors and labour recruiters while the militant Ndebele offered no armed opposition at all. Many whites allowed themselves to believe, indeed, that the Ndebele had realized the implications of their defeat and had accepted white rule. 'It was a glorious scheme to open up such a vast country to Europeans,' wrote the *Bulawayo Sketch* in sentimental mood in 1894; 'glorious for us, but the pathos is there all the same disguise it as we may. Natives selling their beautiful Ostrich Feather Head Gear for a mere song which they offer with a sad smile of deprecating air, saying, "Our Glory is done, our Fighting Days over".' 'Since the war the Matabeles have never given the least trouble,' wrote the missionary Helm in 1896. 'The people have undergone a wonderful change since Lobengula's time and were so submissive that anything in the nature of a revolt seemed out of the question.'

In Mashonaland the whites did not attempt to transform Shona society even though their demands upon it threatened to undermine many of its values. In Matabeleland after the 1893 war there was a deliberate attempt to transform the whole structure of Ndebele society. The monarchy was in effect abolished—Lobengula was dead and his younger sons removed to South Africa to be educated as Rhodes' wards. The regimental towns were broken up and in theory at any rate the regimental system destroyed. None of the Ndebele *indunas* were recognized as authorities for the purpose of administration. The superior Ndebele castes were prevented from exerting their authority over the Holi caste by force; members of the Ndebele aristocracy were compelled to work side by side with the Holi; many members of the Holi caste, though by no means the majority, took the opportunity to move away from the Ndebele settled area. All this, in addition to the confiscation of cattle and land, amounted to an attempt to dismantle the Ndebele system completely.

The Ndebele, therefore, were exposed to pressures quite unlike those experienced by the other peoples of east and central Africa at this time. Most whites were confident, however, that the majority of the old Ndebele nation actually welcomed these changes. They believed that the Holi caste welcomed its new independence; that the young men welcomed freedom from conscription, from military discipline and arbitrary punishments; and that the older members of the aristocracy welcomed an opportunity to acquire wealth and to engage in modern economic activity. Thus the High Commissioner's representatives reported in 1894 that the Ndebele 'seemed greatly relieved when told that the military system of the country had been abolished and that henceforth they were free from all liability to serve as fighting men'. In 1895 Rhodes assured the shareholders of the Company that the 'chiefs of the Matabele . . . were all pleased and naturally so. In the past they have always "walked delicately" because anyone who got to any position in the country and became rich was generally "smelt out" and lost his life. . . . In so far as the bulk of the people were concerned, they were not allowed to hold any cattle, or to possess anything of their own. Now they can hold cattle and the leaders of the people know that they do not walk daily with the fear of death over them.'

The whites were so confident that the Ndebele accepted their defeat and welcomed the new order that they did not take any real precautions against an uprising. They recruited and armed young Ndebele aristocrats as Company Police, training them in the use of modern rifles. And at the end of 1895 Jameson took most of the white Police out of the country on the ill-fated Jameson raid into the Transvaal.

Looking back this confidence seems astonishing. Undoubtedly the majority of the Ndebele were still deeply attached to the old system; the regimental system might be broken up but its members still regarded themselves as bound by its calls on their loyalty; the majority even of the Holi caste continued to regard themselves as Ndebele and to regret the passing of the nation's power. But over and above this there were real individual grievances against the Company administration which more than cancelled out its supposed advantages. The theoretical security of property was cancelled out by the actual loss of nearly all the land in the area of Ndebele settlement and the loss of nearly all the cattle of the nation; the freedom from conscription was cancelled out by the institution of forced labour.

The British Government had tried to prevent a wholesale alienation of land and confiscation of cattle. They established a Land Commission to ensure that adequate land and sufficient cattle were reserved for Ndebele needs and instructed the Company that no permanent grants could be made until the Commission had reported. But the Company easily evaded this attempt at control. The men who had defeated the Ndebele had been promised land and cattle and they were now given land and cattle. Then men who supported the Company in England were also rewarded with land grants. Jameson described all these grants as 'provisional' but by the time the Land Commission reported in October 1894 the greater part of the Ndebele home land had been promised to whites. The Commission therefore tamely recommended that land be reserved for Ndebele occupation to the north and north-east, where few Ndebele had ever lived and in country which turned out to be very unsuitable for grazing or cultivation. The mass of Ndebele found themselves reduced to the status of squatters on European farms and had to pay rent in produce or in labour to avoid eviction. 'One cause of dissatisfaction and unrest,' said the senior *induna* Gambo in 1897, 'is that after we have lived many years in a spot we are told that a white man has purchased it, and we have to go.'

As for the Ndebele cattle the Commission proved equally unable to protect Ndebele rights. It is a complicated story, hard to unravel. Briefly there had been some 250,000 cattle in Ndebele hands before the 1893 war. By the time the reallocation was complete only 40,930 were left in the possession of the Ndebele. Of the others some went to the so-called 'loot-kraals' as payment to the Volunteers; others went for Police rations; others were taken as Company property; others were rustled into South Africa by white adventurers. As far as the Company was concerned the trick was done by maintaining that the majority of the cattle had been royal property in the fullest sense and that as such they had been inherited by the new governing power. As far as the Ndebele were concerned resentment at the confiscation was increased by the fact that the cattle left to them were unequally distributed. Most were handed over to 'reliable' senior indunas while the young men received few or none.

The young men were further aggrieved by the operation of the forced labour system. 'As the demand for labour in the mining districts increased,' reported the Chief Native Commissioner, 'it was deemed advisable to call upon the Abezansi to contribute their share to the labour. In many instances they refused to do so arguing that their slaves should earn money for them. This condition of semi-slavery could not be tolerated by a civilized government and in order to deal equally with all classes the young men of the Abezansi were called upon to work for two months in the year. This they refused to do. . . . In some cases the Native Police had to call out some of the young men to work.'

There is evidence, also, that working conditions were not good. The missionary Carnegie, who had expected so much from the downfall of Lobengula, expressed his disillusionment in 1896. 'A proud and hitherto unconquered Matabele cannot be turned in a month, or a year, into a useful servant by kicks, sjambok and blows. You cannot civilize him by quarrelling with him a few days before his pay is due, by stoning or unjustly beating him, by cursing him for not understanding an order given in English.'

Carnegie went on to criticize the Matabeleland Native Department. 'The wrong men were often chosen for handling such raw material. . . . The whole question of native policy had been left since the war in an unsettled and, therefore, most unsatisfactory condition.' The Native Department in Matabeleland in fact existed almost entirely as a cattle collecting body. It did not establish regular centres of administration in regular contact with the people; the South African political leader, Tengo Jabavu, who visited Matabeleland in 1897, believed that the rising had been mainly caused by the despair of people who did not understand what was happening to them and who had no intermediaries or protectors. We have already seen why it was that the missionaries could not play that role.

There were, then, abundant reasons for Ndebele discontent. Let us end by quoting the most eloquent expression of that discontent, Somabulana's oration at the meeting between the Ndebele leaders and Rhodes in August 1896. 'The MaHoli and the Mashona . . . what are they? Dogs! Sneaking cattle thieves! Slaves! But we, the Amandabili, the sons of Kumalo, the Izulu, Children of the Stars; we are no dogs! You came, you conquered. The strongest takes the land. We accepted your rule. We lived under you. But not as dogs! If we are to be dogs it is better to be

dead . . . I myself once visited Bulawayo. I came to pay my
respects to the Chief Magistrate. I brought my indunas with me,
and my servants. I am a chief. I am expected to travel with
attendants and advisers. I came to Bulawayo early in the morning,
before the sun had dried the dew, and I sat down before the Court
House, sending messages to the Chief Magistrate that I waited
to pay my respects to him. And so I sat until the evening shadows
were long. And then . . . I sent again to the Chief Magistrate and
told him that I did not wish to hurry him in any unmannerly way;
I would wait his pleasure; but my people were hungry; and when
the white men visited me it was my custom to kill that they might
eat. The answer from the Chief Magistrate . . . was that the town
was full of stray dogs; dog to dog; we might kill those and eat
them if we could catch them. So I left Bulawayo that night; and
when next I tried to visit the Chief Magistrate it was with my
impis behind me; no soft words in their mouths; but the assegai
in their hands. Who blames me?'

Notes

I have not attempted to give source references for all the quotations in this
chapter. References for most of them may be found in T. O. Ranger *Revolt in
Southern Rhodesia 1896–7* Heinemann 1967. In the notes below I acknowledge
the secondary sources which I have found most useful and identify the two
African voices which I have quoted at greatest length:

1. I have relied for this section of the chapter mostly on Dr Hilda Kuper's
study in, Kuper, Hughes and Van Velsen *The Shona and Ndebele of Southern
Rhodesia* International African Institute 1955
2. The account given here of the death of the Mambo is taken from the
reminiscences of the old warrior Citsha as recorded in 1898 by Native Commissioner Weale. Citsha was a member of a Swazi contingent which operated
with Zwangendaba but which remained in Rhodesia when he crossed the
Zambezi and later allied itself with the Ndebele. Weale's version of the old
man's memories is full and fascinating even although couched in romantic
nineteenth-century English. It can be found in the National Archives Salisbury
file WE 3/2/6
3. This account of the Ndebele kingship is taken from Hughes and Van
Velsen's study in *The Shona and Ndebele of Southern Rhodesia*
4. I have drawn heavily in this section of the chapter on J. D. Omer-Cooper
The Zulu Aftermath Longmans 1966
5. This passage is again taken from the reminiscences of Citsha
6. Father Christopher Devlin, well known as a historian of English Catholicism,
began work on Shona history before his death. I have found the two articles
which he published on his work extremely stimulating and valuable even
though they are merely first drafts. The articles are: 'The Mashona and the

Portuguese' and 'The Mashona and the British' *The Shield* Salisbury May and June 1961

7. This extract from Johnson's diary is taken, like one or two other quotations in this chapter, from a valuable study of white activity and attitudes in Central Africa, H. A. C. Cairns *Prelude to Imperialism: British Reactions to Central African Society 1840–1890* London 1965

8. For the preceding three paragraphs I have depended upon the work of Richard Brown, 'Aspects of the Scramble for Matabeleland' *The Zambesian Past* (eds.) Stokes and Brown Manchester University Press 1966

9. My quotation is from Stanlake Samkange *The Origins of Rhodesia*, an account of Ndebele relations with the whites (Heinemann, forthcoming)

10. Somabulana was a senior Matabele *induna* and one of the rebel leaders in 1896. He acted as spokesman at the famous first *indaba* with Rhodes. His oration was recorded by the correspondent for *The Times*, De Vere Stent, who was one of the four white men present.

11. For these details concerning the Jesuit and Dominican establishment in Rhodesia I have used Michael Gelfand *Mother Patrick and her nursing sisters* Juta Cape Town 1965

12. I am drawing here upon an unpublished paper, 'The Mashona Rebellion in Oral Tradition: Mazoe District' by C. G. Chivanda

Recommended Reading

Much of the material published on the nineteenth-century history of Rhodesia has really been concerned with the history of white activity in the area. The best classical history is L. H. Gann *A History of Southern Rhodesia, Early Days to 1934* London 1965

Three outstanding books on the African side of nineteenth-century Rhodesian history are:
J. D. Omer-Cooper *The Zulu Aftermath* Longmans 1966
E. T. Stokes and R. Brown *The Zambesian Past* Manchester University Press 1966
P. Mason *The Birth of a Dilemma* Oxford University Press 1958

A lively treatment of Lobengula's dilemma in the form of a novel is:
Stanlake Samkange *On Trial For My Country* Heinemann 1966

7. The political history of twentieth-century Zambia

ANDREW ROBERTS

Introduction. During the nineteenth century, the area now known as Zambia had been rapidly drawn into a wider world. At the end of the century, with the coming of British rule and the creation of Northern Rhodesia, this process entered a new phase. Here, as elsewhere in Africa, colonial rule had two major effects. It continued the extension of contacts with the outside world, so much so indeed that tribal economies became involved in the economy of the world at large. And colonial rule, by imposing a single government over this territory, drew together the various peoples living within it into a larger unity. The most recent stage in this progressive unification and involvement with the outside world was the transformation in 1964 of Northern Rhodesia into Zambia, an independent state under African rule and a member of the United Nations.

Looking back now, this seems a natural and inevitable development; it took place in so many other countries in Africa and Asia. But whereas in most parts of Africa some form of African government was soon seen as the ultimate end—however distant—of colonial rule, the destiny of Northern Rhodesia remained uncertain until quite recently. This uncertainty was due to the country's position between the territories of southern Africa, dominated by Europeans, and those to the north such as the Congo and East Africa where the colonial governments largely denied settlers political power and did envisage, however dimly, an eventual transfer of power to Africans. Northern Rhodesia had been created as an extension of British power in South Africa and Southern Rhodesia, and its main contacts were always with southern Africa. Thus for a time it seemed possible that Northern Rhodesia would move into some form of closer association with its southern neighbours, or at least develop along similar lines, towards self-government by a white minority. On the other hand, the proportion of Europeans to Africans was far smaller in Northern

154

Rhodesia than in Southern Rhodesia, let alone South Africa. As early as 1899 Lord Milner had argued that the Zambezi was the natural frontier to a future British Africa in the southern end of the continent; the country to the north should become a 'black dependency'. In 1924 this view seemed to be confirmed when Northern Rhodesia, unlike Southern Rhodesia, but like the British territories in East and West Africa, came under the control of the Colonial Office. Yet this step was far from decisive. The history of Northern Rhodesia, from 1899 to 1964, can best be understood in terms of the tension between the ties with southern Africa and those with Britain and her theory of imperial trusteeship. At times the first seemed to prevail, especially when the Central African Federation was created in 1953. In the end, however, it was the British factor which counted for most, not so much because of British policy, which had in fact supported Federation, as because of the pressure put upon Britain by popular African nationalism.

These two factors—the South African and the British—also correspond closely to the two main kinds of European influence on Northern Rhodesia, which may be regarded as the heritage of Rhodes the business man and empire builder, and Livingstone the explorer and writer. Rhodes' heritage may be traced in the actual creation of the country, in its close links with the south, the arrival of European settlers, and in the exploitation of the Copperbelt. These served to provide Zambia with an industrial base without parallel among other countries under African rule, except for the Congo which also includes part of the Copperbelt. By contrast the heritage of Livingstone has been, at least until very recently, much less prominent. Perhaps the most impressive achievement so far in this tradition has been the series of studies by European scholars devoted to understanding the condition of Africans in Northern Rhodesia. But the knowledge thus gained, and the spirit informing it, has hitherto had little influence on social policy.

The reasons for this are partly to be sought in financial arrangements which deprived Northern Rhodesia of revenue that could finance social development. But they are also to be sought in the character of European settlement. In terms of African education and social progress, Northern Rhodesia lagged behind not only the countries to the north but also South Africa. In South Africa, and to a much lesser extent in Southern Rhodesia, Europeans felt sufficiently secure in their supremacy to find room for skilled and educated Africans, even if this was only in a segregated 'sub-society' with firm upper limits. Europeans in Northern Rhodesia had no such strength and thus no such security. They had, however, just enough influence to ensure that it was Africans who suffered from the basic uncertainty as to the future of the country and the relative position of Africans and Europeans within it. The Copperbelt attracted white settlers from Europe and South Africa; thus although many Africans also worked on the mines, few were trained to take any part in running them. And because of the European presence, small as it was, there seemed for long to be no prospect of African government; thus African education was neglected. For these reasons, Zambia today, though comparatively rich in financial terms, is poor in developed human skills. It has a 'dual economy', whereby the country, despite an advanced industrial sector, is still largely dependent on subsistence agriculture. The main task facing Zambia today is to redress this imbalance and eliminate the tensions to which it gives rise.

BRITISH SOUTH AFRICA COMPANY RULE (1899–1924)
Economic Development. The British South Africa Company did little with Northern Rhodesia. The stimulus to acquiring it for Britain had come from Rhodes. He died in 1902, and the Company found itself burdened with the administration of a country which offered little hope of economic profit. This was ironical, considering what efforts the Company had made to obtain mining concessions. The Company had failed to gain possession of the minerals of Katanga, and the hopes of finding gold north of the Zambezi came to nothing. Between 1900 and 1905 prospectors examined the surface deposits of copper in Northern Rhodesia, some of which had long been worked by Africans. But in this land-locked country only production on a very large scale would justify the heavy costs of transporting raw materials to the coast. For this, massive invest-ment was needed, but the prospects were too uncertain to be attractive and the Company itself had no capital to spare. It was only after the Company handed over the country to the Colonial Office in 1924 that the deeper copper ores were discovered. For the Company, Northern Rhodesia was no more than a tiresome appendage to its real seat of power in Southern Rhodesia.

Under Company rule Northern Rhodesia was economically

important mainly as a link between the Congo and southern Africa. In 1904 the railway was brought across the Zambezi from Southern Rhodesia, just below the Victoria Falls. By 1909 it had been extended to link up with the Congo system. Henceforward coke from Wankie, in Southern Rhodesia, went to the copper mines in Katanga, which had proved more rewarding than those in Northern Rhodesia; while their copper was exported through the Rhodesias to Beira in Mozambique as the railway from Katanga through Angola to the Atlantic Ocean was not opened until 1931. The only mine of any consequence in Northern Rhodesia was the lead mine at Broken Hill and that did not really get under way until the First World War. Europeans were in any case discouraged from settling in Northern Rhodesia by the prevalence of tsetse fly and malaria. In the more healthy areas, the Company appropriated blocks of land and made allocations from these to Europeans. Thus a few settlers took up land in Tonga country along the railway, which happened to run through a tsetse-free belt. There they raised maize and beef for sale in Katanga. Other European farmers settled in the far north, at the south end of Lake Tanganyika, and near Fort Jameson in the east, where from 1914 tobacco was grown successfully.

Changes in African life. All the same, Company rule brought about important changes in African life. In 1899 its territory north of the Zambezi had been divided into two: North-Eastern Rhodesia with headquarters at Fort Jameson, and North-Western Rhodesia with headquarters, from 1907, at Livingstone by the Victoria Falls. In 1911 the two parts were united to form Northern Rhodesia The days of inter-tribal raiding and warfare were over, and chiefs were now subordinated to a handful of British officials. In theory, the chiefs were now little more than policemen, though they were denied appropriate wages. In practice, they continued to hold courts, and the administration upheld the traditional rules for chiefly succession, though it went so far as to create chiefs among the Tonga, who had never had them before. But the European officials and their small police force had to be paid for by means of local taxes, and these had to be paid in cash. Since Africans grew no cash crops, they had to engage in wage-labour. Some obtained jobs on the railway, others in government or domestic service, but many left the country altogether, seeking work in the mines and towns of Katanga, Southern Rhodesia and

South Africa. The government encouraged this migration; indeed, taxation was regarded as a necessary stimulus to provide the labour needed by Europeans. Recruiting agents from Katanga and Southern Rhodesia were active in Northern Rhodesia until the 1930's, and South African agents recruited in Barotseland and the north-west from 1940 to 1967.

The coming of the *pax britannica* affected different peoples in different ways. The Ngoni perhaps felt the change most severely. Not only was warfare, their way of life, forbidden them, but they lost most of their cattle in the war of 1898 or in the rinderpest epidemic the following year, and transfers of cattle had under-pinned the Ngoni system of social relations. Moreover, Ngoniland was one of the few areas where large blocks of land were alienated from Africans, to the North Charterland Company. In general, Northern Rhodesia was sparsely populated; there may have been little more than a million inhabitants before 1914. But by 1924 overcrowding in the Ngoni area around Fort Jameson was acute; the only other comparable area was the Lozi flood plain, and this was intensively cultivated. In 1941 the Ngoni land shortage was eased when the government reacquired most of the North Charter-land concession and settled Africans on this land. The Bemba, by contrast, were much less affected. They retained almost all their conquests of the previous century, and virtually the only Europeans in their country were the few officials and missionaries. The end of raiding injured their chiefs more than the people themselves, whose traditional freedom of movement now took the new form of long-distance labour migration. As for the smaller or less organized tribes, such as the Mambwe in the north or the Tonga in the south, who had long been harassed by their stronger neigh-bours, they gained under colonial rule a security such as they had seldom known before.

Barotseland. The position of Barotseland was unique. The treaty concluded in 1900 set limits to the Company's authority such as existed nowhere else. Although Lewanika's country was in prac-tice considerably reduced, the Lozi system of government con-tinued to function more or less independently. Lozi chiefs had to collect tax for the Company, but they were the only chiefs to receive a fixed percentage of the taxes paid by their subjects. Moreover, the Lozi gained a head start in education over other Africans in Northern Rhodesia. At first the Company, which had no economic interest in Barotseland, did nothing to provide the various benefits it had once promised Lewanika. Coillard, the missionary, had founded a school and by 1900 there were several young Lozi who could read and write. But Lewanika wanted a school that was independent of mission influence. He attempted to achieve this by collaborating with an American negro church; this scheme broke down, but it scared the Company into setting up in 1906 the Barotse National School, which until 1930 was the only school in the country started by government.

Lewanika's battle for control over Lozi education, for it amounted to this, was perhaps the most serious conflict between Africans and the Company in the years before the First World War. There was, to be sure, unrest among the Lozi aristocracy, especially the ambitious and literate younger men. There was concern that, instead of doing tribute labour in the flood plain which could not now be legally enforced, Lozi men went away to earn wages from European employers. There was also criticism of progressive European encroachment on Lozi power; not only were the borders of Barotseland revised, but the scope of Lozi criminal jurisdiction was reduced considerably in 1905. In 1907 there were rumours of a revolt. But by the time Lewanika died in 1916 this discontent had subsided, though well into the 1920's there was bitter conflict between the British and the new literate, mostly Christian élite headed by Lewanika's son Yeta and his advisers. Elsewhere in Northern Rhodesia, the only important resistance to Company rule occurred among the Gwemba Tonga in the Zambezi valleys in 1909, and the western Lunda in 1912; both were provoked by the imposition of tax and both were unsuccessful.

European opposition. The most determined opposition to Company rule came, paradoxically, not from Africans but from the few European settlers. These were far less powerful than the settlers in Southern Rhodesia who by 1910 had an elected majority in the legislative council there. North of the Zambezi, the farmers and traders found it hard to organize and express their complaints against the Company's restrictive policy on mineral and land rights. The European population rose from 1,500 in 1911 to over 3,500 by 1921; a few rich landowners were able to exert pressure on the Company in London, and in 1918 an Advisory Council was created. But this gave the settlers no real power, and by this time they were quarrelling with the Company over amalgamation. By 1915 the Company was anxious to reduce its expenses in

Northern Rhodesia, especially as it had to bear the cost of defending the country against German troops from East Africa. Amalgamation with Southern Rhodesia would make administration cheaper and more efficient. It would also, so some officials argued, by strengthening both territories, improve the terms on which they might be included in the new Union of South Africa. But amalgamation was opposed by settlers in both Rhodesias. Those in the south thought it would delay their achieving self-government, while those in the north thought it would drain wealth and labour to the south. Nothing came of this scheme, and by the end of the war the Company was ready to hand over its administrative responsibilities altogether, in both countries. The way was now open to self-government in Southern Rhodesia, which came in 1923. But the settlers in the north still had no wish for amalgamation; they thought they would exert more power if Northern Rhodesia became a Crown Colony with a legislative council. Their claim for such representation was strengthened in 1920 when the Company had to impose an income tax. In 1924 the Colonial Office took over Northern Rhodesia from the British South Africa Company and instituted a legislative council. This was dominated by officials, but it included five members elected on a franchise which effectively excluded Africans. The Company retained its mineral rights in North-Western Rhodesia; these were in fact based only on its treaties with Barotseland, which had never extended over all this area. This was thought a minor concession at the time, but it was soon to prove enormously profitable to the Company.

THE ECONOMIC AND SOCIAL BACKGROUND (1924–53)

Exploitation of the Copperbelt. The most important development in Northern Rhodesia between the two world wars was the exploitation of the Copperbelt on a large scale for the first time. In the 1920's the U.S.A. already led the world in the techniques and financing of copper production and was itself the chief producer of copper. But the expansion of electrical and automobile industries during and after the First World War created a sharp rise in demand for copper. Between 1922 and 1926 South African financiers restarted the small mine at Bwana Mkubwa, while a few Americans initiated intensive prospecting for new sources of supply in Northern Rhodesia. Between 1925 and 1928 this revealed the existence of huge ore-bodies of copper sulphide, from which copper could be extracted by a process invented in 1911. Such ores lay several hundred feet deep but, given enough capital outlay, they could be worked far more profitably than the oxide deposits which lay near the surface in Katanga and the similar, but much poorer surface deposits, which had hitherto been worked in Northern Rhodesia. At Nchanga both kinds of ore-body were found: a large copper oxide deposit was found in a swamp, while sulphide-oxides were found at 600 feet. By 1930 five new mines were being rapidly developed; Nchanga and another were owned by the Rhodesian branch of the South African based Anglo-American Corporation and three were owned by Rhodesian Selection Trust, dominated by American capital.

In 1931, just as the first two new mines, Roan Antelope and Nkana, were going into production, the copper industry suffered a catastrophic slump. This was partly due to the effects of the world-wide depression, but also to the over-rapid expansion of world copper supplies. It was not until 1935 that the situation improved decisively. Thereafter, there was a steady advance and smelters at Nchanga and Mufulira were brought into production. Northern Rhodesian copper contributed to both British and German rearmament, and the prosperity of the Copperbelt was assured by the Allies' need for copper during the Second World War. By 1945, Northern Rhodesia was established as one of the world's major copper producers, contributing about one-eighth of the non-communist world's total product.

Migrant labour. We have already seen that, from the first, migrant labour was an important factor in the history of Northern Rhodesia. The rapid exploitation of the Copperbelt provided a new market for migrant labour within the country, while the demand for labour continued to increase in the surrounding territories. The skilled labour on the Copperbelt was provided by Europeans, many of whom came from South Africa. By 1930 the Copperbelt had been cleared of the chief malaria vector; many of the Lamba inhabitants had been moved to new land; and, in 1931 the Europeans there numbered 4,000, which was as many as the total number of Europeans in the country in 1924. The unskilled labour was provided by Africans from Northern Rhodesia, especially from the peoples of the north and east. In 1924, only 1,300 Africans were employed on the Copperbelt. By 1930, when construction was at its height, there were nearly 22,000, which was over a third of the total number of Africans employed in Northern Rhodesia. Thereafter, the slump intervened but by 1937 there were almost 20,000. At the same time, the earlier patterns of migration for work outside Northern Rhodesia persisted; indeed, they were extended by the development in the late 1920's of gold-fields and sisal plantations in Tanganyika. In 1936, these employed about 15,000 Africans from Northern Rhodesia; there were also about 34,000 in Southern Rhodesia and several thousands in Katanga. Thus there were probably as many Africans employed outside Northern Rhodesia as within it. Altogether, it is likely that in 1936 more than half the able-bodied male population of the country was in employment, and most of them were working far from home.

This migrant labour was essentially short-term. Rather than move home to their new places of employment, workers made expeditions lasting a few years at most, and sometimes only a few months. On the Copperbelt, this was true of Europeans as well as Africans. Many Europeans returned to the Rand, for example, when conditions seemed more favourable there. Yet their skills were in short supply and the mining companies boosted European wage-levels to induce them to stay on the Copperbelt. On the other hand, there was no such shortage of African labour, and the Northern Rhodesia Government, like colonial governments elsewhere in eastern and southern Africa, feared the prospect of settled communities of urban Africans. This fear was rationalized in various ways and the slump of 1931–4, which threw thousands of Africans out of work, indicated that prospects of long-term employment were indeed uncertain. But the real reasons for the fear of 'detribalization' lay deeper. The colonial officials, mostly from British middle class backgrounds, were unfamiliar with the problems of industrial and urban growth and their African experience had been gained in rural areas. Moreover, their thinking was dominated by the belief that there was a single correct path for African social evolution—through tribal institutions, developed in the tribal homeland. Besides, if Africans were merely transient labourers, there seemed no need to go to the expense of providing them with proper housing and other facilities, let alone social security. And if they only came to town for a short time, they could be expected to leave their families at home; they were housed as single men and it was a short step from this to paying them as if they had no dependents. Thus, for theoretical and strictly practical reasons, the government did nothing to discourage the pattern whereby an African, having perhaps sampled European employment nearer home, would take a job on a mine for two or three years, save or send home part of his meagre earnings, and then go home himself, perhaps returning later for a second spell.

This pattern was, on a long-term view, highly inefficient since it made it difficult to train Africans in the special skills and habits of industrial work. By 1946, there was some tendency among the mining companies to favour the Belgian pattern in the Congo, where African workers were encouraged to settle with their families in towns and sever their ties with the countryside. From the first, the mining companies had housed their workers, both black and white, in 'company towns' which were much better supplied and regulated than the municipal townships where employees of other businesses and of government were supervised by understaffed and underpaid government officials with inadequate funds. Nonetheless, 'stabilizing' the African labour force would necessarily mean offering Africans greater inducements to stay, in the form of higher wages and more opportunities for skilled employment. This would not only run counter to government policy; it would also threaten the favoured position of the European workers, whom the mining companies could ill afford to antagonize. Thus the Copperbelt continued to be worked by migrant labour, and as late as 1958 the average length of service of Africans was less than five years. And indeed that of Europeans was little more.

The rural situation. The policy of preventing 'detribalization' by using short-term migrant labour was full of contradictions; this has never been clearer than in South Africa today. During the 1930's, the Northern Rhodesia Government introduced a policy of 'indirect rule' in rural administration, whereby the powers of chiefs were extended to include not only the administration of justice but the maintenance of 'native treasuries'. Yet the revival of tribal authority was meaningless unless it involved a corresponding revival in the rural economy, and this was impossible as long as more than half the able-bodied male population was away earning wages. There were, indeed, a few rural areas which profited from the growth of towns. In the 1920's the Tonga began to compete with European farmers in raising maize and livestock for sale, while fish from the Luapula River was bought and frozen by Greeks who sold it in Elisabethville (now Lubumbashi). Elsewhere, however, remittances from relatives working in towns remained the only important source of cash income, while in Ngoni country land shortage was an additional factor driving men to the towns. Subsistence agriculture was gravely handicapped by the absence of men, especially in the woodland region of central and northern Zambia, where men were needed to pollard trees and clear the bush, even if women had always done the actual cultivation. Where, as in Mambwe villages, the remaining men were related to one another, it was possible to reduce the impact of labour migration by increased economic co-operation. In Bemba villages, on the other hand, men were usually related only through their wives; villages frequently split up, and long-term co-operation was difficult. Thus not only was there little rural progress; to some extent the condition of the rural population actually declined. Malnutrition was widespread, resistance to disease was lowered, and the efficiency of both rural and urban labour was seriously impaired.

Taxes and royalties. It was not only shortage of labour which held back rural development; there was also a shortage of capital. This seems paradoxical in view of the enormous sums invested in the Copperbelt and the large profits made there after 1935. From this date, the mining industry was indeed Northern Rhodesia's major source of revenue; taxes from the mining industry formed about 45 per cent of the total revenue in 1937, and perhaps as much as 70 per cent in 1939. But these taxes were much less than they might have been. The mineral rights throughout the Copperbelt belonged to the British South Africa Company. Its legal title to them was negligible; it certainly owned the mineral rights in Barotseland but this had never, except as a convenient fiction, reached within a hundred miles of the Copperbelt. Nonetheless, the mining companies acknowledged the claims of the British South Africa Company, they obtained their mining concessions from it, and they duly paid royalties in return. These royalties varied with the price of copper, but they had to be paid whether the companies made a profit or not. The government, on the other hand, could only raise tax from the mining companies if, despite the burden of royalties, they did make a profit. The profits of both the British South Africa Company, which consisted mainly of royalties, and the mining companies were taxed at the British rate of 5s. in the pound, since all these firms had their headquarters in London. But for the same reason the British Government took half this tax. Thus in 1936–7 after the Copperbelt had recovered from the slump, the mining companies paid over £300,000 in royalties to the British South Africa Company. From the remaining profits of just over £4,000,000 the governments of Britain and Northern Rhodesia took in tax £500,000 each; they also took in tax about £40,000 each from the British South Africa Company in virtue of its income from royalties. The total levy, in royalties and taxation, on the profits from mining was about 30 per cent, but only 12½ per cent went to the Northern Rhodesia Government. In 1939, as copper prices rose, the British South Africa Company drew from the Copperbelt as much, or more, in royalties (about £500,000) as the Northern Rhodesia Government did in taxation. And despite the revenue drawn by Britain from the Copperbelt, virtually the only assistance received from Britain by Northern Rhodesia in the 1930's took the form of loans. In 1943 it was calculated that from 1930 to 1940 Britain received £24,000,000 in taxes from the Copperbelt, while Northern Rhodesia received from Britain £136,000 in grants for development.

African education and development. Thus the prosperity of the Copperbelt was no guarantee of the prosperity of the country as a whole. In 1938, the financial situation was reviewed thoroughly by the Pim Commission which concluded that, as a result of the country's inequitable fiscal arrangements, 'the essential social services are very backward and require to be largely expanded'.[1] The Northern Rhodesia Government had been unable to make any investment in roads, schools, urban housing, secondary industries and agricultural development commensurate with the rapid expansion of modern industry. The Second World War, from 1939 to 1945, maintained copper prices but hindered European immigration and reduced government's administrative and technical staff, which had just begun to make good the cut-backs imposed during the depression.

The imbalance between the phenomenal progress of the Copperbelt and the backwardness of the country at large was, and still is, most clearly reflected in the history of African education. Furthermore, this plainly shows that the slow pace of African development was due not simply to shortage of funds but also to deliberate social policy: Africans could not be allowed to compete for jobs held by Europeans. By 1931 the government spent £15,000 on assisting selected mission schools, but this was remarkable only by comparison with the neglect of education under Company rule. After the depression, expenditure on African education rose fast, and several government schools were founded. But the system was extremely wasteful as very few children stayed at school long enough to become literate even in their own language. In 1942, of 86,300 who were said to be in school, only 3,000 were in the fifth year and a mere 35 received secondary education. The country's first junior secondary school, Munali, had only been opened in 1939. Of the handful who reached the final year of primary education, most became primary school teachers, to give another generation two or three years in school. On the Copperbelt there were by 1944 schools for about half the African children of school age. In 1932 a trades school was started at Lusaka but in 1948 it only had 70 pupils; besides, plans for giving Africans technical training were a hollow mockery when legislation passed in 1943 prevented Africans from becoming industrial apprentices.

African responses (i) *Political.* African responses to colonial rule were inevitably conditioned by the slow pace of real economic and social development. With so few Africans who could read and write, modern-style politics were slow to emerge. Significantly, some of the earliest moves towards political organization owed much to the influence and example of Africans from Nyasaland. There, education had advanced much further, and for many years Nyasas occupied most of those clerical posts and other skilled jobs on the Copperbelt which were open to Africans. But their first political achievement in Northern Rhodesia took place far from the towns. In the far north-east, the Scottish mission at Livingstonia, near Lake Nyasa, had established two stations. One of these, Lubwa, was founded in Bemba country by a Nyasa minister, David Kaunda, father of Zambia's first President. In 1912 the elder Kaunda and his African colleagues founded a Welfare Association at the other Scottish station, Mwenzo. Its constitution, which was modelled on that of the North Nyasa Native Association, stressed that its purpose was not to subvert the authority of government, but rather to be 'one of the helpful means of develop-

ing the country in the hands of the two necessary connecting links
—the government and the governed'.[2]

The Mwenzo Association failed to take root; not because the
government was hostile, but because, as yet, such a group was
indeed too far removed in experience and outlook from the
villagers whose 'desires and needs' it sought to represent. A common interest existed but there was not as yet a basis for popular
participation. In 1928 the Mwenzo Association was dissolved; in
the next few years other welfare societies were formed in rural
districts but these developed as social clubs without any political
character. More important were the welfare associations which
were founded in 1930 at Livingstone, Mazabuka, Broken Hill and
Ndola, all towns lying along the railway line. In Livingstone, the
capital, most of the members were government employees who
knew some of the secrets of power and some were educated young
men from nearby Barotseland. But most of the officials came
from the northern Province, three from the Mwenzo area, and
only three were Nyasas. The association confined itself to making
protests to government; yet these dealt with important and
specific grievances, such as the removal of Africans from land
newly reserved for Europeans along the railway or the more out-
rageous cases of racial discrimination. All the same, when an
attempt was made in 1933 to form a United African Welfare
Association of Northern Rhodesia, there was too little determination to follow up this bold idea. When government denied
it recognition there seems to have been no reaction. As yet, the
few Africans who had some familiarity with the world of Europeans
and of government lacked a cause big enough both to bring themselves together and to draw massive popular support. Details of
colonial rule were criticized, but there was still no idea that it
should go, as there was, by this time, in West Africa. Popular
political leadership first developed, not in the southern towns or
in the rural areas, but at the real centre of political gravity, the
Copperbelt, in the years after 1935.

African responses (ii) Religious. Nonetheless, Africans throughout
the country were aware that much was wrong with colonial rule;
the stresses and strains of labour migration, the consequent weakening of family ties, the decline of chiefs and the increase in rural
poverty. The difficulty was to see just how these misfortunes were
brought about. Faced with the bewildering complexities of social

change, induced by factors beyond their knowledge, let alone control, many Africans sought answers not in political action but in the realm of the supernatural. In many parts of central and north-eastern Zambia between the world wars, much enthusiasm was aroused by millenarian preachers who had been influenced—often through the mediation of Nyasas—by the doctrines of the Watch Tower Bible and Tract Society—an American-based organization also known as Jehovah's Witnesses. These 'African Watchtower' preachers foretold that the end of the world was at hand and when it came, salvation would be for Africans alone while Europeans went to hell. Even so, salvation might have to be earned through baptism and by adhering to special moral codes. Some communities inspired by 'Watchtower', as among the Mambwe and on the Luapula, went so far as to reject the earthly authority of chiefs and officials, and the Mambwe group was forcibly suppressed by government in 1939.

One important element in many 'Watchtower' movements was action against witchcraft and sorcery, for in Northern Rhodesia, as elsewhere in Africa, social tensions and frustrations were commonly ascribed to the action of sorcerers. The government had aggravated these fears by prohibiting the poison ordeal, by which chiefs had in the past tested charges of sorcery. There was thus a widely felt need for new techniques to combat sorcery. The missions, of course, could offer no help, since they refused to admit the reality of sorcery. But there was a strong desire to believe that even so the battle against sorcery could make use of Christianity, or at least elements from it, such as baptism. Besides, the Bible itself greatly strengthened the notion that the world could somehow be released once and for all from the power of evil. The most notorious anti-sorcery movement was that led by Tomo Nyirenda, a Nyasa influenced by 'Watchtower' doctrine who called himself Mwana Lesa (Son of God). Nyirenda practised baptism by total immersion among the Lala in Central Province; this was also an ordeal by water, and his career ended abruptly in 1926 when he was hanged for drowning suspected sorcerers. Less lethal, but no less popular, was the brief campaign in the north-east in 1934 led by the *bamucapi*, who were also Nyasas. Accusations of sorcery were outlawed by the government, but the *bamucapi* sought to eliminate suspicion and accusation by making people give up all their charms, whether malevolent or merely protective, and by issuing them with a medicine (*mucapi*) which conferred immunity to the innocent and death to those who attempted sorcery after taking it. And though the *bamucapi* had no direct connection with 'Watchtower', their routine also showed Christian influences: they spoke in sermons of the washing away of sins and foretold the second coming of their dead founder. The *mucapi* cult did not, as did some 'Watchtower' preachers, openly attack government, but it did, like the popular *beni* dances introduced from Nyasaland and Tanganyika, induce a feeling of successful adjustment to, and participation in, European custom and belief, and it seemed to provide an answer to a perennial African problem. If only for a short time, such cults did provide a means to communal well-being that seemed more effective in colonial conditions than the old tribal rituals.

For many years the Northern Rhodesia Government regarded with suspicion the Watch Tower Bible and Tract Society, which had urged non-co-operation with the war effort in 1914–18 and was the inspiration, even though unintentionally, of the African 'Watchtower' movements. In 1935, however, the Society sent a permanent representative to Northern Rhodesia, and over the next two decades it established control over several communities which had adopted African versions of its doctrines. The Society forbade involvement in politics, and stressed that Witnesses must prepare for the end of earthly kingdoms, but it strongly deplored civil disobedience. Nonetheless, it was far more popular than the mission churches, for its members were only indirectly supervised by Europeans and were left free to organize their own meetings and religious instruction. The impact of missions in Northern Rhodesia should not be discounted; one of the most striking witnesses to 'orthodox' African Christianity was the Union Church of the Copperbelt, which was formed in the late 1920's by African mineworkers, not in reaction against their missions but simply because there were no missionaries in the area. Here, yet again, Nyasa leadership was prominent. All the same, the mission churches were slow to develop an African ministry. The Watch Tower Society offered much more opportunity for leadership and full participation in the life of a Christian community; moreover, it recognized, or at least did not deny, the efficacy of sorcery, even if it offered no immediate remedy other than urging people to forswear it. By 1951, it seemed that the Society's success in Northern Rhodesia accounted for the virtual absence of separatist churches there.

THE GROWTH OF MODERN POLITICS

The modern political history of Northern Rhodesia really began in the late 1930's, when the Copperbelt finally emerged after the depression as the economic heart of the country. The mining towns brought large numbers of Africans into close association and recurrent conflict with a small number of dominant Europeans. In this situation, both sides began to compete in bringing pressure to bear on the government and the mining companies. It was in the mining towns that popular African discontent first found effective expression through recognized leaders; and through the system of migrant labour there was continual movement between town and country, so that the development of African political awareness in the towns was from the first of great significance for Northern Rhodesia as a whole. Moreover, this development gave a new urgency to the long-standing problem of Northern Rhodesia's relationship to Southern Rhodesia, and it was this problem which dominated political controversy up to the emergence of Zambia in 1964.

Townsmen and Tribesmen. African migrants on the Copperbelt had two main roles: they were tribesmen, and they were also mineworkers. As tribesmen, they continued to a large extent to observe traditional tribal law and custom in their relationships with one another. As mineworkers, however, they were involved in a quite new kind of situation, in which they were all, at least potentially, united as Africans in opposition to their European employers and fellow-workers. The government, as we have seen, wished to regard them solely as tribesmen, that is transitory visitors to the towns who remained attached to their tribal land and institutions. On the Copperbelt, as in the bush, some form of African participation in administration seemed necessary, but as far as possible this was to follow traditional lines, regardless of the quite different problems of life in the towns. Thus in 1931 when Native Authorities were being introduced in the rural areas, 'tribal elders' were appointed at the Roan Antelope mine compound and the nearby municipal township, Luanshya. These elders performed a useful function in settling disputes involving tribal custom. But in disputes involving conditions of life and work in the towns they obviously had no authority, either as arbiters or representatives of African interests. Expertise in tribal custom was no help in dealing with the challenges of European custom and innovation.

In 1935, for the first time, African mineworkers went on strike, first at Mufulira, then at Nkana and Roan Antelope. At Roan, incautious use of the police provoked rioting; elsewhere, there was very little violence, and the strikers soon went back to work. Brief and ineffective though it was, the strike served to show that African mineworkers were already conscious of a common interest and were capable of organizing concerted resistance within the urban environment. The immediate cause of the strike was a plan, partly misunderstood, for revising the assessment of poll tax. But the strike crystallized long-standing discontent with living and working conditions. It also exposed the absence of any effective channel of communication between Africans and management: significantly, the tribal elders at Roan were ignored. But though this was noted by the Commission of Enquiry which reported on the disturbances, the response of both government and management was to strengthen the 'tribal' character of urban administration rather than seek new and more appropriate forms. In 1937 tribal elders were introduced at Mufulira, and in 1938 Urban Courts under 'tribal councillors' were set up in the municipal townships. As a channel of communication between Africans and government, Native Advisory Councils were also introduced, but these were far from representative and in any case they did not operate in the mine compounds.

The strike in 1935 showed the potential strength of African miners. And by this time, many of them were efficient enough at their jobs to suggest that before long some at least would be quite capable of taking over jobs reserved for Europeans. The European mineworkers saw this as clearly as anyone, and in 1936 they formed the Northern Rhodesia Mineworkers Union (NRMU) in order to safeguard their interests against their African fellow-workers as much as against their employers. In 1940 the NRMU organized strikes at Mufulira and Nkana in protest against the rise in the cost of living brought about by the war, and its wage claims were largely conceded. This success at once stimulated Africans to stage a strike of their own, and with much greater reason. During the depression, their wages had been reduced and despite the rising cost of living the companies, who by 1940 were making handsome profits, had not even raised wages to their former levels. Rations, housing and medical services were free, but the cash wage was so low that any fall in it was acutely felt. In 1940, the starting wage for Africans underground was 22s. 6d.

for every thirty days of work, whereas in 1929 it was 30s.; and surface workers got 13s. 6d. in 1940 compared with 17s. 6d. in 1929.

As a result of this strike, the wages of African mineworkers were slightly increased. But the basic problem was sidestepped once again. Strikes were a wasteful and cumbersome form of protest; in wartime they might be positively dangerous. Yet there was still no other way for African miners to bring pressure on the companies. They were not considered mature enough to form trade unions; instead from 1941, Urban Advisory Councils were nominated from African elders in both mine compounds and municipal townships. From 1942 tribal elders on the mines were called Tribal Representatives, and were supposed to present workers' complaints 'in a reasonable manner'. But in the sphere of labour relations they were no more representative than they had ever been. The government and most employers refused to admit that Africans had to be regarded as townsmen as well as tribesmen, even though there were now signs in the older towns, such as Broken Hill, that many Africans had lived for several years in towns and were as much at home there as in their tribal areas.

Welfare societies on the Copperbelt. The official structure, then, provided little or no opportunity for Africans to come together and express their views as mineworkers. Instead from 1942 African welfare societies were formed throughout the Copperbelt. These were mostly led by clerks and foremen, but they were very different from the welfare societies which had come and gone in the years between the wars. These had suffered from the difficulty of organizing and maintaining links between people doing different jobs in different places, and they lacked a common and continuing interest which involved them as groups. Such an interest existed, however, in the mining towns, especially in the mine compounds. The new welfare societies not only became important forums for discussion; they also became the means of securing substantial local improvements. The Luanshya Association, for example, whose members were drawn both from the mine compound and from the municipal township, persuaded the mining company to make a road between the two. Though few Europeans were prepared to admit it, the officials of the welfare societies were far more representative leaders than the elders in the Urban Advisory Councils.

In 1946, at the initiative of Dauti Yamba, founder of the Luanshya Association, welfare societies through the territory—from both urban and rural areas—met in Lusaka, the capital since 1935, and formed a Federation of Welfare Societies. This conference 'represented a considerable landmark, since it was the first time an unofficial body of Africans had met together to discuss their problems at a territorial level'.[3] This Federation held several other meetings, and in 1948 it reconstituted itself as the Northern Rhodesia Congress, a forerunner of the nationalist political parties. The rapid progress of the welfare associations provoked the government into providing its own large-scale structures for African political discussion. From 1944, African Provincial Councils were formed from among members of Urban Advisory Councils, welfare societies and rural Native Authorities (that is chiefs). In 1946, these provincial councils were united in a territory-wide African Representative Council. But such councils had a purely advisory role, and like the tribal elders and representatives they were compromised by their semi-official character. The future lay with the Africans' own organizations—with the societies, with Congress and with trade unions.

African trade unions. The welfare societies provided opportunities for common action and for the growth of a new kind of African leadership based on experience of town life. But neither they nor the Urban Advisory Councils had the power to negotiate effectively with employers on the most fundamental questions, wages and terms of employment. The need for African trade unions was made clear by the miners' strikes in 1935 and 1940, and again in 1945 by a strike of African railway workers. Eventually in 1947 the Labour Government in Britain sent out a British trade union leader, Comrie, to assist Africans in forming their own unions. By 1949 there were unions in all the mine compounds and they combined to form the Northern Rhodesia African Mineworkers' Union (NRAMU) led by Lawrence Katilungu, a clerk who had first worked in the mines in 1936. Unions were also formed among other African wage-earners—on the roads and railways, in the building trades, in shops and hotels. But none of these proved so effective as the NRAMU. For example, in any one town, building workers had many different employers, worked in different places and some lived in compounds outside the municipal township. They thus found it hard to organize meetings and recognize a common interest as employees, whereas the mine-workers all lived in the same compound, worked on the same mine, and had a common employer. The strength of this 'unitary structure' was shown in 1952, when mineworkers throughout the Copperbelt went on strike after negotiations for wage increases had broken down. The strike lasted for three weeks; there were no disturbances, and in the end a board of arbitration awarded substantial wage increases, whereby most mineworkers were to earn about 100s. per thirty days. The status of the NRAMU was dramatically confirmed by the abolition of Tribal Repre-sentatives throughout the Copperbelt, at the insistence of more than 80 per cent of the total mining strength.

European politics (1935–53). The growth of African organizations on the Copperbelt had a profound effect on the attitudes of Europeans. We have seen that a European miners' union was formed in 1936, largely in response to the growing strength and efficiency of African labour. And in 1930 Europeans had been alarmed by the British Government's reminder that in Northern Rhodesia, as in other British colonies to the north, African interests were to be paramount. This, and the fear of African economic and social advance, stimulated Europeans in the 1930's and 1940's to make new efforts to obtain more political power. The Europeans had three main objectives: to gain majority representation in the Legislative Council; to amalgamate the two Rhodesias, and thereby to throw off control by the Colonial Office; and to end the payment of mining royalties to the British South Africa Com-pany. They succeeded in none of these aims; instead, the first and the last were eventually achieved by Africans. But they un-doubtedly did increase their influence on government policy.

The two most important European politicians were Roy Welensky and Stewart Gore-Browne (both were later knighted). They came from different backgrounds: Welensky, whose father had gone to South Africa from central Europe, had been a rail-wayman and boxing champion; Gore-Browne was an aristocratic ex-army officer with a large estate in Bemba country. These backgrounds, as much as personal inclinations, led them to adopt different attitudes to European-African relations. Welensky re-garded African advancement from the point of view of a European trade unionist. Gore-Browne, on the other hand, stressed that real concessions must be made to African demands, indeed, he was one of the first people to argue that tribal forms of government were irrelevant for African townsmen. But both he and Welensky were impatient with Colonial Office rule, which seemed to limit the opportunities of both Europeans and Africans; indeed, Gore-Browne proposed a scheme for Central African Federation in 1936. And both men strongly resented the loss of so much of the country's wealth in the form of royalties paid to the British South Africa Company and in taxation levied by Britain. In 1948, the royalties may have amounted to as much as £2,000,000. Objections to the Company's legal title to the royalties made no impression on Britain and they were never taken to court. But in 1949 the British South Africa Company was induced to surrender its royalties in 1986, and meanwhile agreed to pay 20 per cent of them to the Northern Rhodesia Government, as against the previous $12\frac{1}{2}$ per cent.

Efforts to secure settler control over the Legislative Council were unsuccessful. In the 1930's European representation had been increased, and in 1945 a majority of non-official members was created. But this was done by increasing the number of non-officials nominated by government; three represented African interests, of whom Gore-Browne was one for a time, and two represented other interests. But there were still only eight elected members as against nine officials. Thus the prospect of Northern Rhodesia becoming an independent state under white rule seemed remote, which indeed was hardly surprising, since the Europeans formed little more than 1 per cent of the total population. On the other hand, there was considerable progress after 1945 towards the long-term European objective of European domination throughout central Africa, through closer union between the two Rhodesias. In the days of Company rule, Europeans in Northern Rhodesia had feared that amalgamation with Southern Rhodesia would favour the latter's economy, which at that time was much stronger. By the 1940's, however, the development of the Copperbelt had more than redressed the balance and amalgamation, or even federation, seemed to be the only alternative to the eventual development of Northern Rhodesia as an African-controlled territory. Many Europeans in Southern Rhodesia were also in favour of closer union between the Rhodesias. For many years, Rhodesia's destiny had seemed to lie in union with South Africa, but this prospect was abruptly closed in 1948 by the triumph of the South African Nationalist Party. English-speaking settlers had no wish to join a country dominated by Afrikaners who were pledged to reduce its ties with Britain. Moreover union with the north would mean a greater share, through trade and taxation, in the wealth of the Copperbelt.

Since there was no question of handing over power in Northern Rhodesia to a white minority, Britain had always resisted Rhodesian pressure for amalgamation. On the other hand, there was general support among British political leaders for uniting under a Federal Government the settler regime to the south and the Colonial Office regimes to the north of the Zambezi, Northern Rhodesia and Nyasaland. The problem was how far Europeans should be allowed to exert power at the Federal level. The Labour Government, which took office in 1945, supported Federation in principle, mainly on economic grounds, but would only approve it if Africans were given a greater share in political power. In 1951, however, Labour gave way to a Conservative Government which was more willing to accept mere assurances from Rhodesian settlers that they would in due course share their power with Africans. Moreover, the Conservatives were susceptible to pressure for Federation exerted in the City of London by the mining companies and the British South Africa Company. The Conservatives were, like Labour, searching for some way to reduce and eventually bring to an end British responsibilities in central Africa. It was in 1951 that the Gold Coast achieved self-government, under Nkrumah as Prime Minister, and there was clearly no future for British rule in Africa. But unlike Labour, the Conservatives sought to 'decolonize' central Africa by handing over extensive powers to a federation dominated by European settlers. If they formed a 'partnership' with Africans, so much the better. However, the main consideration was that they, not Britain, should have to deal with the massive problems of accommodating African pressure for political and economic advance. Accordingly in August 1953 the Rhodesias and Nyasaland were joined in a Central African Federation.

African politics (1948–53). The Europeans' drive towards political supremacy had largely been prompted by fears of African advance; but their campaign for amalgamation or federation stimulated Africans to make a counter-bid for political power. Africans in Northern Rhodesia feared any form of union with the south for the same reasons that most Europeans welcomed it; such union would strengthen European domination. Africans north of the Zambezi were well aware of European motives in seeking amalgamation, and they sensed that Southern Rhodesia would be the dominant partner. They knew Southern Rhodesia well: many had worked or were still working there, and they knew that land alienation had gone much further there than in Northern Rhodesia, even if the colour bar in the two countries was much the same.

The fear that amalgamation would mean the loss of tribal land to Europeans was widely shared among Africans in Northern Rhodesia. It was not their only reason for opposition, but it carried the greatest emotional force and it crystallized other fears which were perhaps less easily defined. Land was still of absorbing interest to almost all Africans. The growth of industry on the Copperbelt had done nothing to undermine this interest; rather, indeed, it had strengthened it. Rights to the use of tribal land were still a man's only security against unemployment or old age; this was, after all, not simply the attitude of African miners but the deliberate policy of government and the mining companies. Thus fears of large-scale land alienation alarmed African townsmen no less than their relatives at home. And in this sphere both looked for leadership to their chiefs, the traditional trustees of tribal land. This unity of African feeling was expressed in 1937, in testimonies before a Commission which investigated the possibilities of amalgamating the Rhodesias. In 1944 a senior Bemba chief raised his voice against amalgamation in the Northern Provincial Council, and from 1950 several chiefs spoke out firmly against federation. In 1953 a petition to the Houses of Parliament against federation was signed by 120 chiefs, including the Bemba and Ngoni paramounts. In the same year, the Mambwe paramount was deposed, and leading chiefs of the Ushi and Bisa suspended, for organizing resistance to government—in the form of non-compliance with agricultural and conservation measures. Government had long insisted that chiefs were the true leaders of their people; now the Africans were showing government that, in this situation, this was perfectly true; and very awkward for government.

The campaign for amalgamation, then, gave the first stimulus to an African political awakening throughout the territory. But though chiefs might well articulate popular fears and discontent on this issue, they obviously could not provide the basis for political organization on a large enough scale to challenge the Europeans. It was above all for this reason that in 1948, at its annual meeting at Munali school, the Federation of Welfare Societies was transformed into an expressly political body, the Northern Rhodesia Congress. The idea of a Congress had been conceived by Dauti Yamba after a visit to South Africa in 1942. The main strength of Congress lay in the towns, and when trade unions were formed several of their members became prominent in Congress. But during the 1940's welfare associations had been founded or refounded in many rural areas, and these provided bases on which Congress could build up membership throughout the territory. Thus in 1947 Kenneth Kaunda, a teacher who was one of the few graduates of Munali school, was prominent in the Mufulira welfare society and became a member of the local Provincial Council. In 1949 he returned home to Lubwa, the mission founded by his father in Bemba country, and in 1950 he transformed the local welfare association into a Congress branch. Moreover, the cyclical pattern of labour migration to and from the towns meant that between town and country there was a constant flow of news and ideas as well as leadership; such links reinforced the common interest of chiefs and miners in protecting tribal land.

In 1951 the Congress was significantly renamed the Northern Rhodesia African National Congress. Over the next two years, under the leadership of Harry Nkumbula, a former teacher who had studied at Makerere College, Congress did much to unite Africans in Northern Rhodesia in a sense of common purpose; opposition to federation. In 1952 a conference of chiefs and Congress delegates in Lusaka set up a Supreme Action Council, with a majority of trade unionists, to plan and if necessary order mass action. In March 1953, at another conference of chiefs and party officials, Nkumbula burned the British White Paper on Federation, announced that the chiefs had determined not to co-operate with a Federal Government, and called for two days of 'national prayer' in April during which no Africans would go to work. Within the existing political framework, Africans could hardly do more.

The plan for 'national prayer' fell through, Federation was introduced despite African protests, and Congress seemed to many to be discredited. Certainly, 1953 marks the end of a period in the growth of African nationalism in Northern Rhodesia. It was perhaps inevitable that Congress should fail to prevent Federation; the European pressures in both the Rhodesias and in Britain were too strong. Nonetheless, it is worth looking briefly at the reasons why Congress failed to organize a massive act of African resistance. Its most glaring failure was on the Copperbelt, where African miners, except at Mufulira, completely ignored the call to 'national prayer'. This at first seems puzzling in view of the heavy support for Congress in the African Mineworkers' Union. But the mine companies' threats of instant dismissal could not easily be disregarded. Furthermore, as Epstein suggests, the union leaders, being more experienced negotiators than the Congress leaders, probably realized that Federation was inevitable. They feared, perhaps, that the prestige of the Union, solidly based on achievements such as the wage increases in 1952 would greatly suffer if it allied itself with Congress in a major defeat.[4]

FROM NORTHERN RHODESIA TO ZAMBIA (1953-64)

Federation was seen by most Europeans in Northern Rhodesia as a step towards settler control north of the Zambezi. Instead, ironically, it greatly stimulated the growth of African nationalism in both Northern Rhodesia and Nyasaland. As a result, the Federation collapsed and Africans took over in both countries. Even in the short run, Europeans in Northern Rhodesia were disappointed by Federation. Northern Rhodesia remained under the Colonial Office, and there was no significant increase in settler power in the Legislative Council. Their elected membership rose to twelve, but there were now six members representing African interests, four of whom were chosen by the African Representative Council. And at the Federal level, Northern Rhodesia was definitely subordinated to Southern Rhodesia. In the Federal Parliament, out of the twenty-six members elected on a franchise that excluded most Africans, fourteen came from Southern Rhodesia and only eight from the north; there were also two African members for the north, chosen by the African Representative Council. The Federal Government dealt with all matters concerning Europeans and economic development, and the preponderance of southern interests in these fields shortly became very clear.

Federation: the European critique. For Europeans in Northern Rhodesia, the first few years of Federation were hopeful. African resistance had proved a failure, while the preponderance of Southern Rhodesia was not immediately obvious. The Federation attracted both investment and European immigrants, and up to 1956 at least Northern Rhodesia seemed to be doing well. It had certainly entered the Federation on the wave of an economic boom. Between 1946 and 1951 the European population rose from 22,000 to 37,000 and reached 49,000 in 1953. The ratio of Europeans to Africans in that year was thought to be about 1:40, much less than in Southern Rhodesia, where the ratio was 1:13, but more than twice that in 1931, while the ratio for 1911 has been reckoned at 1:548. If the economy could be expanded and diversified, it seemed not inconceivable that Northern Rhodesia could attract enough Europeans to approach the ratio in Southern Rhodesia. To judge from the mines on the Copperbelt and at Broken Hill the prospects for such growth were excellent. In 1945, the total value of minerals produced in Northern Rhodesia was £13,000,000, in 1950 it was £50,000,000, and in 1953 in the boom created by the Korean war £95,000,000. Between 1953 and 1956 the price of copper in London rose from £250 to £420 per long ton, and the ensuing profits were reflected in the rise of European mineworkers' wages from an average of £1,782 to £2,295. Moreover, the European mineworkers enjoyed many facilities and amenities, including schools, that were either free or else heavily subsidized. For a time, they enjoyed material living standards that were as high as any in the world for wage-earners. The copper boom also stimulated the growth of service trades, providing more jobs for Europeans, and by 1958 they numbered 72,000. Thus when in the same year Unofficials obtained a majority in the Executive Council (comprising the Governor and heads of departments), this corresponded to a real growth in the importance of Europeans in Northern Rhodesia.

This spectacular economic advance, however, was unbalanced. Copper alone could not guarantee the country's prosperity; it was necessary to develop agriculture and secondary industries. It was easy for Europeans to come north from South Africa, make a 'killing' on the Copperbelt and return home when copper prices and wages fell, as they did in 1957. But in the long run European prosperity was bound up with that of Africans. The African population, due to improved medical care and hygiene, was rapidly increasing, while more modern industrial methods reduced the demand for unskilled labour. Only a massive increase in jobs for Africans and in the local production of food and cash crops could sustain a continuing inflow of Europeans as supervisors and entrepreneurs, and limit, if not reduce, the dangerous gulf between European wealth and African poverty. And there was little prospect of such expansion. The one serious possibility was cultivation of the Kafue flood plains, and the estimated capital cost of such development seemed prohibitive.

The difficulties of diversifying the Northern Rhodesian economy were not only due to the inaccessibility or actual lack of economic resources, such as land for high-yield production or new kinds of minerals. They were also due to the dominant position of Southern Rhodesia within the Federal economy. Southern Rhodesia, being closer to the sea, was better placed for the distribution of imports, while Federation denied Northern Rhodesia protection against the established secondary industries in the south. Salisbury, the capital of Southern Rhodesia, was also the Federal capital, and it became the business headquarters of the Federation. Africans in Northern Rhodesia bluntly called it 'Bamba Zonke' (take all) and this attitude was shared by many Europeans. Hopes for economic progress in Northern Rhodesia were also set back by the decision in 1955 to build a hydro-electric power station at Kariba, on the Zambezi, instead of on the Kafue. This decision was taken by the Federal Government against expert technical and economic advice. The Kafue scheme would have made possible extensive irrigation; Kariba was in a gorge, and was far too big for any foreseeable demand. But it created 'the biggest man-made lake in the world' and was obviously a more striking advertisement for Federation. Moreover, the power station, a highly strategic point, was sited on the south bank, thus symbolizing the predominance of Southern Rhodesian interests in Federal planning. Finally, this predominance was expressed in Federal financial policy. In 1959 the Northern Rhodesia Minister of Finance, a British civil servant, complained that the country received much less than its due share of Federal revenues; it was calculated that from 1953 to 1959 Northern Rhodesia had suffered a net loss of more than £50,000,000 to the Federal Government.

Federation: the impact on African society. In Northern Rhodesia, then, the economic arguments for Federation seemed more and more doubtful. If most Europeans continued to support it, this was mainly on political grounds, as a protection against the spectre

of black government. As for the Africans, they had of course no
reason to favour Federation on political grounds. They did perhaps
make certain economic and social gains, but these were limited
and belated. African production of cash-crops—mainly maize and
groundnuts—which hitherto had been limited, rose considerably,
due to improved communications and agricultural extension
services. But this only affected a few areas in the Central and
Southern Provinces, within easy reach of the towns. Besides, the
relative gains were slight, since Europeans in the same areas were
able, with more capital and experience, to make much more
rapid progress, and in the Central Province there was a rapid
increase in European settlement on land long since alienated by
government. Over the country as a whole, there was no per-
ceptible progress in the rural economy. The obstacles were indeed
great, but the necessary changes could certainly not be effected
by a government lacking any popular support.

On the Copperbelt, economic opportunities for Africans were
also slightly expanded, but not nearly fast enough to offset the
great increases in European wealth. By the 1950's, the Copperbelt
had clearly established itself as an essential and, so far as could be
seen, permanent feature of the Northern Rhodesian economy. As
a result, it was clear to at least some Europeans that Africans must
be accepted as townsmen and encouraged to form stable urban
communities; this would be in the interests of efficiency, economy
and long-term planning. Africans would only stay on the mines
for more than a few years if they could gain greater rewards and
responsibilities as their experience increased. African skilled
labour would obviously be cheaper than European, and the
arguments of economic self-interest were reinforced by the pressure
exerted from 1950 by the African trade unions. Some of the larger
firms, therefore, were more ready than they had been to risk
antagonizing European employees through African advancement.
In 1946 the European mineworkers' union had protected their
jobs from African competition through a 'closed shop' agreement
with the mining companies, but in 1953 the Rhodesian Selection
Trust (RST) announced that it would seek to end the colour bar
on its mines. In 1955 both RST and the Anglo-American Corporation induced the European miners to accept a new agreement
opening to Africans a number of hitherto 'reserved' posts. And
in 1958, against strong opposition from the Europeans in the
Legislative Council, the government enabled Africans to become

industrial apprentices. From 1960 Africans on the railways could be trained as firemen and engine drivers, although they were still excluded from the workshops.

At the lower levels of industry, Africans were at last beginning to make some headway. But the training of Africans for more senior posts, whether in industry or administration, continued to be grossly neglected. The real key to full African participation in industry was perhaps technical education. But this was a Federal responsibility, and not until 1962 was the Copperbelt Technical Foundation opened to Africans, after years of pressure from the few Africans in the Federal Parliament. As for general education for Africans, this continued to be controlled by Northern Rhodesia. Yet this arrangement had its drawbacks; it suffered from the unequal share of that government in Federal wealth. Besides, the main emphasis continued to be on primary education; in 1958 there were less than 1,000 African children in secondary schools, and only one provided for entrance to universities.

The triumph of African nationalism. There was thus little reason for Africans in Northern Rhodesia to accept the European assurance that Federation meant 'partnership'. Even where, as on the Copperbelt, a few concessions were made to Africans, Europeans were for the most part still reluctant to admit any Africans as social, let alone political, equals. And the Federal political structure certainly did not encourage hopes that any substantial power would be conceded to Africans in the near future. Thus most Africans in Northern Rhodesia continued to oppose Federation, and some now began to work towards a new objective: the creation of an independent state based on majority rule.

In the first few years of Federation, African political progress was slow. Popular enthusiasm for the African National Congress subsided after its failure to prevent Federation, and it took time for new strategies and objectives to emerge. This temporary loss of political purpose was reflected in the rapid growth between 1954 and 1958 of a new religious movement in Bemba country, the Lumpa Church, founded by Alice Lenshina. Lenshina herself was moved by a genuine, if ignorant, religious feeling, and she was more concerned to eradicate sorcery than Federation. But for a few years the Lumpa Church attracted support from a great many people, both in the north-east and on the Copperbelt, who needed some form of organization in which they could feel free of European domination. Significantly, the Lumpa Church gained little or no support in areas where Jehovah's Witnesses were strong.

The Congress was also weakened by its disagreements with the African Mineworkers' Union. The immediate reason was the union's 'betrayal' of Congress in 1953 when it ignored the Congress call for a work stoppage. The underlying reason, however, was perhaps that the AMU, unlike Congress, represented compact and closely knit groups of men bound together both by work and residence. Congress found it hard to obtain any direct control over mineworkers, who tended 'to look to the union for the solution of nearly all their problems'.[5] This tension was exposed in 1954 when the AMU refused to co-operate in a Congress boycott of European butchers shops where the colour bar was especially vicious. The conflict persists to the present day, though it was further complicated by the division of union strength in 1955, when African clerks and foremen gained the approval of the companies for a separate Mines African Staff Association.

By 1958, Congress had revived and once again had a network of branches over most of the country. This revival was largely due to the influx of new leaders, as more young men emerged from secondary schools and obtained further education overseas. Some of these young men, such as Sikota Wina, a son of a former chief minister of the Lozi paramount, or Simon Kapwepwe, a friend of Kaunda's from Lubwa, were committed to the idea of creating an independent African state. This aim, they believed, could only be achieved by refusing to compromise in any way with the Federal political system. They dedicated themselves to uniting Africans, and any Europeans who cared to listen, in a sense of belonging to a new nation to be called Zambia. This ideal was most lucidly expressed by Kenneth Kaunda who had been Secretary-General of Congress since 1953. Nkumbula, the president of Congress, was less clearly committed to this radical approach. In 1958, Nkumbula agreed to take part in elections based on a new constitution for Northern Rhodesia, and this provoked a major split in Congress. Kaunda, Kapwepwe, Sikota Wina and others formed a new party, the Zambia African National Congress (ZANC). Nkumbula retained much support in the Southern Province, in which his home area lay and which had seen more economic progress under Federation than most areas. Elsewhere, however, Africans generally gave their support to the new ZANC. In 1959 a state of emergency was declared in Nyasaland and

Southern Rhodesia, following the unfounded rumours that the Nyasaland African Congress was about to launch a 'murder plot' against Europeans. As a result, the ZANC was banned and several of its leaders gaoled, but this repression only stiffened African resistance. Following further secessions from the ANC, a new party was formed, the United National Independence Party (UNIP). In January 1960, Kaunda was released from gaol; he was greeted as a popular hero and took over the leadership of UNIP.

By this time the British Government realized that there would have to be rapid constitutional advance in Northern Rhodesia, and it also seemed increasingly doubtful whether the Federation could be held together. Not only was the African pressure against it rising fast in Northern Rhodesia and Nyasaland; in Southern Rhodesia, where many Europeans had always opposed any form of union with the north, there was growing white support for the Dominion Party, which aimed at a fully independent Southern Rhodesia. And in Northern Rhodesia, as we have seen, there were powerful economic reasons why at least the more far-sighted Europeans were ready to see the end of Federation. Thus in 1961 the Colonial Office proposed a constitution for Northern Rhodesia which would make possible an African majority in the legislature, even though this was bound to lead before long to Northern Rhodesia seceding from the Federation. Under pressure from the Federal Prime Minister, Sir Roy Welensky, Britain revised this plan in favour of the Europeans. But this concession provoked UNIP to stage a campaign of civil disobedience throughout the northern and eastern parts of the country. This campaign involved a good deal of violence, against government property rather than Europeans, despite Kaunda's personal belief in non-violence. It was amply justified, however, for in 1962 the constitution was revised once again, and this time UNIP agreed to participate.

In the election of October 1962, UNIP and ANC between them gained a majority of seats and their leaders took over a number of government departments. The Federation was now doomed and it was finally broken up at the end of 1963. Early in 1964 another election was held, on a wider franchise and this gave UNIP a decisive majority. Kaunda now became Prime Minister of an all-UNIP government with full control of internal affairs, except for defence. Constitutionally, the way was now clear to full independence and this was arranged for October. But the triumphant force of African nationalism faced two major sources of resistance, and

these were not European but African. The relationship of Barotseland to the nationalist movement was complicated by the fact that
it was a 'protectorate within a protectorate', with its own treaty
relationship to Britain. The Lozi paramount was enticed into
supporting Federation by promises that Barotseland would become
an independent state. The younger Lozi, however, had no sym-
pathy with this idea; they knew that Barotseland had no economic
future on its own. UNIP won massive Lozi support in the elections
in 1962 and 1964 and eventually the paramount agreed reluctantly
to the full integration of Barotseland with the rest of the country.

Much more difficult was the problem posed by the Lumpa
Church. From about 1958 this had begun to lose much of its
support, but in its home area in the north-east there was a hard
core of believers who opposed any outside interference with their
affairs, whether from the colonial administration or from African
politicians. UNIP, however, was committed to obtaining total
support from the whole country; not to support UNIP was to
declare oneself an enemy of the new nation, Zambia. The conflict
between the Lumpa Church and UNIP was peculiarly bitter,
since the centre of Lumpa strength was also a UNIP stronghold;
indeed, the church had originated in a split from the Lubwa
mission where Kaunda and Kapwepwe were educated and where
they had taught for a time. By mid-1964 Lumpa defiance of
government authority had reached a point where an explosion
was inevitable; in the event, a war broke out in which over 700
people were killed. As a result, the Lumpa Church was banned
and its surviving leaders detained indefinitely.

After independence. On 24 October 1964 Northern Rhodesia
obtained full independence as the Republic of Zambia. After more
than half a century of uncertainty, the territory north of the
Zambezi had chosen to align its future, not with the European
supremacies of southern Africa, but with the African countries to
the north. This change of direction was emphasized on the very
eve of independence, when the British South Africa Company
ceded its mineral rights, and thus its royalties, to the embryo
Government of Zambia for a mere £2,000,000; the only alternative was expropriation without compensation. But in other
respects the Zambian economy remained heavily dependent on
the south. The government's determination to lessen this dependence was stimulated when Rhodesia declared itself independent

in 1965. Work is in progress on road and rail links between Zambia and Tanzania, and coal is now being mined in southern Zambia in an attempt to replace the Wankie colliery in Southern Rhodesia as the Copperbelt's main source of coke. But many manufactured goods must still be imported from Rhodesia and South Africa, and there are still many Europeans—especially from these countries—on the Copperbelt. They will be needed for many years to come, just because so few Africans have been trained for the more highly skilled and responsible jobs.

Under African leadership, Zambia is doing its best to make up for the wasted years of colonial rule. Technical and higher education were at once given high priority, and the University of Zambia opened in 1965. But the formidable tasks of economic and social development require a high degree of national unity, and this is threatened not simply by the attitudes of Europeans on the Copperbelt, many of whom support the illegal Rhodesian regime, but by the attitudes of Africans as well. The very progress made by African workers and their increasing stabilization on the Copperbelt has heightened their sense of forming a special interest group distinct from the rest of the country. Understandably, they continue to press for wages closer to European levels, but this removes them still further from villagers dependent on subsistence cultivation. And each concession to the demands of African miners leads to all-round wage increases which the country cannot afford indefinitely. Another pressing problem, common to most African countries, is the large number of unemployed in the towns. In 1936 perhaps half the able-bodied male population was in employment; since then the population has increased by a considerable but unclear amount to nearly four million; but there has been no corresponding increase in employment. Copper production has of course hugely increased, but this never engaged more than a minority of the total number of wage-earners. Industry is never likely to expand far enough to provide work for the ever-growing number of boys and young men who come to the towns after a few years in primary school, too little to make them fully literate but enough to give them aspirations which the countryside cannot satisfy.

These problems are the more keenly felt since Zambia's mineral wealth does give her a unique advantage among other developing nations. But the dependence on copper is dangerous since the demand for copper could easily fall if substitutes now known could be produced more cheaply. This dependence is also a moral embarrassment; the Copperbelt never does so well as in wartime, and directly or indirectly it assists the American war effort in Vietnam. This would be a compromising situation for any anti-colonialist government; it must be especially painful for Kaunda, a disciple of Gandhi. But Zambia's most immediate need is the downfall of the illegal Rhodesian regime, for as long as Zambia's chief supply route runs through Rhodesia, international sanctions against Rhodesia will bear hardly on Zambia, at just the period when it can least afford the consequent strains and shortages.

Notes

1. *Report of the Commission Appointed to Enquire into the Financial and Economic Position of Northern Rhodesia* p. 347 Colonial Office no. 145 London 1938
2. Richard Hall *Zambia* Pall Mall 1965 p. 113
3. A. L. Epstein *Politics in an urban African community* Manchester University Press 1958 p. 71   4. Epstein p. 190   5. Epstein p. 153

Recommended Reading

You should consult works by Gann, Hall and Wills listed in the reading list for Zambia in the nineteenth century, and the four special studies mentioned in that list. The following works are specially relevant for the twentieth century:

Robert E. Baldwin *Economic Development and Export Growth: a study of Northern Rhodesia 1920–1960* University of California Press 1966

R. H. Bates *Unions, Parties and Political Development: a study of mineworkers in Zambia* Yale University Press 1971

Gerald L. Caplan *The Elites of Barotseland 1878–1969: a political history of Zambia's Western Province* C. Hurst 1970
Better for relations between the Lozi and the central government than for developments within Barotseland

Edward Clegg *Race and Politics: Partnership in the Federation of Rhodesia and Nyasaland* Oxford University Press 1960
A critical study of Northern Rhodesia and the Federation by a soil scientist.

Trevor Coombe 'The Origins of Secondary Education in Zambia' (1928–39): three articles in *African Social Research*, nos. 3, 4, 5 (1967–8)

Sholto Cross 'A prophet not without honour: Jeremiah Gondwe' (study of a Watchtower movement in Northern Rhodesia/Zambia) in C. Allen and R. W. Johnson (eds.) *African Perspectives* Cambridge 1970
The Watch Tower Movement in Central Africa (Historical Association of Zambia Paper no. 3) National Educational Company of Zambia, Lusaka, forthcoming

J. Merle Davis *Modern Industry and the African* London 1933

A. L. Epstein *Politics in an Urban African Community* Manchester University Press 1958
The growth of African politics in the Roan Antelope mine compound.

L. H. Gann *Birth of a Plural Society: the development of Northern Rhodesia under the British South Africa Company 1894–1914* Manchester University Press 1958
Valuable scholarly study which takes note of African as well as European factors.

Richard Gray *The Two Nations: Aspects of the Development of Race Relations in the Rhodesias and Nyasaland* Oxford University Press 1960
Stimulating analysis of economic and social history between 1918 and 1953.

Richard Hall *The High Price of Principles: Kaunda and the White South* Hodder and Stoughton 1969
A penetrating study, with special emphasis on UDI.

Ian Henderson 'The role of labour in Zambia' in R. J. Macdonald and A. K. Smith (eds.) *Protest and Resistance in Twentieth Century Africa* University of Syracuse Press 1972

Kenneth Kaunda *Zambia Shall be Free* Heinemann (AWS.) 1963
The autobiography of Zambia's first President. It is available as a paperback.

Patrick Keatley *The Politics of Partnership* Penguin 1963
A long and interesting study of British rule in Central Africa.

Colin Leys and Cranford Pratt (eds.) *A New Deal in Central Africa* Heinemann 1960
A collection of essays criticising Federation from different points of view and specially useful for Northern Rhodesia.

Philip Mason *Year of Decision: Rhodesia and Nyasaland in 1960* Oxford University Press 1960
The history of Federation from 1953 to 1960.

Henry S. Meebelo *Reaction to Colonialism: a Prelude to the Politics of Independence in Northern Zambia 1893–1939* Manchester University Press for University of Zambia 1971

David Mulford *The Northern Rhodesia General Election 1962* Oxford University Press Nairobi 1964
A detailed study by a political scientist; available as a paperback.

David Mulford *Zambia: the Politics of Independence 1957–1964* Oxford University Press 1967

T. O. Ranger *The Agricultural History of Zambia* (Historical Association of Zambia Paper no. 1) National Educational Company of Zambia, Lusaka 1972

T. O. Ranger and J. C. Weller (eds.) *The Christian History of Central Africa* Heinemann 1973
This includes essays by D. J. Cook on Welfare Associations in Zambia 1912–1931; by T. O. Ranger on the Mwana Lesa movement; and by W. Rau on witchcraft and politics among the Ngoni.

Andrew Roberts 'The Lumpa Church of Alice Lenshina' in R. I. Rotberg and A. A. Mazrui (eds.) *Protest and Power in Black Africa* Oxford University Press New York 1970

Robert J. Rotberg *The Rise of Nationalism in Central Africa: the making of Malawi and Zambia 1873–1964* Harvard and Oxford University Presses 1966
Chiefly valuable for the period between 1930 and 1950.

John V. Taylor and Dorothea Lehmann *Christians of the Copperbelt: the growth of the Church in Northern Rhodesia* London 1961
It is mainly concerned with Protestant missions and churches, but includes a valuable section on Jehovah's Witnesses and some independent African churches, such as the Lumpa Church.

William Watson *Tribal Cohesion in a Money Economy* Manchester University Press, 1958
The Mambwe people, in the north-east of Northern Rhodesia, specially concerned with their adjustments to large-scale labour migration.

8. African Politics in twentieth-century Malawi

JOHN McCRACKEN

THE EDUCATIONAL AND ECONOMIC BACKGROUND

To understand the nature of Malawi politics in the twentieth century it is necessary to know something of the educational and economic patterns established there before the First World War, and particularly to recognize the wide differences existing from one region to another. In many parts of Africa educational and economic advance have gone side by side. The paradox of Malawi is that the area of major educational activity was also that in which local economic development in terms of the production of cash-crops was the most retarded.

Educationally the most advanced region by 1900 was the Northern Province. There the response of a variety of local peoples headed by the Tonga, and the superior financial resources and educational zeal of the Livingstonia Mission, combined to produce the most comprehensive educational system at a primary level and the most advanced of any in central Africa in the upper grades, thanks to the foundation in 1894 of the Overtoun Institution at Khondowe. The work of the Blantyre Mission in the Southern Province, particularly after the foundation of the Henry Henderson Institute in 1909, did something to rectify the balance, as did in the Central Province the construction of a network of village schools by the Dutch Reformed Church among the Cewa. However in standard these schools never compared with those further north. As for the Yao round the south end of the lake, their increasing involvement with Islam from the 1880's and 1890's, and consequent rejection of Christian missionary influences, cut them off from significant educational opportunities. By 1928 out of a total population of over 55,000 in the Liwonde District less than 1,000 were getting any sort of education at all. Even the first government schools introduced in that district in that year were sparsely attended, and by 1934 had been abandoned altogether.

Though education was a northern-dominated activity, economic advances took place largely in the south. The existence of European coffee plantations in the Shire Highlands since the 1880's meant that government policy in the 1890's was designed more to further their activities than those of African peasant farmers. Johnston's land policy enabled European settlers to obtain large areas of land at a nominal price. His taxation programme was designed in part to force Africans to work for several months of the year under Europeans rather than on their own plots. His schemes, and those of his successors, for capital aid were centred on the region of European settlement. The first stretch of railway to be opened, in 1908, ran from Blantyre to Port Herald on the lower Shire, a route that made it of primary value only for those farmers situated in the Shire Highlands.

Three consequences can be traced from these developments. Firstly, the concentration of markets and of communication facilities south of the lake ensured that African cash-crop production would take place principally in the Southern and, later, in the Central Province. With the exception of certain lake shore dwellers like the rice-growing Cewa of Kota Kota and the Ngonde, northern peoples concentrated largely on subsistence farming and were forced to meet their growing needs through employment either with the mission or in labour centres in southern Malawi and in other parts of southern, eastern and central Africa. Second, the expansion in size of the administration and of planting and trading concerns opened up a number of opportunities for skilled employment in intermediary positions such as storekeepers, telegraph operators and hospital assistants. These kind of positions were held in Southern Rhodesia and in Kenya by white artisans and Asians respectively. In Malawi, however, both groups were largely absent, and in consequence Africans were frequently employed. The early experience thus gained, when placed beside the educational standards achieved, meant that Malawians travelling farther afield were able to win positions of responsibility and become, in Dr Banda's phrase, 'the intellectual élite of this part of Africa'. Finally, the limited extent of European settlement ensured that African grievances would take different forms in different areas. In the Shire Highlands land alienation was extensive, many Africans were made tenants at will with little or no legal rights to the land they cultivated, and all were subjected to the insults and tensions inherent in the growth of a settler culture. Elsewhere, however, settlers were few and far between, and land alienation was of little consequence. Though almost all the Northern District centred on Karonga was ceded to the British South Africa Company, its claims were never taken up. The distinctions thus created are of crucial importance in explaining the various forms which politics in Malawi have taken.

ELLIOT KAMWANA AND JOHN CHILEMBWE (1898–1915)

Between the end of the period of resistance in 1898 and the suppression of the Chilembwe Rising in 1915, political activities in Malawi followed two courses. In the north the spearhead was provided by the lakeside Tonga, the first people to adapt themselves to colonial rule, and the first to agitate against it from within. As early as 1902 Tonga resistance to the imposition of increased taxes led to the despatch of a company of the King's African Rifles to the nearest government station at Nkata Bay. The essentially rural character of the area, however, and the absence of the more obvious friction consequent to white rule meant that grievances tended to be centred, not on positive government-inspired abuses but rather, in the first phase, on frustrations resulting from the relationship of the Tonga with the Livingstonia Mission. On a popular level these frustrations stemmed principally from the selective nature of the mission's relations with Tonga villages; or rather from the fact that certain villages, notably Marenga's next to Bandawe, gained very much more from the association than did outlying villages at Chinteche, or even a close neighbour of Marenga's like Chifira. Such differences created tension in the 1880's when Livingstonia's educational and economic role were beginning to be appreciated. They grew in importance from the middle 1890's, when for the first time a popular religious movement began among the Tonga, sparked off by the new evangelical revivalistic methods which the younger missionaries had begun to use. From 1895 to 1898, and again from 1903 to 1909, waves of popular religious enthusiasm swept Tongaland, with thousands attending mass meetings and hundreds coming forward to be baptized.

At this point the contradictory character of Livingstonia's policy began to appear. Although they aimed to change the social and economic conditions of a society as a whole, and followed religious policies which had wide popular effects, the missionaries shrank from mass-conversion and believed that admission to the church could only be granted to those who had served lengthy apprenticeships, whose character could be fully attested for and who were fully instructed in their beliefs. With the spread of the popular movement they became yet more cautious in their policies, inserting new grades of catechumen and hearer through which candidates had to pass, and instituting a system of direct and indirect financial levies to test the sincerity of their faith. By 1908 thousands of catechumens had waited two years or more for baptism, most of them from villages not directly connected with the mission's socio-economic network. There was widespread impatience both to attain the status of a church member and to be placed on an equality with those from more fortunate districts.

To these frustrations of the masses must be added the tensions existing among church members, and particularly among the Institution-educated élite who had begun to reach for greater responsibilities. One source of friction was the differing attitudes of white and black Christians towards African institutions and customs. Most African church members were prepared to side with the missionaries in their condemnation of polygamy and certain other customs, but they were rarely able to agree with the missionary who declared that 'sometimes . . . the best way is simply to cut the Gordian knot and make a clean sweep altogether'.[1] Consequently, Xhosa and Fingo teachers sent up from Lovedale Institution in the Cape Colony who were paid at comparable rates to Scottish artisans, ran into a storm of criticism from their Scottish colleagues in the mid-1880's because of their refusal to reject African attitudes and behaviour beyond the station. In northern Ngoniland the missionary Elmslie, accused his Lovedale colleague, George Williams, of spending too much time in villages among Africans who were not working at school. 'Mr W.,' he declared, 'had neither actively nor passively resisted heathen practices, and has given his direct sanction to many of them by attending and taking part in them, e.g. beer drinking and "Ukutomba" (coming of age of girls) dances and marriages within reach. . . . It is utterly fruitless to endeavour to raise the morals of the people if personal countenance of and participation in such scenes are manifested by those who preach the pure Gospel of Christ.'[2] Elders from Loudon Kirk session attempted to change Livingstonia's policy on the marriage of widows to their husbands' brothers, to bring it more into line with Ngoni practice, only to be defeated in council by the more conservative of the Europeans. African dances, condemned outright by the missionaries, had their African supporters. Charles Domingo, the leading African at the mission, read a paper in 1902 praising some aspects of them. Charles Chinula, a teacher, secretly encouraged his pupils to take part in dances at the Loudon schoolhouse, unknown to the resident missionary.

A second source of friction had its roots in the excessive caution shown by the mission in transferring authority to Africans. The basic aim of Livingstonia, constantly repeated, was to create a 'self-supporting, a self-governing, and a self-extending Native Church', and to this end the Lovedale agents were granted positions of considerable responsibility. From the mid-1880's however the increase in British colonial power was resulting in a growing unwillingness to employ Africans on an equal level with Europeans, and hence to the rejection of the Lovedale men and the refusal of missionaries to promote local Africans as speedily as the officials in Scotland would have liked. African clergy-to-be were given the highest training available in the Normal and Theological classes at the Institution; yet again and again their ordination was postponed on the grounds that congregations could not be found which would support them financially. Charles Domingo, having completed a course at Lovedale, finished his Livingstonia theological training in 1900 and was licensed in 1902. Yet when in 1908 he left the mission in frustration, he had still not been ordained. Yesaya Zerenji Mwase, a Tonga, completed his theological training in 1902; not till 1914, with two other ordinands, did he become Livingstonia's first African minister.

These conditions were dramatically exploited by Eliot Kamwana in the 'Watchtower' movement that began among the Tonga in 1909. Kamwana, himself a Tonga from Chifira village, had left the Livingstonia Institution in 1901 as a protest against the introduction of fees. He then became associated with Joseph Booth, the most radical European evangelist to work in Malawi, responsible for the founding of five missions of different sects there, and subsequently turned to the Watch Tower Bible and Tract Society whose millenarian message he carried back with him to Tongaland in 1908 after a spell in South Africa. Within a few months more than ten thousand adherents had been made, most of them from that sector of society which was frustrated by its failure to get into the Church and refused, or perhaps was unable, to pay the financial price of admittance. 'So far as the religious element was concerned,' wrote Elmslie, 'it was no doubt a revolt against our strict system of admission. It could not have succeeded at all had there not been a desire to get a Church standing without having to undergo the prolonged probation we prescribed.' Those immersed, he thought, were primarily 'hearers whose entrance to class had been deferred for various reasons, and catechumens in the same position; then crowds of heathen received without instruction or examination who answered to the cry "free education and books and no *sonko* to the Church" '.³

Political grievances were also articulated in religious guise. Kamwana attacked the introduction of taxes, prophesied that British rule would come to an end in 1914, and declared that out of the millenium an African state would be created. Pointing to the Residency, so George Shepperson and Thomas Price tells us, he would say, 'These people you soon will see no more. . . . We shall build our own ships, make our own powder, and make or import our own guns.'⁴ It was not surprising that the government took alarm at his fiery doctrines. Kamwana was deported late in 1909, and was not allowed to return to the district till 1937.

The removal of its leader did not end the first militant phase of religious protest in northern Malawi. Watch Tower continued as one of the most popular independent sects in the West Nyasa district and spread to many other parts of the Protectorate as well. It was also carried by migrant workers to the urban centres of Southern Rhodesia where it became a popular faith with the semi-educated élite. More important, Charles Domingo, having left Livingstonia for the Seventh Day Baptists, organized a number of separatist churches and independent schools among the northern Ngoni and strikingly exposed the contrast between Christian theory and practice which he found in colonial society. 'There is too much failure among all Europeans in Nyasaland,' he wrote in a leaflet circulated in 1911. 'The three combined bodies, Missionaries, Government and Companies, or gainers of money—do form the same rule to look upon the native with mockery eyes. It sometimes startles us to see that the three combined bodies are from Europe, and along with them there is a title "CHRISTENDOM". . . . If we had power enough to communicate ourselves to Europe we would advise them not to call themselves "Christendom" but "Europeandom". Therefore the life of the three combined bodies is altogether too cheaty, too thefty, too mockery.'[5] To Kamwana's more generalized resentments, Domingo also brought a reasoned criticism of the treatment of labourers on European estates.

In the south grievances were concerned from the first with economic injustices of a planting economy. In many respects the Shire Highlands was a microcosm of Southern Rhodesia. Land for Africans was in short supply. Johnston had attempted to set aside enough for their needs by writing into the certificates of claim given to European settlers a non-disturbance clause which was intended to protect existing villages from molestation. In fact, the eagerness with which Europeans encouraged increased immigration on to their lands as a means of obtaining labour, and the flood of Nguru settlers into the area from the beginning of the century, both conspired to frustrate these aims. By 1903 the non-disturbance clause was said to be a dead letter, and African land rights had virtually disappeared. The pressures of hut tax imposed at an earlier period than in the north and more rigorously collected, was another grievance, the maltreatment of squatters on European estates was a third.

But if the situation in the Shire Highlands was similar to that in Rhodesia, there were also differences which explain why the explosion of resentment there was so long delayed. In terms of intensity, Yao and Nyanja had less to suffer than Shona and Ndebele, for the introduction of settlers took place over a longer period and they were not subjected to the full force of British South Africa Company policies. Moreover, as a result of the conflicts of the late nineteenth century and the wars of attrition fought by Johnston, their political authorities, with few exceptions, were incapable of becoming the focus of resistance; while religious institutions like the rain shrines of Mbona and Makewana had been disrupted and weakened by Ngoni and slave-trading pressures. Not only was the shock of conflict with the Europeans less extreme, the means to resist were not at hand. Where Rhodesia after the original imposition of rule burst again into flames, the Shire Highlands remained quiescent. By the time that armed revolt did break out new classes had arisen and new aspirations been created. The leaders of the Shona and Ndebele rising had been spirit mediums and officials of traditional cults. In Malawi grievances were to be articulated by 'new men' and in particular by the Rev. John Chilembwe.

John Chilembwe is one of the most remarkable figures to have emerged in Malawi in modern times. A Yao from Chiradzulu, he came into contact with Joseph Booth in 1894 and accompanied him to America in 1897. Three years later he returned to Chiradzulu as an ordained minister and rapidly established the Providence Industrial Mission in that area. Chilembwe's aims were originally of the improving, 'modernizing' type, very different from those of Kamwana. For over a decade he attempted to run schools, grow improved crops and encourage the wearing of European clothing. 'He exhorted people from keeping themselves into strong drinks and such like,' his African biographer reported, 'he taught adults and children to keep on work, not to lounge about, even to advise headmen . . . to keep their villages nice and clean telling them that was the key to civilisation, also the key to good health . . . he liked to see his country men work hard and prosper in their undertakings, also to see them smart, such as negro fellows he had seen in America and other countries.'[6]

By 1914, however, Chilembwe's initial desire to work within the colonial framework was being destroyed. Existing economic discontents were deepened by the famine of 1913 and the flood of yet more Nguru immigrants into the Protectorate. The outbreak of the First World War, followed by increased recruiting of askaris and of carriers for service, was the deciding factor. In November 1914 Chilembwe wrote to the local paper complaining of the injustice inherent in forced African participation. 'Let the rich men, bankers, titled men, storekeepers, farmers and landlords go to war and get shot,' he argued. 'Instead the poor Africans who have nothing to own in this present world, who in death leave only a long line of widows and orphans in utter want and dire distress are invited to die for a cause which is not theirs.'[7] Two months later the rising began. Chilembwe's aim, it has been suggested, was less that of overthrowing government than of bringing the grievances of Africans to its attention in the most dramatic form. Only three Europeans were killed and at no time was its success in prospect. Chilembwe himself was shot while trying to escape and his lieutenants were imprisoned or hanged.

Chilembwe's movement was perhaps the first in central Africa to accept completely the attributes of European society while rejecting European control. It also vividly demonstrated the inability in 1915 of the new educated men to attract widespread popular support in order to carry out resistance.

BETTERMENT AND BEYOND (1912–44)

With the failure of the Chilembwe rising went the withdrawal of the 'new men' from schemes of direct military action and the transfer of political initiatives to the Northern Province. For over thirty years the economic discontents of the Shire Highlands were left to simmer almost entirely undisturbed, while new policies were followed of educational and economic betterment and political advancement at the local level.

In Malawi the initial inspiration behind the new policies came from the dependence of the northern peoples on education in obtaining their privileged positions in labour markets throughout eastern and central Africa. Such was the superiority of Livingstonia's system that up to the First World War this dominance went virtually unchallenged. During the 1920's and 1930's, however, the lack of financial resources at the disposal of the Nyasaland Government meant that much less support was given to education in Malawi than was provided in neighbouring territories. At the same time, changes took place in Livingstonia's structure which meant that less financial aid was available for educational expansion, and that what was supplied went more on the village school than on secondary training, however rudimentary. Standards in the central institution were believed by those who had been trained there to have dropped from the mid-1920's. Not only was the educational lead which Malawi had enjoyed being rapidly eroded, it also seemed to many that in absolute standards the country was suffering a decline.

These circumstances led to increased political activity on the part of leading educated Africans in the area, most of them pastors or teachers, and hence intimately concerned with the question of education. They formed a series of organizations, all designed to bring pressure on the central problem of the lack of colonial development; though some aimed to bring particular issues to the notice of the government, while others attempted to supply the facilities which the Europeans had failed to provide. Superficially the differences between the native associations, independent churches and local tribal councils which they formed appear to be great indeed, and friction sometimes existed between one organization and another. In practice, however, in the inter-war period, the overlap in membership from one organization to another was often considerable. In Northern Ngoniland, for example, the composition of the local Native Association was so similar to that of Mbelwa's Council in 1936 that the District Commissioner at a meeting was forced to ask which body was in session. Charles Chinula, a leading Ngoni pastor, was secretary of them both. Moreover as far as plans of betterment was concerned their aims, in contrast to their techniques, were virtually identical.

The most prominent form of organization was the 'native association', so-called, the first of which, the North Nyasa Native Association, held its inaugural meeting at Karonga in 1912. Later in 1914 and 1920 respectively, the West Nyasa Native Association, a largely Tonga body, and the Mombera Native Association, predominantly Ngoni in membership, were founded, and these were followed later in the 1920's by various associations in the south.

These bodies were essentially élitist in form, making it a condition of their membership that members were to be 'persons of good knowledge and character', and seeing their role as 'one of the helpful means of developing the country in the hands of the two necessary connected links—the government and the governed'. Mission teachers and ministers, government clerks, educated headmen and chiefs played the major role in their deliberations which were designed at once to give the new mission-educated élite a platform for their views, and also to circumvent the District Commissioner and gain access direct to the Governor and his senior staff at Zomba.

Many of the topics which they raised with the government were essentially demands for redress from the action of its agents or the laws they had perpetrated; demands that women should not be seized as hostages when their husbands were in default of tax, or that forced labour should not be exacted from men seeking passes to leave the country. A second category was the demand for government economic action, both in improving the conditions for wage labourers and in creating further opportunities in Nyasaland itself. The West Nyasaland Native Association in October 1929 made a series of detailed charges against European employers alleging that they underpaid and overworked their employees and provided inadequate housing and no pensions. 'Whatever pays which does not answer better food, better clothing, better home, better education; more leisure, more ease and more pleasure in life to the workers are not just pays at all,' the minute recorded. Further requests by the North Nyasa Native Association were for government loans to help develop cash-crops, and by Mombera's Native Association for a veterinary surgeon to help protect their cattle, and for government aid in the growing of cotton.

Education, however, was given the highest priority. During the the 1920's and 1930's the inadequacies of an educational system dependent almost entirely on the missions was increasingly plainly spelt out. They were blamed for failing to support their teachers sufficiently comfortably, for refusing education to the children of suspended church members and of those not of their faith, and of closing schools at the whim of an individual missionary. Repeated demands were made for increased government aid, and in 1932 the question of a Government High School was brought to the notice of the Director of Education.

While native associations brought pressure to bear on the government, the new wave of independent churches founded in the late 1920's sought instead to take the process of betterment into their own hands. New churches were founded in every region. In the Northern Province, the African Reformed Presbyterian Church and the Mpingo wa Afipa wa Africa (the Church of the Black People of Africa) were the most important. In the Central Province, Hanock Phiri's branch of the American-based African Methodist Episcopal Church was significant. In the Southern Province, the refounding of Chilembwe's Providence Industrial Mission by his successor, Dr Malekebu, in 1926 brought modernizing Ethiopianism once more to the Shire Highlands.

The new churches differed in a number of important respects from Watch Tower and its successors in the first wave of Ethiopianism in Malawi in 1909. Their leaders were not prophets like Kamwana, foretelling the imminent end of the world, but well-educated ministers like Y. Z. Mwase and Charles Chinula, both of whom had spent many years in Livingstonia's service, and were deeply involved in the activities of native associations and of their local councils. The solutions they sought were not to be found in millenarian and zionist beliefs, but rather in the creation of independent schools directly under African control, which could act as alternative means of improvement to those supplied by the Europeans. All sought to utilize the grant-in-aid system established in 1927 to enlist government financial support for schools which would teach not only in the vernacular but in English as well, and all were anxious to obtain teachers with the highest possible qualifications. All too had schemes for further advance, the most ambitious of which was that drawn up by Y. Z. Mwase in 1934 for a Nyasaland Black-man's Educational Society, whose expressed aim Mwase wrote was 'To improve or Develop the Impoverished Condition of the Blackman religiously, morally, economically, physically and intellectually, by starting a Purely Native Controlled High School or College . . .' The failure of these schemes in practice to match up to their aspirations ensured the continuance into the 1940's of one source of lingering discontent.

The third type of prominent political organization to be used at this period was the various district councils and Native Authority courts to which increased official attention was given after 1933 with the attempt to introduce more vigorously the principles of indirect rule. As organs of the chiefs and their councillors these courts were sometimes regarded as conservative and reactionary. But partly because in practice many official leaders in Malawi themselves had access to education, and partly because even those who did not, often employed mission teachers and their like within their councils, their policies on certain matters were vigorously modernizing. In the decade before the beginning of the Second World War they passed measures in favour of compulsory education in their districts, petitioned for the establishment of government secondary schools and criticized the low standard of teaching materials provided.

At the same time they provided convenient vehicles for the one serious attempt between the wars to change the structure of government in any fundamental way, the attempt to reduce government interference by seeking to increase African powers at a local level. One example, thwarted as attempts at change in this district tended to be, by intense local rivalries, was the plan, engineered principally by Mwase, to have Marenga, descendant of the first chief to be allied with Livingstonia and himself a well-educated man, declared as paramount over the whole Tonga people. Another, drawing this time on customary beliefs and wide popular support, was the successful campaign for the restoration of the northern Ngoni paramountcy.

In 1915 chief Cimtunga was deported to Zomba owing to his refusal to recruit carriers for the government, and Ngoniland was divided out among seven principal headmen. Cimtunga's case was taken up with great enthusiasm by the Mombera's Native Association and, partly through its efforts, he was allowed to return to the district in 1920, though only with the authority of a village headman. In 1924 a widespread movement began, aimed at having him reinstated as paramount, and when he died in that year popular pressure was placed behind the claims of his son Lazaro Jere, a well-educated young man who had spent four years as a clerk in government employment. Petitions were sent to the government both by the Jere (chiefs') council and the Native Association asking it to recognize his position, and when these were ignored, the Ngoni took matters into their own hands, and treated him from 1930 as *de facto* paramount, though it was not till August 1933 that the government accepted the situation and officially appointed him Native Authority. No more than in the Matabele Home Rule Movement, of which T. O. Ranger writes, did the Ngoni paramountcy issue open the way to territorial nationalism. It did however give the politicians of the 1930's some success in strengthening local institutions vis-à-vis the colonial regime.

By 1940 it was evident that the policies of betterment could not of themselves achieve significant political change, and that new techniques were required if political pressure was to be effective. On one hand, the native associations had pointed the way to the future through the success with which they had transcended tribal particularisms and the extent to which they looked towards the centre. Thanks to the efforts of men like Levi Mumba, secretary of the first association in 1912, and architect of many others, the associations, though they were based within separate communal areas, shared identical constitutions, exchanged a constant flow of information, and, in the case of the northern associations, established a loose representative committee based upon Zomba. On the other hand, independent churches, and to a lesser extent the local councils, had stimulated considerable popular enthusiasm for local political reform and educational self-help. But the associations remained élitist bodies representing the interests of their members more than of the masses, and the local councils remained popular only in so far as they represented district or tribal interests. Changes were required if all were to be united in one inclusive movement.

THE ERA OF MASS NATIONALISM (1944–64)

Although no satisfactory analysis has yet been made of the rise of mass nationalism in Malawi, three factors appear to have played an important part in the process. The first of these was evident in the period of transition in the 1940's when growing frustration on the part of members of native associations at their failure to force major concessions out of the government was combined with the increasing interest that sympathetic aliens, both European and South African, were showing in the wider issues of the African political struggle. Both concluded that more effective action depended on wider unity. The result in 1944 was the foundation of the Nyasaland African Congress, the first political organization in central Africa to seek to work on a territorial-wide basis, and one which gained much of its strength by affiliating to it all the associations already in existence, and by transforming them into its branches.

Geographically, Congress marked an interesting change in focus from pre-war days, for whereas earlier initiatives had come almost entirely from the Northern Province, its creation arose out of discussions taking place in the south among members of the Blantyre Native Association like James Frederick Sangala and Charles Matinga, and foreigners such as the British South African, W. H. Timcke. Its leaders included representatives of the former era, notably Levi Mumba, now President of Congress, but they too, tended to come from a slightly different occupational sector than those of the inter-war years. Civil servants, business men and clerks took the place of the pastors and mission-teachers of old. In terms of political content, however, Congress in its early years spoke much the same language as its predecessors. Education and the need for increased government aid remained the major issues. Neither in terms of popular nor of financial support was it much more successful. An organization had been created which could be used by a mass political party but that political party had still to come into being. It was not till the question of Federation broke on the scene that the catalyst was created leading to widespread political activity.

The birth-pangs of the Federation of Rhodesia and Nyasaland undoubtedly provided a major stimulus for action. From the 1890's when Scottish missionaries fought a successful battle against Rhodes' attempts to incorporate Nyasaland within the sphere of the British South Africa Company, schemes for the close association of the country with her central African neighbours were almost invariably opposed by Africans and their supporters. In the 1920's and 1930's plans put forward by settlers for amalgama-

tion were fiercely attacked and, when in 1949 the settlers changed
their aims from amalgamation to federation the resistance
remained as strong as ever. It grew in 1951 when the British
Government accepted the desirability of the scheme, and came
to a climax in 1953 when the Federation was formally launched.

Federation was important to Malawi at once because it
stimulated political action and also because it united the political
movement in a way that few other issues could have done. Not
only were the new leaders opposed to it on the grounds that its
implementation would destroy hopes of political advancement,
many chiefs within the official hierarchy were also antagonistic,
because to them it represented direct rule policies which would
hit at the basis of their power. Thousands of ordinary Malawians,
too, regarded its advent with hostility. Many had first-hand
experience as migrant labourers of Southern Rhodesian conditions.
They were anxious to prevent such influences being extended to
their homeland.

A further influence stimulating the farmers of Malawi to action
was the increased interference by the government in their methods
of agriculture from the late 1940's. After the Second World War,
Britain was faced with a shortage of food supplies which she
attempted to rectify by encouraging increased production in her
colonial territories. Efforts were made in Malawi to stimulate
peasant agriculture and, though they were partly successful, they
brought in their wake further problems of widespread soil erosion
which the government countered by introducing a comprehensive
series of laws dealing with the usage of land. As early as 1946 the
first comprehensive Natural Resources Ordinance was passed. In
1949 it was greatly extended, and in 1952 it was enlarged again,
when in addition to the usual regulations on the control of erosion
and the limitation of stock, a decree was passed ordering that,
except in the Northern Province, all arable land should be
cultivated in ridges of a prescribed form. Regulations such as
these were often clumsily imposed, and sometimes detrimental in
their economic effects. Disliked by many farmers, they were
resisted by some, and often came to be regarded as a practical
manifestation of the influences of Federation. Some Congress
leaders involved themselves in the resistance. Others disassociated
themselves from it. At Ncheu in 1953 chief Phillip Gomani
instructed his people to disobey agricultural and veterinary rules.
At Kasungu in the same year chief Mwase, though a fervent

opponent of Federation, supported government measures. But whether or not Congress was intimately concerned, the effects were the same. The groundswell of rural discontent gave a marked impetus to nationalist politics.

Although widespread discontent existed by the early 1950's the leadership of Congress was still too ineffective to articulate it in a dynamic nationalist guise. In August 1953 riots broke out in the Cholo district of the Shire Highlands, generated in part by mounting grievances against the iniquities of the plantation system. Dissension spread throughout the Southern Province. But though leaders of Congress may have given limited aid to the rioters, officially they rejected their action out of hand and turned whole-heartedly to the constitutional path. Lacking central control, the disturbances were isolated and sporadic and eventually petered out.

The failure of Cholo opened the way to the next stage of political advance. By 1955 changes in the character of Congress could be noted in the growing influence of a group of young radicals headed by H. B. M. Chipembere and Kanyama Chiume, by the increasingly militant demands for self-government and universal suffrage, and, above, all, by the novel emphasis on obtaining recruits at a popular level and in the rural areas. As the movement gathered strength—by April 1957 some 60,000 members were claimed—so it developed the techniques and symbols of the mass political party—the slogan of *kwaca* (the dawn), the national flag, and the monthly, later weekly, news-sheet. So too, it came to recognize the relevance of earlier resistances in linking the past with the struggles of the present. Laudatory articles on Charles Domingo and Eliot Kamwana were written, and the role of John Chilembwe in particular was emphasized. '. . . he struggled almost in solitude for his people, determined to lay down his life as a price for human rights and liberty', wrote Orton Chirwa. 'His body was defeated, but his soul goes marching on.'[8]

All that was lacking, Chipembere wrote, was a charismatic leader to give substance to the mass of inchoate emotions: 'human nature is such that it needs a kind of hero to be hero-worshipped if a political struggle is to succeed'.[9] He, Chiume and the other radicals were too young and inexperienced to take on the burden. Instead they turned to Dr Hastings Kamuzu Banda who, though he had spent over forty years in the United States and Britain, had still managed to keep closely in touch with developments in Malawi over much of that period. In July 1958 Banda arrived back in Malawi to take over the leadership of Congress and to initiate the final phase of direct action. His vigorous denunciations of Federation, combined with the forceful campaigning of his lieutenants, provoked a series of clashes between congressmen and colonial officials, particularly in the Northern Province where the government's authority was at its weakest, leading to a declaration of a state of emergency in March 1959, the banning of the party and the arrest of its leaders.

That mass nationalism does not inevitably result in political independence can be seen from the situation in Southern Rhodesia where the success of the N.D.P. was frustrated by determined settler coercion. In Malawi, however, the imperial government was still directly responsible. Its political plans for central Africa had been frustrated by opposition to Federation. Its economic plans for the production of increased foodstuffs had been hindered by resistance to conservation measures. Now, with the rise of the new Malawi Congress Party from July 1959 on the ashes of the old, its coercive measures were seen to be equally ineffective. Faced with the dilemma of maintaining control through the continued use of armed force (fifty-two Africans had been killed during the Emergency) or of getting out altogether, the British Colonial Secretary, Iain Macleod, decided on the second alternative. Dr Banda was released in April 1960 and invited to talks in London. The elections of August 1961 brought the Malawi Congress Party sweeping victory, and these were followed in January 1963 by the attainment of responsible self-government. On 6 July 1964 six years to the day from Dr Banda's return to the country, the protectorate of Nyasaland became the independent state of Malawi.

AFTERMATH TO INDEPENDENCE

Thanks to the absence of major economic or tribal divisions within Malawi her nationalist movement was one of the most united and well organized in east and central Africa. Nevertheless, within weeks of the attainment of independence, its unity had been shattered following the crisis in the cabinet leading to the dismissal or resignation of six senior ministers, in September 1964.

On one level these divisions resulted from differences on questions of policy among ministers which reflected above all the gap of a generation between Banda and his lieutenants. While he believed that Malawi's geographical position necessitated the establishment of fairly close ties with Portugal, they wanted a rather more militantly Pan-Africanist line. While he attempted to maintain standards and prevent the growth of corruption and privilege by pegging back salaries and delaying Africanization, they believed that a more vigorous policy was justified. And while they looked for some degree of independence in the running of their own ministries, he stressed their immaturity, and treated them, even publicly, as subordinates required to defer to him on many issues.

On a deeper level, however, it soon became apparent that the divisions reflected inter-regional tensions whose roots lay back in the 1880's with the first contacts of African societies and European missionaries. Just as the contrast between the high educational achievements and the small number of local economic opportunities available in the Northern Province in the 1920's and 1930's had led many Northerners to attempt to obtain clerical situations elsewhere, so the same situation in the early 1960's caused them to regard the Civil Service as the major target for their aspirations. When Banda set in reverse the policies of Africanization from 1961 and placed a ceiling on salaries they reacted with resentment and alarm. It was natural that they should provide the bulk of the most articulate and educated supporters of the ministers.

Natural too, was the fact that the Central Province, the homeland of Banda's own Cewa people, should provide the majority of his own most staunch supporters. Educationally they lagged badly behind their Northern neighbours, though Banda himself had grown up in the Kasungu district when it still came within Livingstonia's sphere of activities; they tended to resent their success in obtaining positions of responsibility open to competition. With little possibility of moving quickly themselves into new posts they were unaffected by the civil servants' grievances. On a more positive plane they welcomed the emergence of an outstanding Cewa political leader after decades in which initiatives had come either from the north or the south.

To this division between the *evoluées* and the less well-educated, a second source of tension was added in the reactions of the Yao of the Fort Johnston area. To an extent even greater than that among the Cewa, they were deprived of educational contacts and of the posts that went with them. Grievances over promotions in the Civil Service can hardly have affected them intimately. They were deprived, too, of a significant share in peasant cash-crop production, the major occupation of the Cewa in the Central Province and one which has expanded appreciably in the years since the attainment of self-government. Cut off from the economic as well as from the educational benefits to be gained from independence, the Yao were understandably sceptical of the existing government, and turned to their own local leader, Chipembere, even though as the son of an Anglican archdeacon, his background was markedly different from their own. By October 1964 Chipembere controlled much of the eastern section of the district in the face of opposition from government forces. From there in February 1965 the one major assault on Banda's position was made, leading to the temporary capture of Fort Johnston, the subsequent rebuff at Liwonde ferry and the eventual withdrawal many issues.

In this way, the rejection of missionary influences by the Yao chiefs of the area from 1875, the increasing involvement with Islam, even perhaps the failure of the government in the late 1920's to find suitable Muslim teachers for their schools, all contributed to the political crisis of the immediate post-independence period.

Notes

1. *Proceedings of the Nyasaland Missionary Conference* 1900
2. Elmslie to Laws 18 September 1888 Livingstonia Archives
3. Livingtonia Mission Report 1909 pp. 34–5; Elmslie to Hetherwick 12 July 1912 Hetherwick papers
4. R. D. MacMinn 'The First Wave of Ethiopianism in Central Africa' *Livingstonia News* August 1909 p. 47 quoted in George Shepperson and Thomas Price *Independent African* Edinburgh University Press 1958 p. 156
5. *Independent African* pp. 163–4
6. George Simeon Mwase 'A dialogue of Nyasaland, Record of Past Events, Environments and Present Outlook within the Protectorate' quoted in Robert I. Rotberg *The Rise of Nationalism in Central Africa* Harvard and Oxford University Presses 1966 p. 64
7. Quoted in *Independent African* p. 235
8. Grigg Jones *Britain and Nyasaland* Allen and Unwin 1964 p. 95
9. *Report of the Nyasaland Commission of Inquiry* 1959 Cmd. 814 (Devlin Report) p. 12

Recommended Reading

Robert I. Rotberg *The Rise of Nationalism in Central Africa* Harvard and Oxford University Presses 1966
  The best account available for the development of politics in Malawi (and in Zambia).
George Shepperson and Thomas Price *Independent African* Edinburgh University Press 1958
  An account of the Chilembwe Rising and of the circumstances surrounding it. One of the very few great works of African history. Indispensable reading for the period up to the First World War.
J. Van Velsen 'Some Early Pressure Groups in Malawi' in E. T. Stokes and R. Brown (eds.) *The Zambesian Past* Manchester University Press 1966
  A useful supplement to Rotberg for the inter-war years.
Grigg Jones *Britain and Nyasaland* Allen and Unwin 1964
  Survey by a former colonial official. Some interesting insights, particularly for the most recent period.
Report of the Nyasaland Commission of Enquiry 1959 Cmd. 814 (Devlin Report)
  Not easy to obtain, but still one of the best written and most exciting descriptions that we have of mass nationalism in action.

9. African Politics in twentieth-century Southern Rhodesia

TERENCE RANGER

THE ORGANIZATION AND EFFECTS OF THE RISINGS OF 1896–7

There were so many reasons for the Ndebele and the Shona to take up arms against the whites in 1896 that it is easy to take their uprising too much for granted. We should not forget that it was not easy to organize such a rising. The Ndebele nation had lost its king, the essential focus of all national activity; in any case, even under the leadership of its king it had been swept aside in 1893. The Shona people no longer enjoyed the centralizing influence of the Rozwi empire and had continued their rivalries and feuds even after the arrival of the whites in 1890. So it was remarkable enough that so many of the Ndebele aristocracy and of their old subject peoples and so many of the western, central and eastern Shona came out against the whites in 1896. It was even more remarkable that their rising was organized, that in each province it was planned to attack whites in all districts at the same time, and that a degree of co-operation was achieved between the various elements on the African side.

We should remember also that the 1896–7 uprisings were not merely one of a series of similar resistances throughout central and east Africa. They were in fact by far the biggest challenge to the whites made in the 1890's and in the later period were rivalled only by the Maji-Maji war in Tanganyika. Even in comparison to Maji-Maji the 1896–7 risings were impressive; they were much more highly organized and they did more damage to the whites. 'The settlers lost something like ten per cent of their total number, a staggeringly high figure, infinitely greater than the proportion of casualties suffered by white colonists in the Algerian national uprising or the Mau Mau war in Kenya.'[1]

As far as central Africa is concerned these risings were different from resistances elsewhere not only because of their much greater scale and intensity but also because they involved so many of the old agricultural peoples of Southern Rhodesia who had occupied the area before the upheavals of the nineteenth century. In Malawi, for example, the old agricultural peoples of the Malawi confederation did not resist the coming of the whites; resistance rather came from the intruders of the nineteenth century, the Ngoni, Yao, Arabs. But in Southern Rhodesia the majority of the fighters of 1896–7 were Shona speakers.

Not only did these risings involve both Shona and Ndebele, they also involved almost everybody in the rebel areas. They were not only a matter of the soldier class fighting and the old ruling class leading. The 1896–7 clash involved children and women and old men; the lower castes and the subject peoples as well as the Ndebele aristocracy. And where traditional leadership was not sufficient or efficient it was sometimes challenged. As Dr Stokes says, 'Here the Zambesian historian encounters a concerted movement of popular resistance unique in scope and intensity . . . what can be described as genuinely national revolutions in which for a time the traditional political leaders were set aside'.[2]

Because the Ndebele and the Shona risings were in so many ways remarkable any account of African politics in Southern Rhodesia must begin with them. Part of the reason for the formidable character of the movements lies in the Ndebele and Shona past—so different from the history of most of the peoples who took part in the Maji-Maji rising, for example. We have already seen that the Ndebele system was remarkably strong and successful and now it showed that it was resilient in defeat. And we have already seen that the Shona survived the pressures of the nineteenth century much better than is usually thought and they they had a great deal of relevant history to call upon. It is easy to see that during the risings much use was made of an appeal to history. In Matabeleland the two main leaders of the rising were Umlugulu, the chief priest of the Ndebele nation who had been entrusted by the dying Lobengula with the task of restoring the monarchy, and Lobengula's eldest son, Nyamanda. Many fighters in Matabeleland believed that Lobengula himself was not dead and would return from the north with an army. The military organization of the rising took the form of a revival of the old regimental system. In Mashonaland there was an attempt at the end of 1896 to revive the authority of the Rozwi Mambo and the best claimant to the position was brought up out of a neutral area in order to lead a force of Rozwi who were gathered together from all over Mashonaland and eastern Matabeleland. This attempt failed with the arrest of the claimant by the whites but the prestige of the Rozwi was important in bringing many Shona people out into rebellion. The Rozwi were still believed to have the special protection of God and to be invulnerable. Military organization in Mashonaland was under the traditional leadership of the paramount chief and his sons.

Even the divisions inside the revolt had historical roots. In Matabeleland the rebels were divided into two factions. One was grouped around Bulawayo; the other around Inyati. This reflected the two parties which had disputed the succession issue on Mzilikazi's death. One was led mainly by older indunas; the other by young men. This reflected the tensions of Lobengula's last years when the two young men wanted to attack the whites and the older indunas supported the king's policy of peace. Among the Shona some paramount chiefs kept out of the rising because old rivals joined it.

And yet as we have already said the risings were revolutionary. Something more than an appeal to history was needed to make Ndebele aristocrats and subject peoples and the Shona groups who had been raided by the Ndebele combine together; and something more than memories of the nineteenth century were needed to bring the Shona chiefs together on the very large scale that happened in 1896. People came together partly because white pressure compelled them to do so; but they came together also because the emergency threw up a revolutionary leadership appealing to unity and promising victory.

This leadership was given by men claiming religious authority. They were not 'new' men. They were officers in one or other of two old Shona religious systems. As we have seen these systems had roots deep in Shona history. The spirit mediums had been part of the whole Mutapa structure and had given support to the king; the Mwari cult was closely linked with the Rozwi empire. In one way, therefore, the religious leaders were appealing back to a golden past of unity. But there were other elements in their leadership. They claimed to lead not only the Shona but also the Ndebele. The influence of the Mwari cult had spread far and wide among the Ndebele, especially after 1893. Moreover, the main leaders in 1896 added new claims to spiritual authority over and above their place in the old religious systems, claims to possess new revelations, to be able to promise invulnerability to European weapons and to be able to guarantee success. The religious leaders, Mkwati in Matabeleland, Kagubi in Mashonaland, were allies of the indunas and the chiefs but they were prepared to challenge the authority of any induna or chief who thought the time had come to make a self-interested peace with the whites. Over and above their appeal to the Shona past these leaders stood for total commitment, for the unity of black men against white men. These leaders were killed and their following broken up; in different ways both the whites and the Ndebele indunas regained authority. But it was important that the African peoples of Rhodesia had combined together under such leadership. Later on other leaders who wanted to unite the African peoples and who wanted to commit them against the white men would be able to look back to the memory of the leaders of the 1896–7 risings; this was one part of the history of Southern Rhodesia that could be used without creating tribal divisions.

We cannot describe the events of the risings here. There were many heroic episodes long remembered. The outbreak was a great blow to the whites and seriously threatened the continued authority of the British South Africa Company. But there was no real hope of success. The enthusiasm created by the religious leaders which made people prepared to face machine guns brought together the great numbers of the Africans against the small numbers of white settlers. If these had been the only whites concerned in the matter the Africans would have won; supplies were difficult, the settlers were not strong enough to move out of the towns, and life would soon have become impossible for them. But the whites in Rhodesia could call upon the help of the whites in English-speaking South Africa and upon the help of Britain. Reinforcements were rushed up by land and sea and more were prepared when the Ndebele were able to defend their hills and caves even against this larger number. The defeat of the risings cost a lot of money, quite a number of white lives, and large numbers of African lives. But the white thrust into Rhodesia was strong and its supporters were rich. The cost could be met.

As more white troops and supplies poured in and as the rebels were pushed back from the towns and the road systems and forced on to the defensive, the various leaders of the rebellion took stock of the situation. The religious leaders still wished the fight to go on to the end and they managed to carry most of the Shona chiefs

and people with them. When the whites offered surrender terms
to the Shona chiefs at the end of 1896 they were refused. Fighting
went on in Mashonaland throughout most of 1897 and only ended
with the arrest of the main religious leaders. In Matabeleland,
however, the leaders of the Matopos faction, under Umlugulu,
decided that they must treat for peace. They did not persuade
everyone of this even in Matabeleland. Some of their younger
followers sided with the Mwari priests to demand continued war;
and in the north-east Mkwati and his followers resisted to the last
and went on fighting until they were driven out of Matabeleland
and into Mashonaland at the end of 1896. But the greater part of
the Ndebele aristocracy was now concentrated in the Matopos
Hills under Umlugulu and the older indunas and they believed
that the only way to save the Ndebele nation was to end the war.
In this way the unity of the rebels, such as it was, came to an end.

On the white side Rhodes also wanted peace. The Company
could not afford more money and more white lives because if the
war went on it would either go bankrupt or lose its Charter; the
British commanders were asking for more and more men and
supplies to win the war in 1897. So Rhodes sent messengers into
the hills to contact the Ndebele and when contact had been made
and he knew that there was a Ndebele peace party he went into
the hills himself to meet them. These negotiations were unpopular
with the whites because they wanted the Ndebele forced to
surrender unconditionally. As it was Rhodes promised a good
many things. He promised that the administration would be
reformed, he promised that the Ndebele would be allowed to come
out of the hills and settle down on the land they had occupied
before 1893, though he did not promise legal title to it. He
promised that some of the rebel leaders would be given official
posts and paid a salary as recognized indunas and that none of the
senior indunas would be punished. Many of these promises were
kept though before long the Ndebele discovered that whites still
owned the land to which they returned. But the terms were a
small victory for the Ndebele and did result in some improvement
by comparison with what had been going on in 1894 and 1895.

As for the Shona rebels they were hunted down throughout
1897; stronghold by stronghold. They were dynamited out of
their caves and chased from one place to another. In the end
most of them surrendered unconditionally, especially after the
capture of the religious leaders. The Shona rebel chiefs were given

no terms and promised nothing. Many of them were put on trial for murder and a number were hanged. Their place was taken by rival claimants who had shown 'loyalty' to the Company. In this way the Ndebele indunas came out of the rising with a good deal of authority still left, but most Shona chiefs no longer appeared as leaders of their people in the old sense. In 1964 the old white leader, Sir Godfrey Huggins, then Lord Malvern, spoke a belated epitaph on the Shona chiefs. The attempt by the Rhodesia Front to claim that the chiefs were the real leaders of the Shona, he said, 'was a swindle. . . . Many of the Shona chiefs are rather dodderers. Their real powers and influence were destroyed at the time of the rebellion—1896.'

One last word is necessary on the rebellions in general, however. They did not win the really important victory which, in the context of the times, was not the evacuation of the whites but the end of Company rule. We can now see that if the British Government had been forced to come into Southern Rhodesia in 1897 many things would have been different. But at least the risings showed that Africans could not be taken for granted, that they could hit back. In this way even the defeated Shona did win better treatment; they were still subjected to a system built in the interests of the whites but the open abuses and outrages of the past were brought to an end. And when new measures were planned which affected Africans, like an increase of tax, the British Resident Commissioner asked whether they would provoke another rising. Sometimes as a result of this question plans were dropped.

SHONA REACTION AFTER THE RISINGS OF 1896-7

The Shona in the rebel areas were left in a bewildered state after 1897. Their total commitment to the rising had failed and many of their leaders were dead. Some turned to the missionaries for a new solution. Others took to the woods and the hills as followers of the die-hard rebels who would not surrender. Most lapsed into a dull acceptance of defeat.

It was difficult for new forms of political protest or action to grow up amongst them. There had been virtually no Shona converts to Christianity before the risings and so there were now very few literate Shona in touch with the new world. The educational breakthrough was a slow process; Shona leaders were not really produced by it for twenty or thirty years after the risings.

In practice, therefore, politics in the ex-rebel areas of Mashonaland reverted to tribal politics, embittered in many cases by the
hostility between those who supported the new 'loyal' chief and
those who remained faithful to the dead or deposed rebel paramount. There were some signs of a desire to keep alive the ideal
of wider Shona unity expressed in the risings; thus chief Kunzwi-
Nyandoro, a prominent rebel chief who survived into the later
period, was accepted as a leader by many Shona who lived outside
his paramountcy and was consulted by them on the most effective
way to demonstrate opposition to hut tax increase. Yet a man like
Kunzwi-Nyandoro was unable, for all his shrewdness and courage,
to offer effective leadership in the new age; he embodied a
tradition of resistance and that was important but open armed
resistance was out of the question in most of Mashonaland after
1897. So he spent the rest of his life, closely watched by the
suspicious administration, planning or half-planning resistance on
the old lines, in alliance with spirit mediums and hoping to take
advantage of Rhodesian involvement in the Boer or the World
War.

The hold that the old tradition of resistance had on Shona
imagination is easy to understand. After all, during this period
Shona-speaking people were still standing out against the white
man in arms. There were a series of risings after 1897 in the
Shona-speaking areas of Portuguese East Africa, reaching a
climax in the great Makombe rising of 1917. These are not
usually treated as part of Rhodesian history. But they were part
of Shona history. The peoples involved had shared the same
political experiences as the central and eastern Shona right into
the 1890's; men from the Shona paramountcies had gone to help
Makombe of Barwe against Gouveia then and they could not be
indifferent to later battles in Barwe against the Portuguese. One
of these later resistances directly affected Rhodesia and in some
ways can be regarded as a continuation or an extension of the
1896-7 revolt. This was the so-called Mapondera rising of 1900
to 1903. It is so little known that it seems worthwhile to give some
account of it.

Mapondera had lived in south Mazoe before 1890; his people
were involved in the 1896 rising. Mapondera himself was not
because he had moved out of the Company sphere of influence
before the rising. Mapondera was a proud man, a famous war-
leader who had defeated even the Ndebele. He was one of those

who had declared in Selous' concession that he was independent of both Lobengula and the Portuguese. He would not tolerate interference from the white settlers who moved into his area and went away to Makombe's country to fight the Portuguese until the Company had moved on and Mazoe was once more left to the Shona. Instead there came the rising in which his relatives were killed and his cattle seized by the whites. In 1900 Mapondera returned to take his revenge. He raided into south Mazoe but found it impossible to rekindle rebellion there. So he moved north into the old Mutapa heartland. There he found many people resentful of the white administration which was affecting them for the first time, demanding tax, threatening disarmament, and disturbing trade patterns. Mapondera allied himself to the last Mutapa, Chioco Dambamutupe, who lived with a well-armed following just inside Portuguese East Africa. At the head of a force drawn from the whole area of the Mutapa's surviving influence Mapondera invaded Rhodesia and marched on the administrative centre of Mount Darwin. His attack was beaten off and Mapondera returned to Portuguese territory to help his allies fight off the Portuguese advance. In 1902 Mutapa Chioco died and the Portuguese entered his kraal; Makombe in Barwe was defeated and his country occupied. The old Shona world was vanishing. Mapondera returned to Rhodesia in 1903 and surrendered himself to the authorities; jailed for seven years, he died in jail while on hunger strike.

Mapondera's adventures were not the last episode in Shona armed resistance. In 1917 a great revolt broke out among the Shona-speaking peoples of Portuguese East Africa in protest against Portuguese maladministration, particularly conscription for service as carriers in the war against the Germans. Portuguese authority was swept away once more in the Zambezi valley and in Barwe and the revolt was suppressed only after many months of hard fighting. This Shona rising of 1917 reminds us once again of the remarkable capacity of the Shona people for more or less co-ordinated resistance.

By 1917, of course, conditions in most of Mashonaland were already very different from those in the Shona-speaking areas of Portuguese East Africa. The Shona of Rhodesia were being drawn more and more into a modern economy, and they were being influenced more and more by missionary teaching and education; already in some areas some Shona were moving towards Christian independency as a vehicle of opposition. But as yet the leaders of Christian sects and still less the leaders of political organizations had not supplanted the spirit mediums or the memories of the rebel chiefs in the imagination of the Shona masses.

POLITICS IN MATEBELELAND 1898–1923

It was easier to move into more modern styles of political activity in Matabeleland. There were several reasons for this. One was that in Matabeleland some of the most respected leaders of the rising had become recognized indunas and were able to give their people some leadership inside the new system. Another was that Ndebele politics was bound to centre upon the desire to restore the kingship. This gave the Ndebele a target which could be aimed at in a variety of ways—petitions, collections of money, the organization of associations and so on. It also meant that many Ndebele recognized the leadership of the young sons of Lobengula who had been sent to school in South Africa and who were now by far the best educated Africans from Southern Rhodesia. These young men, who completed secondary school and one of whom began university, were able to attract support from the old indunas but also from the younger men, from educated Ndebele and even from Africans from South Africa. The kingship issue was also a good issue on which to appeal for help from outside. At this period many African politicians in South Africa were lawyers and they took a legal approach to politics; it seemed possible that something might be gained by appealing to Britain or the World on the basis of the legal rights of the Lobengula family and on the grounds that the Company had defrauded them. In this way the Ndebele kingship movement attracted the support of South African Congress leaders. In any case Matabeleland always interested these South African leaders more than Mashonaland; the Ndebele and the Zulu were one stock. Like Rhodes in the 1880's they approached Rhodesia by way of Bulawayo and knew little about the Shona.

All these things combined to produce political movements in Matabeleland which it would have been impossible to create in Mashonaland. But it is important to stress that it was not outside influence which made these movements important. Outside influence suggested ways of proceeding; the African Congress of South Africa was able to take Ndebele grievances to the world and did so in 1919 when they sent a delegation to Paris. The words of

Ndebele petitions were probably drawn up by Congress lawyers. But the force of the movements came from Ndebele hopes and grievances. Another reason which made African politics in Matabeleland different from those in Mashonaland was that the Ndebele had a more concrete and pressing grievance. That grievance was land. Most Shona had hardly begun to feel the threat of land alienation or the dangers of land fragmentation by the early 1920's, though some areas in Mashonaland already had serious land problems. But the Ndebele had lost virtually all their land in 1894 and had not recovered it in 1896. As white farmers began to take up the land so Ndebele settlements were disturbed, rents were demanded and thousands of people were evicted. Among them were important Ndebele dignitaries, senior indunas, members of the royal family. These men Rhodes had tried to conciliate after 1896; some of them were quite wealthy by Ndebele standards and owned large herds of cattle. But they found themselves and their herds and their people turned off land and they refused to accept land in the Reserves.

It was the land issue which gave the Ndebele kingship movement its wide base of support. The leader of the movement in its significant period was Lobengula's eldest son, Nyamanda. He became a claimant to the kingship after the death of one of his younger brothers and the mental breakdown of the other. He was not an educated man as they had been. But he was of royal blood, he had been a leader in 1896, he had contacts with some of the new men and was sending his sons to an independent church school in South Africa. He was able to maintain the alliance with the educated and with the Congress movement in South Africa. And he was able to speak to the memories of the Ndebele.

Nyamanda's movement became important in the years at the end of and immediately after the First World War. Various things helped to make this a period of activity in Ndebele politics. Land grievances were mounting. Returning Ndebele servicemen joined the movement; their service in the war seemed to the Ndebele generally a good reason to expect concessions from the whites. And at this time the whole legal question was very much in people's minds. A legal action was being heard in the Privy Council in London to decide the ownership of land in Southern Rhodesia; in 1919 the Privy Council decided that the British South Africa Company did not own the land and that it had no claim to it through Lobengula's concessions. It was true that the

Privy Council went on to say that the British Crown now owned the land through conquest, but the whole decision seemed to reopen the question of the rights of Lobengula's heirs. Finally, at this time whites in Rhodesia were campaigning for self-government and an end to Company rule and it was obviously important that an African view be heard.

Nyamanda really aimed at Lobengula's ideal of Ndebele Home Rule. He dreamed of a restoration of the Ndebele kingship and of the Ndebele homeland; he wanted Protectorate status under the direct supervision of the British Crown. It was not a programme that today we should call nationalist and it ignored altogether the interests of the Shona. Like Lobengula, Nyamanda was content to let the whites take Mashonaland, and a considerable bit of Matabeleland, provided the Ndebele National Home was left in peace. His movement was an expression of Ndebele nationalism. But at the same time it was not exclusively a tribal-conservative movement. Nyamanda enjoyed the support of many of the educated Ndebele, the preachers, teachers and the rest. He also gained the support of the South African Congress because his movement offered a way of attacking Company claims to the ownership of land and of trying to obstruct settler progress to self-government. And Nyamanda was supported and advised by groups of would-be modernizing Africans inside Southern Rhodesia. Most of these were migrants from South Africa who had originally been brought in as a reliable civilized work force whose presence would act as a restraint on the Ndebele. These men were now frustrated by the limitations placed on their economic enterprises and particularly on their ability to buy and farm land. Thus they had it in common with Nyamanda that both they and he wished to purchase land even though he was thinking in terms of communal purchase and they in terms of individual. It was members of this frustrated modernizing group who put Nyamanda in touch with the South African Congress. Finally, Nyamanda's movement enjoyed the support of bodies overseas, like the Aborigines' Protection Society in Britain, who welcomed it as an assertion of African rights.

Nyamanda's movement collected money from the Ndebele and tried to prove that it was representative of Ndebele opinion; it joined with Congress lawyers and Ethiopian churches in South Africa to petition the King and the High Commissioner; Nyamanda hoped to travel to England to make a personal appeal to King George. Quotations from two very different documents of the movement will give some idea of its complicated character; first, extracts from Nyamanda's letters to the Ndebele *indunas*:

> I write this paper of mine to you, all Chiefs of the Regiments. I say to you, all nations that have been conquered by the English the Government gave them Chiefs to whom they pay their tax. Look at Khama! He has his country, and Lewanika, he has his plot. His country is settled well and Mosheshe he has his land. Also the son of Dinizula has his country. All natives have their bit of ground where they pay their taxes. They pay taxes they know and are not like you who pay for what you know not. You do not know what is done with your money. It is like money that is lost because you pay so greatly and do not know what your money does. At the same time you undergo tribulation . . . I want to hear your word. We remain in a scattered state all the time. Even if people have been conquered may they not abide in one place? For myself I ask of you, ye owners of the territory, inasmuch as you are the nation. I do not say it is war, my compatriots, I only inquire. You also know that all black tribes in great numbers were overcome by white people, but they have their piece of land to stay on happily. We, forsooth, pay only for staying on white men's farms and for what reason?

Nyamanda's petition to King George V of March 1919 speaks a different language.

> Referring to Native laws and treatment, Your Petitioners have experienced with great regret that High Commissioners and Governors General, who are the true representatives of Your Majesty, have merely acted as disinterested spectators whilst Responsible Government parties of various names and associations are interpreting the Laws in class legislation to suit their purpose. Your Petitioners pray that in case Rhodesia is granted any form of Government the Imperial Government take over the Administration of Native Affairs in that country . . . Your Petitioners are further aware that the Judicial Committee of Your Majesty's Privy Council has found that the so-called unalienated land belongs to the Crown by reason of an alleged right of conquest and the de-thronement of the late King Lobengula. The right or justification of that alleged conquest Your Petitioners do not seek to discuss here; but in the interest of right and justice, and in pursuance of the fact that the right of conquest . . . is now repudiated by the civilised world, Your Petitioners pray that Your Majesty be pleased to hand back the so-called unalienated land to the family of the late King Lobengula in trust for the tribe according to Bantu custom, and the right of chieftainship therein to be restored and acknowledged.[3]

Nyamanda's movement did not achieve any of its objects. But it was the only African voice to make itself heard at a key moment in Rhodesian politics—the achievement by the white settlers of political control. The movement can be compared with others which took place at much the same time. In Zambia, for instance, the first 'modern' political movement began in Barotseland in support of the claims of the paramount chief. This Lozi nationalist movement also attacked the Company's claims to land and asked for direct imperial protection; it also used the techniques of petition and of lobbying supporters overseas; and it also combined a traditional aristocracy with educated modernizers. We cannot consider either of these movements as forerunners of territorial nationalism but both of them were pioneers of new political techniques.

THE WHITES ACHIEVE POWER:
THE CONSEQUENCES FOR AFRICAN POLITICS

Although we can compare these early African movements in Rhodesia and Zambia we must remember that the two countries were in one important way different from each other. The Nyamanda movement got none of the things it asked for; control of Matabeleland as of the rest of Rhodesia went to a white settler government in 1923; and so did the control of land. In Zambia, on the other hand, the British Government took over in 1923; land was largely reserved for African use; and Barotseland got its direct imperial protection. These different results came about not because the Lozi movement was much stronger than the Ndebele but because in Southern Rhodesia the white settlers were much stronger than in Northern Rhodesia.

When Nyamanda and his allies attacked the idea of white settler government, in fact they were attacking something which had been decided long ago. There had been white settler representatives in the Southern Rhodesian Legislative Assembly since 1898; Rhodes had promised that the territory would proceed to settler self-government; the British Government had committed itself to the idea before the First World War. When the Company decided to give up the administration the only real decision left to take was whether the whites would vote to join the Union of South Africa or to run Southern Rhodesia on its own under what was called Responsible Government.

For these reasons some Africans began to challenge the basic idea of the Nyamanda movement. They said quite rightly that it was bound to fail and that appeals to Britain would be useless. One of these men, a South African resident in Rhodesia called Abraham Twala, put it very clearly in a letter to the press. 'Experience has taught us,' he wrote, 'that our salvation does not lie in Downing street. I strongly advise our native fledglings in Southern Rhodesia, indulging in politics, to find out and make their friends in Southern Rhodesia. When this has been done we shall see what the harvest shall be.'[4]

Twala was profoundly influenced by South African examples, particularly the example of Jabavu's leadership in the Cape. In the Cape there were sufficient number of African voters registered on the common roll for them to have a considerable influence in elections; under Jabavu's leadership this influence was used to bargain with the white parties for concessions. In Rhodesia also the franchise was in theory colour-blind; a very small number of Africans were already registered as voters on the common roll. Twala and his allies, among them one or two educated Ndebele and Shona, decided to try to organize the African voters of Rhodesia in the same way as Jabavu had done in the Cape. Twala decided to offer the support of African voters to the Responsible Government Party in exchange for promises of justice to Africans after they came to power. On 20 January 1923 the Rhodesian Bantu Voters Association was formed in Gwelo; two white candidates of the Responsible Government faction were present and the meeting decided to 'co-operate as much as necessary with the present M.L.Cs who carried out Responsible Government propaganda' and at the same time asked them for a promise that, after Responsible Government, Africans would be allowed to purchase land freely, that higher education would be provided, that African voters should be exempt from certain restrictions, and so on. The founders of the RBVA hoped a great deal from their organization. In June 1923 its Ndebele secretary, Ernest Dube, wrote to Jabavu's paper that 'In Rhodesia the year 1923 will be a year of events beyond past years, for on January 20th 1923 the brown voter of Rhodesia formed a Union . . . to aim and strive for the betterment of the Brown Race in School and Government. . . . The brown people of this country are very backward, we still await a little, a lot, a movement forward, but we hope with the help we will get from our brothers in the South of Africa things will right themselves.'[5]

As things turned out the RBVA was not able to exercise the influence it had hoped. The numbers of African voters were too small and there was no readiness on the white side to accept educated Africans as allies. 'An impression is abroad,' an RBVA general meeting minuted in 1929, 'that educated and progressive natives are not in favour in some quarters.' The new settler government were determined not to encourage the African élite to claim rights as spokesmen for the mass of the people. So the RBVA won few concessions. And in any case it is tempting to dismiss it as very much an élitist and selfish organization, trying to use its special status to win concessions which were of interest only to the emerging middle class. To that extent Nyamanda's movement was much more genuinely a mass movement and so, it might be argued, more directly in the line of ancestry of modern nationalism.

Things were not as simple as that, however. The RBVA was important as the first association to focus on politics at the centre and to concern itself with the territorial parliament instead of thinking about a Ndebele National Home or dreaming of a new Shona rising. And some of its leaders did see themselves as speaking for the masses and made real efforts to reach a mass audience. Here the outstanding figure was Martha Ngano, a Fingo who had come up to Rhodesia in 1897. Well educated, an outstanding speaker and organizer, Martha Ngano was the life and soul of the RBVA in the 1920's. She took its claim seriously. In meetings in the rural areas she attacked the leadership of drunken and illiterate chiefs calling upon Africans 'to combine in an attempt to become as clever as the white man'. As the hopes of a fruitful alliance with white politicians faded Ngano became more radical in her approach. She realized that the only way in which the RBVA could become powerful was by registering many more voters. She therefore attacked the way in which the franchise qualifications were interpreted; in 1924 she pointed out that literacy in English was a qualification but that English was not taught in African schools and that communal property should be allowed instead of a demand for a high money wage. 'Why can't we vote our live-stock?' In Matabeleland she did succeed in setting up a number of rural branches and establishing a legal defence fund for farmers. In appealing to this new audience she became concerned with mass issues; her speeches came to centre around destocking and dipping and land shortage as well as around the need for higher education. Martha Ngano deserves to be better remembered as a pioneer of the sort of contact between educated modernizers and the masses which developed in later nationalism.

LAND APPORTIONMENT AND AFRICAN POLITICS

With all its limitations the political future seemed to lie in the 1920's with the RBVA and the other associations rather than with the Nyamanda movement or with Shona dreams of revolt. Many of the Ndebele remained devoted to the ideal of a National Home and a restored monarchy and the cause was taken up by the Matabele Home Society. But after 1923 it became more and more obviously a tribal cause and the commitment of the Ndebele aristocracy to it prevented them from moving on into new forms of nationalist protest. As for the Shona, a report on attitudes in the Belingwe area in 1923 stressed that their response to white pressures had become one of fatalistic and despairing acceptance; the futility of old forms of resistance was understood. But the new associations also had serious weaknesses. The RBVA, the Gwelo Native Welfare Association, the Rhodesia Native Association and the others that came into existence at this time were especially open to the charge of being unrepresentative. Unlike the Native Associations of the same period in Malawi they were mainly led by foreigners—Fingos, Sothos, Nyasas. This was because African education in Rhodesia lagged far behind African education in Malawi in the early period of contact. Large numbers of Nyasas were already literate before the first Shona went to school, and some sort of higher education was avilable in Malawi decades before it was available in Rhodesia. It was inevitable that educated Africans from South Africa and Malawi should take a leading role in these early associations. Exactly the same thing happened, for example, in the early political associations of Zambia and Tanganyika. But it was also inevitable that this should make it difficult for them to establish contact with the Shona and Ndebele masses; not everyone was a Martha Ngano.

The Rhodesian administration thought that it could safely disregard such unrepresentative associations. Prime Minister Moffat thought that their pretensions were more 'pathetic' than they were dangerous. In any case, even if these associations had spoken with an indigenous voice the Rhodesian Government was much less likely to listen to them than the Colonial Government in Malawi.

And all these associations depended upon being listened to; they had no other effective means of applying pressure. The motto of the RBVA expressed the faith of them all: 'Not by might, nor by power, but by My Spirit, saith the Lord of Hosts'. Southern Rhodesia showed little signs of the working of the spirit in the 1920's and 1930's.

The land issue came as a test case for all these associations. Land was the one issue upon which they might hope to rally wide support. And the new settler government had promised British philanthropic organizations that it would reopen the land question and seek for a final and just settlement. One of the aims of the RBVA was to ensure that African opinions were heard when the land issue was reopened. And the other associations were equally concerned with land. They all asked for the right to purchase land freehold and they all asked for more land to be added to the Reserves to be held communally. The whites also wanted the land issue discussed because they hoped to achieve a system of segregation. Up until the appointment of the Carter Commission in 1925 all parties were equally delighted with the prospect of a land inquiry. The RBVA boasted that its representations had been responsible for the appointment of a Commission. And the hearings of the Commission were the most important political event for Rhodesian Africans since the risings. Hundreds of African witnesses testified to the Commission; African views were sounded in a way that had never happened before. Chiefs and elders and church ministers and independent church leaders and school teachers and members of the Ndebele royal family and the leaders of the new associations all gave evidence. Their evidence varied a good deal but certain things came out of it; Africans wanted more land, and to get it they were prepared to accept the idea of segregation. The land left to the whites was to be for whites only. Rhodesian Africans were falling once again for the old Home Rule trick that Rhodes had played on Lobengula.

Some African voices warned against the idea of segregation, pointing out that it would mean that all the towns fell in the white area. But the real disillusionment came with the publication of the Commission report. Segregation was indeed recommended; so also was an addition to African land. But this addition was a small one. The Reserves were not significantly increased, and the new African area, the so-called Native Purchase area, was to be reserved for Africans who could afford freehold plots.

Those who had wanted to be able to buy land were no better pleased. The new Native Purchase areas were remote, and often waterless and unsurveyed. They suspected a swindle, and their suspicions were fully justified since the greater part of the land remained undistributed for decades. Only 893 farmers had been settled in the Native Purchase Areas by 1939; 'many of the successful applicants were retired BSA policemen, evangelists and teachers from Missions . . . many of them were old and many had their origins in Nyasaland, Mozambique or South Africa'. As Roger Woods tells us 'the evidence is that progressive natives (i.e. those with capital) met nothing but frustration in trying to acquire land'. In short, the whites had got segregation and neither the tribal Africans nor the progressive leaders of the associations had got their share of the bargain.[6]

In July 1929 various African associations of Southern Rhodesia held a combined meeting in a mood of bitterness and disillusionment. On issue after issue they voted against the 'Home Rule trick', those policies of parallel development which did not offer a fair share to the African, which gave him no real power in his own areas, and which debarred him from education and opportunity. The 'Congress' of associations unanimously voted to reject the Land Apportionment Bill. A Shona speaker drove the rejection home. 'Let us tell the Government that this bill is wrong. Our people have been driven to lands where they cannot live. Our cattle die for want of water . . . Let us tell the Government that the bill is no good. It is all for the white man. Rhodesia is big. Let them cut the land in half and let us live on the one side and the white man on the other. If they cannot do this they should at least give us a place for reserves where there is water.' The 'Congress' went on to reject the proposed Local Councils Bill which purported to give a measure of local self-government. Delegates objected above all to the provision that the Native Commissioner was to be Chairman of the Local Council: 'He is a European, how can he understand the domestic affairs of natives? Only a native can do that.' And the 'Congress' also attacked an educational policy which provide Government schools for white children but not for black. 'Do we not pay taxes to the Government? Then we want a proper Government school, we want to see something for our money, we want proper schooling for our children.' Their disillusioning experience had driven the polite associations into a much more radical position. But even then they could only reiterate: 'If we talk sensibly as we have done today the Government will take notice of us'.[7]

EARLY TRADE UNIONISM

At the end of the 1920's the first attempts to organize the African workers of Bulawayo, Salisbury and other urban centres were made. They also were inspired by the example of the Union of South Africa. There the remarkable Nyasa leader, Clemens Kadalie, had created the most spectacular mass movement ever known in South African politics: the Industrial and Commercial Workers Union. The ICU seemed to offer a solution to the essential dilemma—how to produce a modern movement with effective mass support and with a weapon in its hands. The unity of the worker would replace the division of the tribesman. In 1927 Kadalie sent another Nyasa, Robert Sambo, to start ICU activity in Rhodesia.

Sambo was an extremely interesting and unusual man. In addition to his interest in the organization of urban workers he was concerned with the condition of the agricultural labourers who worked on white farms in Rhodesia. This question had not hitherto interested African organizations in Rhodesia mainly because a large proportion of this agricultural labour force were migrants from Nyasaland and Portuguese East Africa. Sambo, however, compiled facts and figures about the poor conditions of work and the low wages customary on Rhodesian farms as well as attempting to stimulate urban trade unionism. This combination alarmed the Rhodesian authorities who deported Sambo and did what they could to destroy the infant ICU organisation which he had created.

Sambo and Kadalie were confident that the seed had been well sown. 'In spite of your ban,' wrote Kadalie to the Rhodesian Prime Minister, 'we shall find means, as we have done in the past, to get our message to our fellow workers, and we shall find men and women in your colony to raise and uphold the banner of freedom from all forms of oppression.' And a handful of men and women did, indeed, continue to raise the banner of the ICU. Branches were formed in Bulawayo and Salisbury and efforts were made to carry the message of the movement into the mining compounds and townships of Rhodesia.[8]

The ICU brought something new into Rhodesian African politics. It worked through the public meeting; every Saturday and Sunday in both Bulawayo and Salisbury such meetings were held. It struck a new note of radicalism, appealing to working-class solidarity, attacking the missions as well as the government, and demanding basic rights. Here are a few extracts from CID reports of the early meetings of the ICU in 1929 and 1930. 'If the White people did not believe in uplifting the native they should have left us in darkness. We are workers suffering. You must all understand that. Your perspiration is coming out for nothing. Everything is worked by natives. You are digging gold out of the earth and are making holes in mines . . . All roads are made by natives but if you walk there you are arrested.' 'You cannot conquer the white people because they are united. If you fight one white man the whole group will come upon you. Do not say "I am a Blantyrer or a Sindebele". Then we shall obtain our country.' 'Why are you black people asleep? Wake up and come to see your true God. The white man has brought another God. That God is money. Everyone is praying to money. If money is our God let us get money. I do not want to go to Europe for it, it is in the ground.' 'I am not separating you young men into tribes. Our prophets were killed for speaking truth. Today it is the ICU.' 'All the workers of the world are united and we must also unite our forces together and so achieve something and have freedom in Africa . . . If they do not want us to join the Communist party and other parties not friendly to the Government they must treat us better.'[9]

This was certainly a new voice. It seemed to offer a good chance of modernizing mass Ndebele and Shona discontent with the ICU playing the role that 'our prophets' had played in the risings of 1896–7. The ICU would succeed because it had the secret of proletarian unity which Lobengula did not possess. But the ICU was weak in practice. In Rhodesia it never became a strong mass organization as it was in South Africa; it attracted crowds to its meetings but collected little in membership dues. Moreover it disavowed any intention of using the strike weapon even though the parent organization had employed that weapon effectively in South Africa. The Rhodesian ICU mocked at the polite associations—'You must not think that Angels will come to the Europeans and tell them to give you more wages. No, we must agitate.' But it did not offer any convincing alternative. If the associations believed that an articulate statement of grievances would be heard the ICU believed that the voice of an organized working-class movement would be listened to. In any case, the fact was that African workers in Rhodesia were not ready for strike action; too few of them had roots in the towns; too many were from outside Rhodesia altogether. So the ICU was unable to build up effective mass support; when the Rhodesian Government moved against its leaders in the early 1930's and imprisoned some of them for subversion the movement dwindled away.

Nevertheless the ICU was important in many ways. It really was not so much a trade union as the forerunner of the urban mass party; it expressed itself through public meetings rather than works committees. It did offer the most outspoken challege yet to white policies. And it did take seriously the task of overcoming tribal divisions. Thus it used a Shona organizer, Masoja Ndlovu, in Bulawayo, and a Ndebele organizer, Charles Mzingeli, in Salisbury. Moreover the people who entered politics through the ICU stayed in radical politics for decades afterwards. Mzingeli as leader of the Reformed ICU dominated Salisbury politics after 1945; Masoja Ndlovu was one of those arrested when Congress was banned in 1959 and in 1967 is in restriction as a ZANU supporter.

THE 1930'S

In some ways the patterns of African political activity in Rhodesia had already been set by the 1930's. Ndebele nationalism had been expressed and had not succeeded; exploitation of the vote had been tried and had not succeeded; organization of the workers had been tried and had not succeeded; polite lobbying had been tried and had not succeeded. There was nothing much else to do but patiently to try them out again. And that is really what happened in the 1930's.

Two important things also happened in this period, however. One of them was that in the 1930's leadership in the various associations began to be taken over more and more by Ndebele and Shona educated men. One such man was the Rev. Douglas Thompson Samkange, a Shona minister of the Methodist Church who spent much time in Matabeleland. Samkange became the leading light in the two most important élite organizations of the 1930's—the African section of the Southern Rhodesian Missionary Conference and the Southern Rhodesia African National Congress. Congress, founded by Aaron Jacha in 1934, became the main exponent of the idea of concentration on territorial constitutional politics. It did not limit its appeal to voters or potential voters but tried to organize Africans more generally, especially in the urban areas. It was neither much bolder nor more successful than the RBVA. But it was the first Congress movement in central Africa. And it did survive to run into modern nationalism in much the same way as did the Tanganyika African Association survived to run into TANU. When the young radicals sought in 1957 to create a radical movement of modern nationalism they did so in the name of Congress, sought out and brought into the new movement the surviving branches of the older organization, and accepted the leadership of Joshua Nkomo, an office holder in the old Congress.

Congress, then, may be regarded as the ancestor of part of modern nationalism in Southern Rhodesia—the centralizing and directing part. But modern nationalism is more than a development out of the élite associations of the 1930's; it is also characterized by enthusiastic mass support. The second important development of the 1930's remotely foretold such mass support. What happened in the early 1930's was that the Shona masses in the rural areas showed that they could move out of their dreams of the past and break away from their old ideas of resistance; that they could accept other visions and other leaders. This did not mean that men like chief Kunzwi-Nyandoro were now replaced by men like Samkange and that the Shona masses began to support Congress; there was still a long way to go before the coming together of the masses and élite modernizing leadership. What took place was a development among the Shona of various independent church movements. Some of these, like Matthew Zwimba's Church of the White Bird, were above all Shona movements which tried to combine ideas of Christianity with older Shona beliefs. Such movements had a limited sort of success in providing a leadership which could speak for the rural Shona; Matthew Zwimba, for instance, was entrusted by the chiefs and people of the Zwimba Reserve to act as their spokesman to the Carter Commission on Land Apportionment. But more important, perhaps, was the sudden Shona commitment to movements which came from outside. One of these movements was the Watch Tower Church which was introduced into the Shona rural areas in the late 1920's and early 1930's by domestic servants from Malawi. The Watch Tower Church appealed to Nyasa heroes, like John Chilembwe and Kenan Kamwana; its hymns

were sung in Nyasa languages. Thus it did not make an appeal
back to the Shona past. But it did promise a miraculous divine
intervention which would overturn the Rhodesian situation and
put white power and wealth into the hands of the Africans. For
a few years the movement swept through north-western Mashonaland, creating congregations which repudiated the authority of
the chiefs and headmen and departed from tribal customs. Then
it faded again as its Nyasa leaders were deported. But the episode
had shown that the Shona were responsive to radical promises of
a transformation of the Rhodesian situation and that they would
follow leaders other than their chiefs and elders.

In the late 1930's there was a simmering Shona discontent in
the rural areas provoked especially by such things as destocking
and cattle-dipping. Every now and then this discontent was expressed openly, as when chief Nyandoro of Chiota Reserve
publicly opposed destocking in the late 1930's and was deposed for
doing so. But as yet these Shona grievances had found no effective
outlet; neither had they been harnessed to any centrally directed
political movement.

THE NEW SITUATION AFTER 1945

During the Second World War politics in Rhodesia as in other
parts of east and central Africa appeared to mark time. When the
war ended the pattern of African political activity in Rhodesia
seemed much the same as it had been in the years before the war.
In fact the same movements and the tactical choices which they
stood for persisted; though as we shall see the situation in which
they operated was being transformed.

Thus the Matabele Home Society still existed in Bulawayo and
the Ndebele countryside. Few of its members can any longer have
expected that the kingship would be restored. The Society had
become in effect the defender of Ndebele values and as such was
supported especially by the Ndebele artistocracy. In Bulawayo it
also acted as an urban welfare association and for this reason
attracted the membership of younger and potentially more radical
men who later left it to join the nationalist parties.

Congress was revived in 1945 and continued with its policy of
representation of grievances to government. It could now draw
upon an increasing number of educated Rhodesian Africans. The
ICU tradition continued in the person of Charles Mzingeli. There

were some developments in his thinking also. The old idea of the solidarity of all African workers had been extended to include the idea of the solidarity of all workers of whatever race; Mzingeli was increasingly working with a small group of radical whites who tried to lead European labour in Rhodesia into an alliance with African labour.

Finally Shona resentment continued to express itself in the form of sporadic and scattered opposition to destocking and dipping. And the growth of the independent church movement among the Shona accelerated greatly. In the twenty years after the war Mashonaland became one of the major centres of independency in Africa, until today there are probably more African members of independent churches in Mashonaland than members of mission churches. These independent churches varied greatly; some were modernizing churches which copied mission organization and forms of service; others were prophetic, faith-healing, millenarian, bringing in the ideas and symbols of older Shona religion. Both types of church had political significance. The first type offered opportunity for African leadership and modernizing enterprise; it was often seen as an African response to the white challenge, as a proof that the African also could run a modern institution. Ndabaningi Sithole, now the leader of the Zimbabwe African National Union, worked for some time as a preacher in one of these modernizing African churches. He tells us about its founder, Rev. E. T. J. Nemapare. 'He was seriously accused of "breaking the body of Christ", and in his defence he stated, "No Protestant has any right to accuse me of breaking the body of Christ. It is my Protestant right to protest, and I do not see what's wrong with exercising my birth-right." He remained unmoved and went ahead with his indigenous church.' Sithole tells us how the teaching and hymns of churches of this type emphasized Africa's unity and the need to plan for Africa's future. And in his own work for Nemapare's church he came into contact with the rural masses as a leader. 'For the first time in my life I saw with my own eyes how gospel-starved the people were in the rural areas away from mission stations. Great crowds came if they heard that I was going to preach to them.' There was still a long way to go before Sithole was to preach the political gospel of nationalism to equally hungry crowds but there is a sense in which his political career began in Nemapare's church.[10]

The millenarian churches, on the other hand, offered the same sort of hope to the Shona that the spirit mediums had held out in 1896–7 and the Watch Tower leaders in the 1930's. The most important of these churches, the Guta Ra Jehovah of the prophetess Mai Chaza, turned boldly to the Shona past; at its holy village the *shiri chena*, white birds, of Mwari pecked the grain; Mai Chaza was supposed to have summoned the spirits of the dead founders of Rhodesia, such as Lobengula, Chaminuka and Rhodes, to Zimbabwe and there to have reconciled them and released them from Purgatory; her followers adopted uniform and looked forward to the aid of spirit soldiers. It was no wonder that timid observers compared her to the female religious leaders who had been important in 1896.

But these various movements seemed as far as ever from being able to offer an effective challenge to the whites and still further from being able to unite in one inclusive movement. Ndebele nationalism; the worker organized as an interest distinct from the peasant-farmer; an élitist Congress; the apparently contradictory tendencies of the independent church movements; all this seemed unlikely to add up. To over-simplify, some people seemed to be demanding more modernization, more changes, and more involvement in the new economy. Others seemed to be demanding less involvement. Some people seemed to be moved with the ideal of a single Rhodesia or Zimbabwe; others were still preoccupied with the old 'Home Rule' idea and wished to be left alone.

Yet under the surface many things were happening to bring these tendencies together and to sharpen the conflict of black and white. Father Devlin in a striking way indicates the essentials of the new situation. After the war, he suggests, there was a Second Occupation of Mashonaland and a Second Shona Uprising. 'The Second Occupation was the large-scale European immigration which began in 1946, a net average of 10,000 a year. Three quarters of the present Europeans of Southern Rhodesia have settled since 1946.' 'The Second Mashona Uprising also began in 1946, or a little earlier. It was the rush for education. It increased every year, doubling or trebling the increase in schools, until by 1958 the children had rushed the Government off its feet and exhausted its allocated funds.'

All sorts of things were associated with the Second Occupation. The Rhodesian economy had been stimulated by the war, and the boom continued afterwards. Fairly rapid industrial development took place until secondary industry overtook both mining and agriculture and became the largest sector of the Rhodesian economy. The industrial areas of Bulawayo and Salisbury and of the towns along the road between them grew in size; the number of African workers and the number of African townships grew. The discontent of the African urban population became a significant thing for the first time. At the same time new white farmers began to take up and develop land in the 'white' areas of Rhodesia. Many thousands of Africans had been living on land which was in theory 'white' under the Land Apportionment Act but which had not been taken up or developed. Now they found themselves obliged to move into the Reserves which were already feeling the pressure of an increasing human and animal population. Rural grievances became more intense; land hunger was felt as acutely in most of Mashonaland in the 1950's as it had been felt by Nyamanda and his followers. To try and cope with the problem of the Reserves government endeavoured to enforce agricultural rules, tried to extend destocking, and in 1951 moved into a revolutionary attempt to change the whole method of tenure and farming in African areas. This 1951 Land Husbandry Act brought home the real position of the Africans of Southern Rhodesia; the Act gave land rights to individuals and broke away from the old communal ownership of land; many Africans living in the towns would lose land-rights and yet they had no security in the towns which were 'white' areas and no status as workers. Only white labour was defined as 'workers' under the Industrial Conciliation Act; African labour was controlled by the Masters and Servants Act. So both urban and rural grievances grew; or to put it better it became clearer that rural and urban grievances were part of the same problem.

All sorts of things were associated also with the Second Shona Uprising. As Father Devlin says, one of these was the rush for education. In the 1930's Nathan Shamuyarira tells us, his father, a teacher, still had to go round with his dog chasing up the children to make up the numbers of his classes. By the late 1940's the education fever had reached the area where Shamuyarira was teaching; villagers used to flock to competitions of English recitation and oratory between the pupils of different schools and to wonder at the youngsters' command of the new world. In addition to more education and more demand for it, there were other developments in the Shona countryside, slow as these were. Teachers and ministers were joined by traders and Native Purchase farmers as potential leaders and articulators of opinion.

Within this situation all the materials lay to hand for the creation of a mass nationalist movement. The potentialities were revealed soon after the end of the war. In Bulawayo the African railway workers were growing strong. In 1945 they staged a strike which was successful enough to gain a wage increase and some degree of official recognition of workers' movements. This strike demonstrated to Africans that action was possible. Both in Bulawayo and Salisbury organizations were set up to co-ordinate the demands of the workers. In Salisbury Mzingeli founded the Reformed Industrial and Commercial Workers Union to carry on the work of the ICU in this more favourable age. The African National Congress leaders were also involved in this attempt to organize urban workers. And in Bulawayo a new figure emerged to take over the mantle of the old ICU. This was Benjamin Burumbo with his African Voice Association. Burumbo linked the newly confident urban discontent with the grievances of the rural areas and was as much concerned with such matters as destocking as with wages.

In 1948 this new period of activity reached a climax in the general strike in which workers in Bulawayo and Salisbury were joined by domestic servants. The initiative was taken by workers themselves, who repudiated the advice of the various leaders to negotiate further. But the strike was another exhilarating sign of new times—the first effective mass action since the risings. The leaders of the associations supported the workers' demands.

The linking up of urban and rural mass grievances with élite leadership was to be the pattern of the future mass nationalist parties. But the strike of 1948 promised more than it could achieve. The wage increases which were eventually granted were much lower than the strikers had expected and there was a reaction of profound disillusionment. Moreover, Burumbo's radical leadership in the rural areas which contested removals under the Land Apportionment Act and later contested the Land Husbandry Act was also only momentarily successful. The loopholes which Burumbo found in the law were soon filled in. Disillusionment and renewed apathy followed in the rural areas. The immediate result of the flowering of African activity after 1945 seemed to many to rub in the essential powerlessness of Africans. This was one reason why after 1953 and the coming of Federation most African leaders turned again to co-operation rather than to opposition.

FEDERATION AND SOUTHERN RHODESIAN AFRICAN POLITICS

In Zambia and Malawi the issue of Federation acted as a decisive stimulus to nationalist politics. Africans in those territories were determined to resist the extension of Southern Rhodesian influence at all costs. It could hardly be seen in the same way in Southern Rhodesia. In Southern Rhodesia the coming of Federation and its doctrine of 'partnership' in fact delayed the formation of the sort of united movement foreshadowed in 1948.

It is true that in the two years before Federation an apparent stimulus was given to Rhodesian associations. In 1951 Congress participated in a meeting of African leaders from all three territories designed to plan opposition to Federation. As a result an All African Convention was formed in Rhodesia. This was joined by Enoch Dumbutshena and Stanlake Samkange, two representatives of the new generation of Congress leaders; Joshua Nkomo, general secretary of the Railway African Workers Union and President of the TUC; and Charles Mzingeli of the RICU. It seemed a strong combination. But Burumbo, the real man of the people as far as the rural areas were concerned, did not waste his time on Federation but continued his campaign against the Land Husbandry Act. And the All African Convention fell apart when Federation was actually introduced.

In fact 1953 is a date of similar significance in Rhodesian African politics to 1923. We have seen how in 1923 some Africans decided to try and work within the system. This happened again in 1953. For the first time Africans were being elected to special seats in the Federal Parliament; in the first elections both Joshua Nkomo and Stanlake Samkange stood for seats as independents. They were defeated but their decision to stand was not compatible with all-out opposition to Federation. Meanwhile even in Southern Rhodesia a new era seemed to be dawning under the banner of Partnership. The new Prime Minister, Garfield Todd, wanted to take the sting out of African grievances. He aimed to amend the Industrial Conciliation Act so as to call the African also a worker; he aimed to expand African education and build up a rural and urban middle class in harmony with the whites. For the first time Africans were welcomed as members of the ruling white party; and delegates from the African township branches appeared at United Rhodesia Party Congresses and moved resolutions for the removal of discrimination. More idealistic whites formed multi-racial pressure groups of various kinds.

It was a heady environment. After the apparent show of strength with the All African Convention the various trade unions and political associations almost fell into abeyance while their leaders tried again to work from within. 'By 1955 only Mzingeli was still active. The Bulawayo branch of the ANC kept going after Federation, but mostly as a social organisation running concerts . . . Everyone else was rushing to join multi-racial organisations, imbued with the new spirit of partnership and believing it would change their whole lives and bring equality.' It would perhaps be too easy to condemn this a betrayal by the African leadership. African politics in Rhodesia has always had to choose between resistance and participation and the hopes of Africans have moved from one course to the other. This was the golden age of participation.[11]

THE RISE OF THE NATIONALIST PARTIES

But this participation did not change the underlying realities. As it was more widely and more vigorously enforced the Land Husbandry Act aroused wider and more vigorous opposition. It was disliked by those living in the Reserves because it threatened to change the whole pattern of social and economic life. But above all it struck at the interests of the young unmarried wage workers in the towns whose ambitions were not to settle permanently there but to return to the countryside to set up their families. These young men now found themselves threatened with the loss of all land rights. In them African politics found a group of embittered activists who linked urban and rural discontent.

It was this group which provided the first support for the new radical organizations of the later 1950's. In 1955 George Nyandoro, James Chikerema, and other young and educated men, withdrew from the participant associations and founded the City Youth League in Salisbury. Influenced by the successes of nationalism in West Africa, they challenged the leadership both of Charles Mzingeli with his classical trade unionism and of the participant élite. Their challenge was backed at once by the group of young men who stood to lose most from the implementation of Land Husbandry. They were not primarily concerned with trade union issues since they did not see themselves as members of a permanent working class; they were still less concerned with the privileges which the participant élite were extracting from membership of the white parties. They joined in the attack on Mzingeli and helped to destroy his influence. Through them, and also through the example of Burumbo, the leaders of the City Youth League made contact with the discontent of the rural areas themselves.

In 1957 a further step was taken. The Youth League now combined with the Bulawayo branch of the old Congress to form a revived Southern Rhodesian African National Congress under the presidency of Joshua Nkomo. Other elements were thus brought into the radical movement. With Nkomo came the trade union tradition of Bulawayo. With the survivors of the old Congress came some of the sort of men who were needed as organizers of branches in the rural areas. But in the later 1950's it was not so much teachers and ministers of religion who performed this role—both were subject to reprimand or dismissal for involvement in political activity—as African traders.

Congress thus established itself in both Bulawayo and Salisbury and began to spread out further into the rural areas. Once again the activists in this expansion were often the landless young men returning from the towns to their home areas to preach the Congress gospel. But in very many places Congress found an eager acceptance within the Reserves themselves. The long smouldering rural resentments were at last being brought into modern politics.

Meanwhile other developments were taking place which were to lead to the disillusionment of the participant élite. In 1958 Garfield Todd was forced out of office by his cabinet colleagues. His fall and the elimination of his party at the subsequent elections brought home to many that participation could not succeed. The life went out of bodies like the Inter-racial Association and the Capricorn Africa Society which up to that time had commanded significant African support. Early in 1959 Congress was banned and severe repressive legislation introduced by the government which had succeeded Todd.

In the months after the ban on Congress it seemed that the new radicalism had been dealt a crushing blow. There was widespread fear and dismay among Africans, few of whom had anticipated so rapid a clash with authority as a result of Congress activity. For months there were no steps to establish a successor movement. Meanwhile the Prime Minister, Sir Edgar Whitehead, was calling for a new era of participant politics, and launching his 'Build a Nation' campaign to win the hearts of the African middle class. In reality the Congress ban merely completed the discrediting of the participation policy. When the National Democratic Party was founded in 1960 it rapidly attracted into it many of the leading intellectual élite.

By 1960, then, a mass movement of a new and formidable kind was emerging. It retained the support of the landless young men, the trade unionists, the peasants, the rural traders, and added to it the support of the most highly educated, the schoolboys and the students. It attempted a wide range of tactics, such as appealing for overseas support, producing cogently argued criticisms of the constitutional proposals of the Rhodesian Government, organizing urban strikes and demonstrations, organizing weekly mass meetings in town and country, and encouraging rural resistance to the implementation of Land Husbandry and destocking. In July 1960 this movement demonstrated in an impressive way its hold on the masses with the great march through the Salisbury townships; in 1961 it gave a further demonstration with the referendum organized by the Party in which its members voted overwhelmingly against the new Southern Rhodesian constitution.

The National Democratic Party and its successor, the Zimbabwe African Peoples Union, were recognizably mass populist parties of the same sort as the Malawi Congress Party, UNIP and TANU. Their emergence took people in Rhodesia by surprise. Everything seemed to have happened suddenly. Commentators regarded the new movements as mushroom growths with no roots in the past. They were explained in terms of Ghanian, Nyasa, Egyptian or Marxist influence. And they were held to be attacking previous traditions of African politics in Rhodesia.

It should have become clear in this chapter that this interpretation was superficial. Of course there were new elements in the situation which produced the mass nationalist parties and of course these parties were not like anything that had existed in Rhodesia before. But in other ways they drew heavily upon certain traditions of African response in Rhodesia; in fact they succeeded partly because they combined in one movement the majority of those traditions. The name Congress was chosen to demonstrate continuity; Rev. Samkange's son, Sketchley, was one of the founders of the National Democratic Party; the old ICU leader, Masoja Ndhlovu was an office-bearer of Congress and

detained in the 1959 emergency. At the same time these movements drew not only upon a tradition of coherent centralized
organization—upon the tradition of the old Congress and the
ICU—but also upon the tradition of the deep-running resentments
and dreams of the rural areas. The Shona expectation of radical
change now expressed itself through membership of the NDP or
ZAPU rather than through membership of Watch Tower. George
Nyandoro, whose ancestors had led in the risings of 1896–7 and
opposed destocking in the 1930's, emerged as a natural spokesman for rural discontent. So, as we have seen, there came
together within the movement the urban worker, the peasant,
the trader, the disillusioned intellectual; the traditions of the
RBVA and the old Congress, of the ICU and of the Shona
millenarians.

The coming together of these elements produced a new and
fascinating mixture. The intellectuals, who had begun by using
Ghanian examples and songs, now found that they had a ready
store of local resistance tradition to tap. People began to sing
again the songs of the 1896–7 risings. The central political leaders
no longer wanted Africans to model themselves upon the whites as
the RBVA had done. There was an appeal back to African
culture, especially to Shona culture since these movements were
pre-eminently Shona mass movements. It was an exciting period
of rediscovery. The rural masses rediscovered, or thought they had
rediscovered the secret of effective action; the new movements
promised them many things and seemed to have the power to
bring them about. The leaders rediscovered their roots in the past
of an African Rhodesia—or Zimbabwe. Everyone was intoxicated
with the great achievement of bringing all this together. The great
mass rallies of 20,000 or 30,000 people seemed to release an
unbeatable force. As Nathan Shamuyarira tells us the nationalist
parties were engaging in something more fundamental than
politics. They were engaging in the creation of a new society and
a new sense of nationhood. This they were able to do because they
had deep roots right back into Shona history and African history
generally.

Of course there were still many limitations upon the effectiveness of these mass nationalist movements. They drew their strength
from bringing so many traditions together. But this combination
of interests also produced problems. Thus there was not complete
co-operation between the Trade Union movement and the

nationalist parties. There were a number of reasons for this. One was that the main energy of the nationalist movements in the towns came from the young men who did not primarily regard themselves as urban workers but who were more concerned with what happened in the Reserves; the mass parties were never workers' parties as such. Another was that the aims of the Trade Unions—improvement of wages and working conditions—seemed at times to clash with the aims and tactics of the mass nationalist movement, most obviously so during the NDP's campaign to 'destroy industry' in Rhodesia on the grounds that only the industrial sophistication of Rhodesia's economy prevented Britain from accepting majority rule. Finally, workers did not always respond to nationalist appeals to go on strike, largely because these were sometimes made in the name of abstract constitutional issues apparently remote from day-to-day urban life.

Another problem which faced the nationalist parties was the problem of holding mass support in the rural areas. In some ways the nationalist parties were the successors of former millenarian movements. In order to improve morale and to ensure commitment their spokesmen promised the rapid attainment of African rule. The parties were, in fact, remarkably successful in creating the impression of rapid forward movement. But they inherited the dilemma of other millenarian movements. So, indeed, did the mass parties of Zambia and Malawi. But there the dilemma was that independence when it came did not seem millenial; the new African governments faced a crisis of expectations. In Rhodesia the mass parties faced a crisis of expectations before the attainment of majority rule; people did not question that majority rule would bring the millenium but the problem was how to achieve it. Rhodesian mass parties had to stimulate expectations which they could not fulfill. Thus after the nationalists had successfully brought the Rhodesian problem to the United Nations there was a widespread expectation that majority rule would automatically follow. The problem was how to prevent disillusionment and cynicism when success was postponed.

Finally there was the problem of the relationship of the urban and rural masses to the intellectuals who played an increasingly important role from the days of the NDP onwards. Many of these intellectuals had been involved in the great age of participation and came into the NDP from the Capricorn Africa Society or the Inter-Racial Association. As a result there was much suspicion of the extent of their commitment to the nationalist cause. This came out clearly in the debates within the party after the 1961 Constitutional Conference. Very many ordinary members argued against participation in the new constitution mainly on the grounds that once the leaders had been returned to Parliament they could not be trusted not to return to the politics of participation.

Such tensions, together with regional and tribal feelings, were bound to exist. They came out into the open in 1963 when the nationalist leadership split and there was a contest for support between Nkomo and Sithole, leaders of the Zimbabwe African Peoples Union and the Zimbabwe African National Union respectively.

But despite these tensions, and despite the ZAPU-ZANU split, it must still be said that the creation of the mass nationalist parties was an important and remarkable achievement.

THE DILEMMA OF AFRICAN POLITICS

If I had been writing this chapter in 1963 I would have ended with the last paragraph. In 1963 it was easy enough to assume that the whole of African political history in Rhodesia was leading to the emergence of the mass nationalist parties and that they were the final, triumphant form of organization. This has not proved to be so. The creation of these mass parties was a great achievement. But the mass party and the public meeting are not suitable instruments for an actual resistance by force. The mass party can apply a great deal of moral pressure and can in addition organize widespread disobedience and sabotage in the African rural areas. In Zambia and Malawi this moral pressure and rural disorder was sufficient to achieve independence. In Rhodesia these pressures were not enough. White settlers have been in control of government there since 1923. Moral pressure by itself does not impress them; disorder in the segregated rural areas of Rhodesia can be contained and even disregarded so long as it remains within the Reserves. The NDP and ZAPU were able to demonstrate that they had mass support and to precipitate rural unrest. But they were not able to go beyond this. For the purposes of underground resistance the mass movements were ill-fitted. They were too open in their organization depending as they did upon the mass public meeting and so they were too open to attack. African leaders were slow to realize this and during the contest for influence between ZAPU and ZANU in 1963 both sides revealed all too much of their organization and support to the Rhodesia Front government. When that government moved in to break the mass movements hundreds of leaders at every level were arrested. The great majority of them are still in prison or in restriction.

It is hard to foresee the future of African politics in Rhodesia in the next few years. It may lie in a revived uprising; a new form of guerilla warfare drawing upon the heroic memories of 1896 and of Mapondera. ZAPU and ZANU guerillas are operating within Rhodesia just as guerillas of Mozambique liberation movements have been operating in the Shona areas of Portuguese East Africa. The nationalists in exile are calling their violent confrontation with the whites by the name *ChiMurenga*, the Shona title for the 1896 rebellion. On the other hand should Harold Wilson's plans for Rhodesia succeed, should sanctions bring down the Rhodesia Front regime and British over-rule be established, there may be another period of participation, in which Africans are drawn into another attempt to work from within the Rhodesian political system. At some time in the future the mass party will undoubtedly rise again. But it is clear that there is still some repetition of the basic themes of Rhodesian African politics to come before the new problems which follow African majority rule replace them.

And to round the thing off neatly the Rhodesia Front government is once again playing the Home Rule trick. Its answer to the nationalist challenge is to revive the power of the chiefs and indunas; to increase their salaries; to give them powers of arrest and trial; to give them representation in Parliament; and generally to treat them as the representatives of their people. The Reserves have been left alone since the Unilateral Declaration of Independence by the Rhodesia Front government. The Land Husbandry Act is not being implemented; no attempt is being made to enforce agricultural rules. The government hopes that the rural masses will be content to be left to themselves. There is some attempt also to play on potential divisions between the Shona and the Ndebele; the government constantly predicts war between the two groups on the coming of majority rule; some of the strongest supporters of the government are drawn from among the Ndebele indunas. Perhaps we shall yet see a government supported revival of the Ndebele kingship and even, perhaps, a Ndebele National Home. But this time, I believe, the Home Rule trick will fail.

Notes

1. L. H. Gann *A History of Southern Rhodesia* Chatto and Windus 1965
2. Eric Stokes 'Introduction' E. T. Stokes and R. Brown (eds.) *The Zambesian Past* Manchester University Press 1966
3. These documents of the Nyamanda movement are quoted in T. O. Ranger 'Traditional Authorities and the Rise of Modern Politics in Southern Rhodesia 1898–1930' *The Zambesian Past*
4. Twala's letter is in the *Rhodesia Herald* 31 March 1922
5. Dube's letter is in *Abantu Batho* June 1923
6. The quotation is from an unpublished paper by Roger Woods who is working on the Native Purchase Areas of Southern Rhodesia
7. The proceedings of the meeting of Associations in July 1929 are described in CID reports in file S 84/A/261 in the National Archives, Salisbury
8. Kadalie's letter to the Prime Minister is quoted in a Malawi police report in the National Archives, Zomba
9. These extracts from ICU speeches are given in CID reports in file S 84/A/300
10. N. Sithole *African Nationalism* Oxford University Press Cape Town 1959
11. N. Shamuyarira *Crisis in Rhodesia* Deutsch 1965

Recommended Reading

So far few studies of African politics in Rhodesia have been published. Two books by Rhodesian Africans are useful for the later period:

Ndabaningi Sithole *African Nationalism* Oxford University Press, Cape Town 1959 (Second edition in preparation)

Ndabaningi Sithole has written in restriction an extremely interesting biographical study of a rural ZANU activist which relates his nationalist committment to his whole life and to the life of his ancestors. This book is to be published by Oxford University Press.

Nathan Shamuyarira *Crisis in Rhodesia* Deutsch 1965

For the rebellions and their connection with later politics there is,

T. O. Ranger *Revolt in Southern Rhodesia 1896–7* Heinemann 1967

For African politics in the period before 1939 see,

T. O. Ranger *The African Voice in Southern Rhodesia 1898 to 1930* Heinemann and East African Publishing House (forthcoming)

Much light is thrown on the activities of the ICU, the South African A.N.C. and other political organizations in South Africa in:

Edward Roux *Time Longer Than Rope* The University of Wisconsin Press 1964

Mary Benson *The African Patriots* Faber and Faber 1963

Mary Benson *The Struggle for a Birthright* Penguin 1966

A valuable background to Rhodesian African politics is:

Richard Gray *The Two Nations* Oxford University Press 1960

10. African politics in Congo-Kinshasa to independence

JOHN MASARE

I. INTRODUCTION

Location: The Democratic Republic of the Congo-Kinshasa (formerly Leopoldville) covers an area of about 905,000 square miles; it extends from the Central African Republic and the Sudan in the north to Angola and Rhodesia in the south; from Lake Tanganyika in the east to the Atlantic ocean in the west. This huge area was never united politically before the colonial period, when it came to be called the Belgian Congo.

Population: The 1962 population was estimated at 14,700,000, while the present figure could be around 15,000,000. This population is made up of at least 200 ethnic groups which, when sub-divided into smaller tribes, speak about 700 dialects. The major ethnic groups, such as the Bakongo, Baluba, Mongo, Kuba, Mangbetu-Azande and Warega, are in turn sub-divided into smaller tribes and sub-tribes; for instance, the Bakongo ethnic group is made up of the Bantandu, Bandibu, Manyanga and Mayombe.

Communications: Apart from the airways, not only are the other means of transport and communication not enough for the country but the majority of them—river, roads and railways—run from an east-west direction; that is from the interior towards the capital, Kinshasa, and out to the Atlantic ocean. There are few important routes running along a north-south direction and this has limited the possible contacts between some of the major ethnic groups of the Congo.

Hence in considering the rise of African nationalism in the Congo, it is important to bear in mind some of the basic facts mentioned above—the immensity of the country, the diversity of the ethic groups sometimes of different cultural backgrounds, and the inadequacy of the transport and communication systems.

There has been a long tradition of resistance to colonial rule in many parts of the Congo but as we shall see the creation of a

Congolese nationalism as such has faced hitherto almost insuperable difficulties.

II. STAGES IN THE GROWTH OF NATIONALISM IN THE CONGO

In describing the development of nationalist movements in the Congo, I should like to make it clear that there are no sharp and clear-cut frontiers between one stage and the next; on the contrary there is a great deal of overlapping. Some movements have in fact changed from one stage to the next, as when a tribal association developed into a political party. Hence I set out the stages of the rise of nationalism in the Congo only in the hope of facilitating the study of the problem. Of course from the Congolese standpoint the fundamental problem was always one and the same thing, namely, to get rid of foreign domination under whatever form it presented itself.

A. PRIMARY RESISTANCE

According to Young, primary resistance is defined as 'armed opposition to the establishment of Colonial occupation . . .' In order to stage such a resistance the following minimum conditions have to be met:

first—there must be a certain military power to warrant such an attempt

secondly—there must be a recognized leader, chief or elder who directs the action of the group, tribe or clan which is making the resistance

thirdly—there must be at least some hope of winning the struggle.

Thus most of the primary resistances in the Congo were staged among the well-structured traditional societies with organized political institutions. There were a considerable number of them such as:

i. *The Azande:* 1892–1912. This resistance occurred among the tribes of the north-eastern corner of the country along the Congo-Sudan frontier. The Azande are a Nilotic people who speak Sudanese languages.

ii. *The Bayaka* in 1895, 1902 and 1906 rose in arms against foreign domination. They are found in the south-western corner of the Congo, along the Congo-Angola frontier.

iii. *The Baluba Shankadi of Kasongo Nyembo*, 1907–17, skirmished

with the Belgian authorities. This people are found in the south-
eastern corner of the Congo.

iv. *The Bashi-lele*, 1900–16, found in the eastern part of the
country, staged a resistance against the colonial occupation of
their country.

Apart from these primary resistance movements there were a
number of uprisings and revolts. These were usually directed
against the harsh treatment of the Congolese by the officials of
the Congo Free State regime, particularly their forced labour
practices to collect rubber and ivory. Examples are the uprisings
of the Babua in the north, 1903–4 and in 1910; and the Budja
uprising of 1903–5. Young points out that: 'Neither of these were
centralized systems; both felt the harshly enforced rubber and
ivory deliveries of the "red rubber" era. These were peasant
uprisings of a sort, a reaction of the entire society to the severities
of the Free State. There were many more localized insurrections
of this nature, or even individual acts of resistance. For example
the Abir rubber company reported that no less than 142 of its
Congolese "sentries" were assassinated in the first seven months
of 1905.'[1]

Besides the primary resistance movements as such and uprisings
like those of the Babua and the Budja, there were mutinies—for
instance, the Luluabourg Garrison Mutiny of 1895 and that of
the Batetela of 1897–1908. The common element in both was a
revolt against European Officers as the representatives of foreign
domination.

B. SYNCRETIC RELIGIOUS MOVEMENTS

By the beginning of the First World War, only two major uprisings
still opposed the Belgian authorities; the Bashi-lele and the
Kasongo-Nyembo which were suppressed in 1916 and 1917
respectively. The only major armed resistance after the First
World War was that of the Bapende in 1931. The primary
resistance movements therefore proved a failure in face of the
superior weapons of the invaders. But the physical defeat of the
Congolese people did not mean that they accepted the servitude
to which they were subjected by force by their conquerors; their
spirits were just as opposed to foreign domination before and after
defeat. They looked therefore for other channels of externalizing
their opposition and frustration with foreign domination. One
way was by establishing messianic, millenial and syncretic

religious movements. There are two major movements of this kind in the Congo; Kimbanguism, in the Lower Congo and Kitawala in the Eastern Congo. 'Fundamentally,' according to Young, 'the motor force in these movements was an apocalyptic reaction to a colonial situation which seemed beyond any secular remedy. The millenial vision provided the means for transcending a temporal situation which was intolerable yet beyond the power of the African to alter . . . This is most conspicuous in the Kimbanguist movement among the Bakongo.'[2]

i. *Kimbanguism's Historical Background*

The name comes from that of the founder of the movement, Simon Kimbangu. According to the catechism of this movement, he began his public mission on 8 April 1921. Before 1956, little is known about Kimbanguism in the Lower Congo due to the Government ban on such activities. Kimbangu himself only worked for his movement for six months, because in September 1921, he was arrested and imprisoned in Elizabethville where he died on 10 October 1951. From 1921 to 1956 the movement was obliged to work underground for fear of persecution. As a result the movement was composed of several small groups or cells which met secretly and which had little contact among themselves—since open organization and propaganda would have led the leaders to be detained or imprisoned. It was after the lifting of the ban in 1956 that these cells came together to form what is now known as the Kimbanguist movement or 'L'Eglise de Jésus-Christ sur la Terre par le prophète Simon Kimbangu'—that is the Church of Jesus Christ on Earth interpreted by the prophet Simon Kimbangu.

According to Paul Raymaekers, 'The EJCSK reveals itself therefore as being at once an extension and an organized assemblage of a series of these minor prophetic movements which have never ceased to proliferate in the Lower Congo since April 1921, the time when a certain Simon Kimbangu declared himself as sent with heavenly messages. Historically one could define the EJCSK or Kimbanguism, as being a religious movement placed under the authority of the sons and the contemporary disciples of Simon Kimbangu resulting from the regrouping effected since 1956 . . . of the disseminated sects in the Lower Congo; sects which claim to identify themselves with the name and the principles of Simon Kimbangu.'[3]

The Kimbanguist doctrine. From the doctrinal standpoint, Kimbanguism is an offshoot of protestantism, 'particularly the baptist sect of Wathen. In the present EJSCK, in spite of numerous consecutive deviations due to the dispersion of the first converts—a dispersion resulting from a long period of secrecy, one finds a number of traces of the baptist origin. It is in the natural pool formed by the "Jordan" at Nkamba (Nkamba is the birth-place of Simon Kimbangu, and is referred to by his followers as the New Jerusalem) that the converts receive baptism by immersion, just like the baptists of Wathen.'4

Emphasis is placed on the reading of the protestant Bible of the British and Foreign Bible Society. Most of the Kimbanguist hymns have similar tunes to protestant ones. Finally the free interpretation of the Bible and public confessions are some of the Kimbanguist characteristics which place it close to protestantism. As to the person of Simon Kimbangu, the following questions and answers, taken from the Kimbanguist catechism, give the general belief about him:

1. Who is Tata (father) Simon Kimbangu?
Tata Simon Kimbangu is the messenger of our Lord Jesus Christ.
2. How do we know that Tata Simon Kimbangu is the messenger of our Lord Jesus Christ?
Jesus Christ himself has promised us to ask his Father to send us another consoler to continue with His work. (John XIV Verses 12–18.)
3. What has Tata Simon Kimbangu realized?
Tata Simon Kimbangu has resuscitated the dead; he made the blind see; he made the paralytic walk; he made the dumb talk . . . (Matthew VIII Verses 1–10.)
19. Why is it that the name of Tata Simon Kimbangu is put in the first place—is Tata Simon Kimbangu God?
No, Tata Simon Kimbangu is not God, but God in all epochs chooses a man to enlighten his people.5 (Exodus III Verses 7–17.)

The Development of the Kimbanguist Movement. Immediately after the lifting of the ban on Kimbanguist activities in 1956, it gained momentum and spread rapidly in the Lower Congo where, by 1959, it was the strongest and the most dynamic messianic movement. Raymaekers gives the following reasons which contributed to that rapid growth:
—The remarkable improvement of education in the Lower Congo at that time helped the movement to get technically trained

adepts and propagandists who have laid the foundations of the
organization which characterizes Kimbanguism today.

—The rapid increase of population in urban areas due to new
arrivals from the rural areas helped to raise the membership of
the movement. These new arrivals, having been separated from
their customary groupings, found in the movement a new channel
for expressing their spiritual sentiments.

—The economic boom of the time in the Lower Congo helped
the members of the movement to be self-reliant in financial
matters.

—Lastly, there was at the time a 'prise de conscience' of a
'potential nation', the Bakongo, which made the people of the
area more sympathetic to the movement.[6]

The membership of the movement was increasing rapidly by
1959, particularly after the January riots in Leopoldville when
many Congolese left the protestant sects and the Catholic Church
to join Kimbanguism. For many Congolese considered the
Catholic Church as working in collaboration with the Belgian
Colonial Administration. By December 1958 there were about
60,000 members and by August 1959 there were about 100,000.[7]
Today the EJSCK is the largest of all the African churches of
central Africa.

Political Aspects of Kimbanguism. Today, Kimbanguism is not a
political movement—nor did its founders state that it was such.
However, some aspects of the movement indicate clearly its
political side. Before the establishment of proper political parties
there was no regular way of expressing political views. Hence as
Paul Raymaekers pointed out: 'it is not surprising to find out that
very rapidly, not to say immediately, the religious movement
launched by Simon Kimbangu—the first movement of an ex-
teriorized reaction—saw an infinite number of other reactions
towards European influences crystallizing themselves upon it, and
this was the cause of prejudices on the part of the established
authority who quickly crushed these tendencies'.[8]

These other tendencies of protest sprang from political, social
and economic roots. But it was not until the time when the
Belgian authorities showed a more tolerant attitude towards expression of such grievances that a decrystallization took place and
non-religious activities were left to the care of political movements, Kimbanguism occupying itself more and more with

religious affairs. However, sometimes there was an overlap even in this later period. For instance, as late as 1956, a group of Kimbanguists from Leopoldville sent a memorandum to the United Nations denouncing the 'Colonialist Governments of Belgium and Portugal . . . who introduced themselves illegally into the ancient Kongo Kingdom', and suggested that they be replaced by a Kimbanguist government. Here clearly, Kimbanguism was entering the political arena.[9]

Kimbanguism and Abako. Kimbanguism stood in a close relation to the traditions and aspirations of the Bakongo people; it sprang from a long line of Bakongo millenerian movements and appealed to the memory of the old Kongo Kingdom. Thus it was bound to be associated with the powerful Bakongo ethnic association, Abako. In a way the leaders of these movements were regarded as working for the same goal, the emancipation of the Bakongo people from external domination. The difference was that, while Abako concentrated on political and cultural matters, Kimbanguism was primarily interested in religious and spiritual affairs. Yet as spiritual powers are considered to be superior to political powers the political leaders are believed to depend upon the spiritual leaders. Thus Lemarchand points out that 'after the riots of January 1959, Kasavubu seems to have been regarded by some Bakongo as the reincarnation of Simon Kambangu, and pictures that were circulated among the African population of Leopoldville showed Kasavubu receiving his powers from Jesus Christ at the request of Kimbangu. This kind of imagery is not only indicative of the immense prestige enjoyed by Kasavubu but it also helps to explain the rapid rise to prominence of a party like Abako'.

ii. *Kitawala*
Kitawala, the other major syncretic religious movement is an offshoot, indirectly, of the Watch Tower movement, founded in America in 1874 by Charles Taze Russell and, directly of the African controlled Watch Tower churches of Zambia and Malawi.

From the doctrinal standpoint, Kitawala is similar to Kimbanguism in such things as its reliance on the Bible and its opposition to spiritual foreign domination. Perhaps it is politically more radical and less tribally associated than Kimbanguism for its slogan is 'Africa for Africans'.

The Development of Kitawala. 'The influence of Kitawala manifested itself in the Congo for the first time in 1923, when a group of propagandists from Nyasaland and Northern Rhodesia attempted to set up local branches in the southern part of the Katanga. Similar attempts were made in 1925 in the district of Sakania and in 1927 in Elizabethville. From the beginning of 1930's, the movement underwent rapid expansion, recruiting and increasing the number of adherents in Elizabethville, Kipushi, Manono, Shinkolobwe, Jadotville and Albertville as well as in many rural areas of the Katanga . . .'

By 1932 the movement claimed a thousand members in Elizabethville alone and by 1936 the workers' camps of the Union Minière in Jadotville were reported to be 'infected' by Kitawalist cells. 'Their propagandists preach equality of races, equality of salaries and Africa for Africans.'

In 1937, one of the adepts of the Kitawala movement, expressed his idea of equality from the point of view of the Bible and linked it to the need for political freedom:

We blacks are here in our country and what we want is to be considered as Europeans, for the Bible makes no distinctions between the whites and the blacks. Our Watch Tower movement seeks to put an end to all this, for it is only here in the Congo that the Government considers the natives as slaves. We are fed up with this, and the new God of the Kitawalist doctrine is here to help us . . . Look at this man on the brochure of Watch Tower: 'Toward deliverance'; this man laden with chains represents all the natives.

Conclusion

These syncretic religious movements had a considerable influence upon the subsequent political developments in the Congo:

[First] By creating a climate of social and political unrest which in turn invited stringent repressions, they provoked intense nationalist feelings among the local populations. And at a later stage these feelings were capitalized by political leaders to mobilize support . . .

[Secondly as was the case with Kasabuvu after the riots of January 1959 in Leopoldville.] Such movements afforded subsequent generations of nationalists ways and means of furthering their immediate political goals . . . by a curious process of identification, the magico-religious qualities of a prophet were attributed to a political leader, hence adding an element of mysticism to his personal prestige . . .

[Thirdly] . . . these movements sometimes contributed to the cultural revival that attended the emergence of some political groups. The continued diffusion of the Kimbanguist faith, with its emphasis on the traditional aspects of the Bakongo culture, probably stimulated the rise of cultural nationalism among the Bakongo.[16] [This indirectly resulted in the formation of the Abako.]

Thus as Young points out:

. . . the messianic sects had a dual role: on the one hand by providing a channel for the externalization of radical hostility for the colonial regime, they created a pre-disposition toward subsequent diffusion of explicitly nationalist ideas, on the other hand, they served to catalyze a sense of ethnic unity and identity.[10]

This was especially so for the Kimbanguist movement among the Bakongo people. There seems no doubt, indeed, that Kimbanguism was the most politically significant of the independent churches of central Africa.

C. PRE-POLITICAL ASSOCIATIONS

But the religious syncretist movements were not the only preparation for later politics. Various other forms of association also played an important role.

There are three main types of pre-political organizations—the alumni associations, the *cercles d'évolués*, and the *associations des ressortissants*.

i. *The alumni associations*

Many of these were sponsored by religious congregations in order to instill christian spirit among their members. The *Association des Anciens Elèves des Pères de Scheut, Association des Anciens Elèves des Ecoles Chrétienes* and the *Union des Anciens Elèves des Frères Maristes* were leading associations. That of *Pères de Scheut* became active in the recruitment of members and in 1945 claimed 15,000. 'While many of them failed to resist the pressure of tribal particularisms,' as Lemarchand points out, 'they nevertheless contributed to the political awakening of their members.'[11]

ii. *Cercles d'évolués*

These were organized under the patronage of the administration and their numbers grew rapidly after the Second World War. Their membership was restricted to the westernized Africans, those who have sometimes been referred to as the 'detribalised' elements. As these cut across the tribal lines, they were strongest in the urban areas. 'By 1947,' Lemarchand wrote, '113 *cercles d'évolués* with a total membership of 5,609, had been organized in the several towns of the Congo. Between 1952 and 1956, however, their number increased from 131 to 317, and their membership from 7,661 to 15,345.' These *cercles* helped to decrease the problem of tribalism, and according to Lemarchand, 'one result of the de-emphasis on tribal ties is that it favored the rise of broadly based parties led by modernist, westernized elites. Among the more prominent leaders of such groups were Patrice Lumumba, at one time President of the *Association des Evolués de Stanleyville*, Cleophas Kamitatu, a leading personality of the *Cercle des Evolués de Kikwit*, Chrysostome Weregemere, President of the *Cercle des Evolués de Costermansville*, etc'.

iii. *The associations des ressortissants*

These were formed by the Congolese themselves who were living in the urban areas. As their name implies, they are associations composed of people coming from one tribe, and sometimes from one district or region; as such their membership was limited to a particular group of people. They were initially formed in order to help their members in case of financial, social or other type of difficulty. They had a special role in bringing together the *évolués* and the masses, the modern and ancient, for they were not based on financial educational or professional standing but on the tribe, district or region and as such included people of all levels of social and economic standing. As one Bonaventure Mukoya put it in the Elizabethville newspaper, *Etoile-Nyota* of 11 July 1957:

They (i.e. the tribal associations) are an inescapable reality emanating from the entire people. They unite the uprooted (i.e. those who had left their places of origin) and those who have remained in their places of origin, the *évolués* to the masses. They unite no more at the clanic but at the tribal level . . . due to the efforts of the white man—promoter of the vast agglomerations facilitating the meeting of the members of the same tribes for long separated by time and distances. They do away with the notion of customary and extra-customary to form but one sole group harnessed to one and the same task: the systematic evolution of all the inhabitants of one and the same country. [The Congo.]

Their main goal, however, as we have pointed out was the establishment of mutual aid among their members. Grevisse puts it:

In all circumstances, pleasant or otherwise the members [of these associations] unite around the one among themselves who suffers or rejoices. They organize themselves and they make subscriptions to care for the hospitalized and the women who have given birth. They take the trouble to receive, lodge and to direct new arrivals, to settle family troubles, to intervene in case of a prolonged sickness and that of non-voluntary unemployment; or during the ceremonies of birth, marriages or deaths; to contribute to the fares for the journeys of those who would like to go home during the holidays and to help the widows and the orphans.[22]

[These associations helped to] set important limits on the range of political goals and activities . . . thus preparing the way for the emergence of political parties based on cultural, historical and ethnic ties or a combination of these.[23]

Before Abako turned into a political party it was one of the strongest of these pre-political tribal associations in the Lower Congo area. Young points out that:

The pre-political association has traditionally served as the organizational apprenticeship for the modern élite which subsequently assumes the lead in nationalist political parties. This was equally true in the Congo; nearly all the leadership which emerged in 1959–60 had occupied posts of responsibility in one or more of the organizations which proliferated in the major towns . . . Lumumba, for example, was either president or secretary of no less than seven associations in Stanleyville in 1953—testimony to his boundless energy and skill in organizational situations.[12]

On the whole the same could be said of the role of the Congolese trade unions of pre-independence days—as Lemarchand points out:

On the whole the main contribution of these associations (i.e. satellite organizations attached to trade unions) to the development of Congolese parties was not ideological but educational. They were the agencies through which a number of future Congolese leaders, including Cyrille Adoula, Joseph Ileo, and Patrice Lumumba received their initial political education, and learned the techniques of propaganda and agitation.[13]

D. URBAN RIOTS

In addition to the expression of urban discontent and aspirations through such associations there were a series of outbursts of rioting and looting in the major cities of the Congo which had an important political effect. These were in part the result of the economic frustration among the unemployed in the urban areas, particularly in Leopoldville. 'According to Ritner, 40 per cent of adult male Congolese lived in towns. In 1959, Belgian sources placed the number of the unemployed in Leopoldville at 15,937 as at June 30, 1958, a figure which the same source says had increased to 19,000 by the end of August and 25,000 by February 1959.'[14]

In 1941, the African workers of the Union Minière staged a revolt and rioting took place. The Belgian authorities called on troops who suppressed the workers' revolt by firearms, resulting in the death of at least sixty people. In 1945 the African dockworkers staged a demonstration at Matadi. Again troops were used, seven workers died and nineteen were wounded. These revolts, as can be judged from their nature, were related to the urban life and conditions of employment of the Africans. The army also staged a revolt at Luluabourg in 1944. But of all the urban riots none is more famous than that of January 1959 in Leopoldville. The immediate cause of the rioting was the banning of an Abako meeting on 4 January 1959:

The Abako supporters . . . grew excited and talked wildly of independence; Mr Kasavubu, who was also present, failed to calm them. The police arrived and resorted to the use of fire-arms; anger spread throughout the native city, and the cry of independence was taken up; the pent-up fury of many months was unloosed; Europeans were attacked and churches, schools, hospitals and social centres destroyed. The Europeans gave way to panic, the army was called in and the repression was violent.

The official list of casualties in the Leopoldville riots of 4, 5 and 6 January 1959 were given as 'on the European side there were 49 wounded, 15 of whom were hospitalized and 34 returned home after first-aid treatment . . . As for the Congolese 49 were killed (including 12 wounded who later died in hospital), 101 wounded and hospitalized, and 140 slightly wounded who were not taken to hospital'.

After the riots Belgium immediately formed a parliamentary commission of inquiry. It found that the important causes were:

Social causes: . . . Human relationships between Europeans and Natives; the irregular migration of the rural population towards the cities and the resultant over-crowding and unhygienic living conditions; the unemployment arising out of the recession; insufficient schools for chidlren and young people; labour conditions and the influence exerted by the trade unions.

. . . Political causes: Government incompetence, inefficient administration, the various nationalist movements, religious friction, inadequate news services and foreign influence (such as the Accra Conference).

The second major consequence of the riots, 'was the dissolution of the Abako movement and the arrest of its principal leaders. Those arrested, however, were never brought to trial, and instead were gradually released. On 14 March 1959 the last six were liberated, Joseph Kasavubu, Daniel Kanza and Simon Nzeza were suddenly sent to Belgium where they arrived on March 17'.

On 13 January 1959 the Belgian Government issued a statement about the future of the Congo which said, among other things:

Belgium intends to organize in the Congo a democracy capable of exercising its prerogatives of sovereignty and of deciding on its independence. As a co-signator of the Charter of the United Nations our country has moreover confirmed its wish to lead the people of the Congo to the point where they will be capable of governing themselves. All our action in the Congo is directed toward this line of conduct.

According to Young:

It is appropriate that January 4 has been designated as a national holiday since independence, in memory of the martyrs of independence. It was at once the most decisive single event in the surge of independence and singularly prophetic of the revolution without revolutionaries which followed in 1960.[15]

On 30 and 31 October 1959 there were also violent riots in Stanleyville, where tension among African and European populations of the city was high; thirty Congolese were killed in the two day disorders.

III. SOME FACTORS WHICH CONTRIBUTED TO THE RISE OF AFRICAN NATIONALISM IN THE CONGO

Thus by the 1950's Congolese discontent was expressing itself in a series of demonstrations. It remained to be seen whether it could express itself nationally. Despite the obstacles to national feeling already described there were also factors operating in the 1950's in favour of the growth of Congolese nationalism.

A. THE IMPACT OF POLITICAL DEVELOPMENTS
IN THE NEIGHBOURING COUNTRIES

To a certain extent political developments in other African countries reminded the Congolese to examine their own political situation. For instance, when in 1953 the British Government adopted measures to Africanize the civil service in the Gold Coast (now Ghana), a Congolese commented bitterly in *Congo Pratique* of March 1953: 'When will it be the turn for the Congolese? Will it be when the chickens will have grown teeth?'[16] However, due to the language problem and other political reasons, the greatest influence upon the development of the Congolese politics, came not from the former British territories in Africa, but from the French possessions—particularly from Congo-Brazzaville—just on the other side of the Congo River.

Congo-Brazzaville

If contacts between the Congolese of Congo-Leopoldville and the outside world were strictly controlled, Brazzaville had always been easily accessible to the Congolese living in Leopoldville. As Young commented, 'this was the one small leak in the dike of isolation built around the Congo'. What most impressed the Congolese who visited Brazzaville was the relatively low degree of racial discrimination by the French against the Africans. In Leopoldville during the colonial era one could see notices such as '*Ni chiens ni noirs*'—meaning 'No dogs nor blacks' in front of the European recreational centres, so one is not surprised to learn that, 'Lumumba confided to a European friend that a visit to Brazzaville in 1947, where he was served a glass of mineral water in a European cafe, was one of the traumatic experiences of his youth'.[17]

Some Belgians were also aware of the differences of social relations between Africans and Europeans in the two countries. One of them noted in 1948: 'The example of neighbouring territories has produced a strong impression on our blacks. The Belgians have evidently gone far beyond the French in the way of social benefits for the Africans. But the French are more humane. In Brazzaville the whites and the blacks commingle in the same cafés. In the stores the whites stand in line behind the blacks. There are no racial priorities.'[18]

Congolese leaders in Leopoldville were closely following political developments in Brazzaville. Thus on the occasion of the election of Abbé Foulbert Youlou as mayor of Brazzaville in late 1956, Abako sent him a letter of congratulations in which was said:

It is not without enthusiasm that the Bakongo, assembled in the Abako, have followed the development of the last elections which have resulted in a free expression of the will of the Congolese people.

That outright success promises a future of peace and justice for which the Africans are longing and for the establishment of which they are uniting themselves more and more.[19]

On 24 August 1958 General de Gaulle was speaking in Brazzaville of the choice of total independence or of joining the French Community. The General was outlining the pros and cons of the two choices. The Congolese leaders in Leopoldville were just as intensely interested in the words of the General as their counterparts in Brazzaville. Their reaction was 'Why don't the Belgians speak this way to us?' Two days later after General de Gaulle's speech in Brazzaville, leading Congolese politicians sent a petition to the Belgian Minister for the Congo, M. Petillon. The first object of the motion was to ask the Belgian authorities to include Africans among the members who were going to form a study group which was then being established in Brussels, to examine the political, economic and social situation of the Congo. The study group was to report to the Belgian Government as to the possible modifications which would accelerate the general development of the Congo. Secondly the motion demanded a statement from Belgium of the stages with dates of 'decolonization and the total emancipation' of the Congo.[20]

Political Development in Ruanda-Urundi
To some extent political developments in these countries influenced the rise of African nationalism in the Congo. For instance when, in August 1956, it was announced that popular elections to the Collèges de Sous-Chefferies, were to replace the old method of designation, Lumumba commented:

The fact that Ruanda-Urundi, a territory which has been under Belgian mandate since 31st August 1923, is more favorably situated than the Congo from the Administrative point of view is not without influence on the Congolese. Whereas Ruanda-Urundi which had the good fortune to be placed under international trusteeship in 1923, is taking giant strides towards autonomy, we Congolese, who have been under the same Belgian administration for more than three-quarters of a century—much longer than Ruanda-Urundi—are far behind our neighbour.[21]

B. VAN BILSEN'S 'THIRTY YEARS' PLAN FOR THE POLITICAL EMANCIPATION OF BELGIAN AFRICA'

In December 1955 Van Bilsen, at that time Professor of Colonial legislation at the University Institute for Overseas Territories at Antwerp, published his book, giving reasons and suggesting methods for bringing the Congo to complete political emancipation in thirty years' time.

The general reaction among the Belgians was one of disapproval, particularly over the fixing of a date for independence —'once the influence of Van Bilsen's ideas on the Congolese came to be realized, however, the Minister of the Congo did not hesitate to heap scorn on the irresponsible strategists who fix dates, such an attitude shows either that they know nothing or that they understand nothing of Africa'.

The general reaction among the Congolese who knew of the plan was to increase enthusiasm for the political problems, related to independence and self-determination. 'Several students at Lovanium,' wrote Lemarchand, 'sent him [Van Bilsen] wheedling letters asking for copies of the plan.'[22]

i. *Conscience Africaine Manifesto*

In 1953, Abbé Joseph Malula (now Archbishop of Kinshasa) organized a small intellectual group to discuss social, political and cultural problems facing the Congolese. The group began publishing a paper called the *Conscience Africaine*. It was in a special issue of their paper of July-August 1956, that the group showed that it was in general in agreement with Van Bilsen's Plan. Their manifesto declared, 'We believe that such a plan has become a necessity . . . This plan should express the sincere will of Belgium to lead the Congo to its complete political emancipation in a period of thirty years.'[23]

ii. *Abako: Alliance des Bakongo*

On 24 August 1956 Abako leaders issued what came to be known as the counter-manifesto to that of the *Conscience Africaine*. Abako was almost for the total rejection of the plan and refused to participate in its elaboration. They declared: 'Our patience is already exhausted. Since the hour has come, emancipation should be granted us this very day rather than delayed for another thirty years.'[24]

However, whether the Congolese agreed or disagreed with

Bilsen's plan, the fact remains that the plan gave the Congolese one of the important points of starting political discussion. As Lemarchand points out; 'unquestionably the most important of such influences was the Van Bilsen proposal. Because it created the issue that provided the initial stimulus to the rise of nationalist assertions, it may well be regarded as the starting point of political developments in the Congo'.[25]

iii. *The Brussels Exhibition May-October 1958*

Hundreds of the Congolese who were invited to the Exhibition, had the opportunity of meeting one another and of discussing the political problems facing their country. Though the Mouvement pour le progrès National Congolais—which resulted directly from the meeting of the Congolese leaders at the Exhibition—was short-lived, its influence lived in the minds of those who attended the Exhibition. As Young points out: 'The effects of the meetings of the Congolese at the Expo 58 have been somewhat under-estimated in the past. Surely this first opportunity for contact among emerging politicians who had never previously met each other or indeed even been exposed to each other's ideas, was of capital importance to the future of the Congo.[26]

In the course of the Exhibition a *groupe de travail* was formed to elaborate a plan for decolonization. That working party was a catalyst for the formation of both the Mouvement National Congolais and the Conakat in the Katanga.[27] The African politicians in the Congo realized the importance of organization in order to present a common front to the Belgian authorities.

iv. *The All African People's Conference, Accra, December 1958*

Three delegates from MNC-Lumumba attended the AAPC in Accra in December 1958. Lumumba as the President of MNC-L gave a short speech on 11 December 1958. The influence of the contacts they made with other African political leaders can hardly be overestimated. The Congolese leaders saw that they were not alone in the struggle for the liberation of Africa—this gave them assurance. Immediately after their return to Leopold-ville, Lumumba spoke to a crowd of about 7,000 people and declared: 'The independence that we claim in the name of peace cannot be considered any longer by Belgium as a gift, but on the contrary . . . it is a right that the Congolese people have lost.'[28]

IV. POLITICAL PARTIES AND INDEPENDENCE

In the late 1950's, then, popular discontent was finding spontane-
ous expression in a variety of ways. Belgian response to this was
opening up a whole range of new political opportunities. And the
Congolese élite was realizing the possibility and the desirability
of putting pressure on the Belgians by the creation of formal
political movements. The question was whether the élite would
be able to harness mass discontent to such political parties and
if so whether they would be able to bring together the many
different interests, such as ethnic and regional groups, into which
mass discontent was divided so as to form an effective party or
parties on a Congolese national scale.

At the same period in Malawi, Zambia and Rhodesia the
characteristic form of expression of the new nationalism was the
single mass populist Congress party. Nothing like this emerged in
the Congo. Indeed the numerical expansion of political parties in
the Congo just before independence was phenomenal. Merriam
points out: 'As of September 1, 1959, De Backer listed thirty-one
political parties in the Congo, but by January 11, 1960, this had
grown to fifty-one and by May 20, 1960, Artique listed no fewer
than 120 Congolese political organisations.'

A good deal of this expansion was ephemeral and insignificant.
Many of these so-called parties were *ad hoc* and short-lived, lasting
often only a few months. As Merriam points out 'this fluidity can
be laid in part at least to the fact that Congolese leaders had
virtually no political experience, and once they formed a party
they sometimes found that after a few months it no longer represented their own desires or that their own desires had changed
and the party refused to change with them. In some instances,
political leaders learned that other parties formed in other parts
of the Congo were organised around similar principles and
were perhaps stronger, thus dictating political fusion for self-
preservation'. Thus many organizations were merged into larger
groupings or absorbed into bigger parties. But even after allow-
ance is made for all this the fact remains that a considerable
number of significant parties emerged and that no one party was
able to dominate Congolese politics by operating at the national
level.[29]

It is impossible to examine all the significant Congolese parties.
But an examination of two—Abako and the MNC-Lumumba—
will bring out some of the basic themes of modern Congolese

political history. Abako is the classic example of the mass party based on historical memory, linguistic and cultural unity and a whole series of previous movements of economic and religious opposition to colonial rule. MNC-Lumumba, on the other hand, is an example of a party which sees the need for a genuine and full territorial existence but which cannot depend upon an appeal to the past and which has to seek to create its mass support by other means.

A. ABAKO: HISTORICAL BACKGROUND

As we have seen Abako began as a cultural organization, concerned with the defence of the Bakongo language and way of life. These were felt to be under threat mainly from the movement into Leopoldville of the Bangala people. The Belgians were believed to favour the Bangala settlers and their language, Lingala, was widely used as a medium of instruction in Leopoldville schools. 'Many of our children who go to the schools in town,' complained the founder of Abako M. E. Nzeza-Landu in 1950, 'are instructed in a heteroclite African language and ignore the beauty and infinite richness of their proper literature . . . Experience shows to observers that our children thus formed in that heteroclite language lose more and more the delicacy, modesty and gentleness characteristic to the Kukongo people.'

Abako began with three sub-committees: one to compose a Kikongo dictionary, another to organize a library of works in Kikongo and to produce a history of the Bakongo and the third to work for the protection of the 'civilisation, morals and arts of the Bakongo'.[30] It also published three widely read newspapers in Leopoldville and the Lower Congo where the literacy rate was much higher than anywhere else in the Congo.

In March 1954 Joseph Kasabuvu was elected as president of Abako. Thereafter the movement began to take more explicitly political action. Thus in August 1954 Abako presented five candidates for the municipal elections in Leopoldville, declaring that it did so as the representative organization of the Bakongo majority in the city.[31]

In 1956 Abako stated more clearly than anyone else had yet done the need for politics. Repudiating both the Van Bilsen plan and the *Conscience Africaine* group which had accepted it, Abako challenged that group's non-political position. 'Do they not realise that by trampling politics or even political parties under foot they become enemies of their own projects? Can one participate in government by dispensing with politics? And what do they understand politics to mean? Is it not the art of governing a state? And this union they hope for; do you believe that we will realise it outside the realm of politics?'[32]

As Abako moved into open political activity it was concerned with two problems: the relationship between Belgians and Congolese and the relationship between the Bakongo and other Congolese. As far as the Belgians were concerned Abako was a radical movement, in the forefront of nationalist demands. But during 1957 the movement was more concerned to establish supremacy in Leopoldville over the Bangala and their allies. The communal elections in December 1957 were fiercely contested, arousing in many observers 'fear of a return to the inter-tribal wars which ravaged our country before the arrival of the Belgians'. These elections were a resounding triumph for Abako.[33]

Abako and Bakongo politics

With its local base thus secure Abako openly entered into provincial and national politics. In April 1958 Kasabuvu, newly elected bourgmaster of Dendale suburb, made a strong attack on Belgian policy.

Democracy will only be established when we obtain autonomy. Democracy is not present when functionaries continue to be named instead of being elected by the people ... Democracy is not established when we see no Congolese police Commissioners in the police force. And similarly in the militia we do not know of any Congolese officers ... There is no democracy when the vote is not general ... we demand general elections and internal autonomy.[34]

By September 1958 Abako was demanding

'the recognition and proclamation of the Independence of the Congo'. 'Has the American President not cried "America for the Americans"? We are repeating the same cry; the Congo is for us blacks ... We are Africans, we have to have African leaders who will administer us as the Belgians are administered by European leaders who are Belgians'.[35]

Abako politics in 1959

The beginning of 1959 was marked by the January disturbances in Leopoldville. Immediately after the riots, for which the

Belgians held Abako responsible, its leaders crossed the river into
Brazzaville and founded the 'National Defence Committee of
Abako in exile'. Meanwhile Kasabuvu, Kanza and Nzeza were
arrested and flown to Belgium and Abako members in Leopoldville were harassed by the administration. In this showdown
between the Belgians and Abako the Bakongo association won.
The influence of the association had clearly not been destroyed
by repression. 'We confirm it to you that our dear Abako exists',
ran one ultimatum, 'and continues to function normally . . . If
you have a Belgian Abako in Belgium it is that one there that
you are going to dissolve and not ours; understand?' 'The
Bakongo is a people and cannot be eliminated . . . Therefore
Abako exists and will exist till the end of the world. But you speak
like little children; to dissolve the Abako, a people, how?'[36]

It soon became clear to the Belgians that they would have to
release and negotiate with the Abako leaders held in Belgium.

Abako and the Politics of Federalism

Abako was acting like a nationalist movement. But how did it
see the nation? Clearly its main loyalty was to the Bakongo
'people'. In 1959 Abako came out strongly for a federal solution
to the problem of Congo independence which would allow the
Bakongo to dominate the Lower Congo. It is important to realize
that at this point the federal demand was neither seen as conservative nor as in any way agreeable to Belgium. 'We affirm to
you', ran the manifesto of the Movement of Bakongo Resistance
in April 1959, 'once more our faith in immediate independence.
We demand the return with the least delay of our leaders; the
partition of Belgian Africa following our conception . . .'[37] If the
Belgian Government refused to pay attention to this demand
Abako would resist it with all means in its power.

In Belgium Kasabuvu took the same line. He and the other
Abako leaders pronounced in favour of 'Unity in Diversity', 'a
sort of federation of autonomous entities'. In June, after his
reinstatement as bourgmaster of Dendale, Kasabuvu declared:

> Federal conceptions are the most appropriate to permit the develop-
> ment of local autonomous powers linked together at the top by
> institutions collectively accepted. It is under that form, and that form
> only, that the unity of the country could be maintained. Powers which
> are too much centralised and too authoritarian, contrary to what their
> advocates think, will fatally lead to secession.[38]

Abako becomes a political party

In July 1959 the central committee announced that 'Abako has been transformed into a political party'. This announcement followed logically from Abako's obvious ambition to form the provincial government. In June 1959, indeed, the leaders were thinking in yet more ambitious terms and were writing to the Minister of the Congo about the formation of a Republic of Kongo Central which would revive the glories of the old empire of Kongo.[39]

The Belgian authorities were not impressed with this idea and Abako sought to bring further pressure to bear on them. In July 1959 Abako declared a boycott of all elections. It denounced all those groups which were prepared to negotiate with the administration:

> The Republic of Kongo Central recognises only two political parties: Parti Solidaire Africain [with whom Abako had now formed an alliance] and the Abako. All those who form political parties in Leopoldville who are not Bakongo may consider themselves as strangers and anyone from the Republic of Kongo Central who lets himself be attracted by these other political parties will make a false step and consequently will be regarded as a stranger.[40]

Abako seeks support from other federalist parties

Although its main concern was with 'Kongo Central' Abako realized that it would have to form alliances with parties in other regions in order to avoid control of the central government falling into the hands of parties opposed to the federal solution. Thus in December 1959 Abako attended a congress at Kisantu together with other federalist parties such as the Parti de la Défense du Peuple Lulua. The Congress demanded immediate independence and the recognition of federalism as 'the only form of government which can assure the harmonious development and the normal flowering of all the people'. Their aim was 'autonomous provincial states which will enjoy absolute powers' but they desired 'to assemble the different federated states under one central government'.[41]

By the end of 1959 Abako had attained its major objectives. It was firmly established throughout the Bakongo area; its chief leader, Kasabuvu, was seen as the heir of Kimbangu and the whole tradition of Bakongo independence; and it had played a leading role at the Kisantu Congress.

B. MOUVEMENT NATIONAL CONGOLAIS:
HISTORICAL BACKGROUND

Abako was thus able to draw upon the whole tradition of Bakongo cultural nationalism and of the Kimbanguist protest. Parties committed to a unitary Congolese state had shallower roots. MNC is a case in point.

The MNC came into existence after De Gaulle's 1958 speech in Brazzaville. Seventeen Congolese leaders thereupon sent a letter to the Belgian Minister for the Congo pointing out that reforms in the French territories gave rise to hopes that 'the Congo, which is in the forefront with regard to social and economic progress may not be indefinitely maintained as an anachronistic political regime'.[42] In September 1958 the signatories of this letter formed themselves into a Provisional Committee under the name of the Mouvement National Congolais. But there was little thought that this committee would lead to anything permanent since its members were drawn from a wide diversity of political groups. It included members of Abako, representatives of the Bangala, the leaders of the Socialist Action Party, the editor of *Conscience Africaine* and Patrice Lumumba.

Despite its incongruous membership, however, Lumumba saw the MNC as the nucleus of a national political party; after his return from Accra in December 1958, for example, he announced that 'the Movement National Congolaise, of completely African origin, has for its fundamental aim the liberation of the Congolese people from the colonial regime . . . to unite and organise the Congolese masses in the struggle for the amelioration of their lot, the liquidation of the colonial regime and the exploitation of man by man'.[43]

In May 1959 the MNC issued a statement of policy. It declared for 'the installation of an independent democratic state'; for 'the equal distribution of the Congolese national revenue' for 'a system of social security that guarantees the individual's welfare from the cradle to the grave'. The party began to establish branches throughout Leopoldville.[44]

The split in the MNC

So far the MNC had shown an unexpected effectiveness. But now the tensions of this attempt to create a genuine national movement began to assert themselves. In July 1959 Ileo and Kalonji broke away to form the MNC-Kalonji. The MNC-K moved rapidly away from a unitary concept of the Congo; indeed at one time Kalonji moved into a secessionist position and declared the independence of his 'State of Kasai'. Kalonji attended the federalist Kisantu Congress and was elected as the first vice-president of the Cartel formed by Abako, MNC-K and other groups. The MNC-Lumumba remained the foremost advocate of a Congolese unitary state.

MNC-Lumumba Congress, Stanleyville, 27–31 October 1959

But MNC-Lumumba was faced with severe problems of organization in attempting to compete with the federalist bloc. Unlike them it could not appeal to ready-made mass emotions and organizational structures; it had to build up a Congo-wide organization if it was to make its aspirations a reality. For this reason the speed of the movement of the Congo to independence was a grave disadvantage to the MNC and to any other group concerned to create new Congolese political machinery. In 1959 MNC-L demanded the postponement of the December elections and announced that they would refuse to take part in 'anti-democratic and anti-national elections prepared by the Belgian Government in the sole aim of perpetuating the Colonial regime in the Congo by artificial means'.[45]

At the same time the MNC-L, as a radical party, could not afford to appear to be advocating a delay in the coming of independence. Its Stanleyville Congress of October 1959 announced that the decision to boycott elections was 'supported by the masses which have decided to gain their immediate independence'. The aftermath of the Congress was the Stanleyville riots of 30 and 31 October 1959. These riots did for MNC-L what the Leopoldville riots had done for Abako. Lumumba was arrested and jailed for allegedly inciting the mob. But in January 1960 he was 'provisionally' freed so that he could attend the Round Table Conference at Brussels. At this conference the key decisions on Congolese independence were taken.

C. THE ROUND TABLE CONFERENCE
AT BRUSSELS

The major figures at Brussels were Kasabuvu and Lumumba, both so recently jailed and so dramatically freed by the Belgians —Lumumba displayed the handcuff scars on his wrist to his fellow delegates. The divisions between them were deep. Kasabuvu was pledged to the position of the Kisuntu Congress on federalism; Lumumba to the counter position which had been once again spelt out in January 1960 at Bukavu. Federalism, so the delegates at Bakavu agreed, was 'the source of the balkanisation of the Congolese territory'.

Both men and their movements, however, agreed to take part in the common front which demanded immediate independence from the Belgians. And both fell into the 'radical' rather than into the 'moderate' group in the divisions of opinion which ensued. Thus both Abako and MNC-L voted for universal suffrage at all levels, to deny eligibility to Belgian citizens, and to refuse to recognize the King of the Belgians as head of state. A considerable group of 'moderates' voted in the opposite sense on all these issues.

In many ways, indeed, Abako and MNC-L were similar to each other. Both appealed to mass support, both saw themselves as modernizers; and both had honourable traditions of radical opposition to colonial rule. But the differences between them were in the long run more important than the Brussels division between radicals and moderates.

D. THE PARTIES AFTER THE
BRUSSELS CONFERENCE

Immediately after the Brussels conference the parties began a complex process of regrouping for the independence elections. Abako entered the elections alone; its temporary alliance with the PSA broke up. The MNC-L, on the other hand, tried hard to widen and consolidate its support. Thus in March 1960 a conference was held at Lodja on MNC-L initiative. The aim was 'to reconsistute the unity of the Bakutshu, Batelela and the related tribes'. The MNC-L was here seeking to use cultural relations to defeat the tribal politics of Abako. 'While seeking to infuse a sense of inner unity into a group of tribally diverse but culturally related people, the MNC also aimed at the construction of a national community out of a group of different cultural entities.'[46]

In this way the MNC-L sought to gather mass support as well as the support of the urban élites.

E. THE RESULTS OF THE
GENERAL ELECTIONS MAY 1960

We have so far described Congolese politics in terms of Abako and the MNC-L. It is now time again to remind ourselves of the complexity of the situation. Not only were there very many parties contesting the elections but also very large numbers of independent candidates who were not identified with any of the parties. No one party or alliance of parties could hope to dominate.

In the result Abako won 33 seats in Leopoldville Province and none outside it. MNC-L won 10 seats in Equateur, 58 seats in Orientale, 17 in Kivu, 17 in Kasai where its allies controlled a further 18, and a number of Katanga where it was allied to the Balubakat. MNC-L thus won seats in all six provincial assemblies and commanded by far the largest bloc of any single party in the National Assembly. Under the circumstances this was a considerable achievement. But it was not enough to enable them to form a Congolese government or to enable them to refuse to negotiate with other regional groupings. Abako commanded support only in one province but this was still enough to give it the third largest number of members in the National Assembly.

On 23 June 1960 the Chamber of Representatives and the Senate approved the formation of the first Congolese government. It was headed by Patrice Lumumba, leader of MNC-L. On 24 June 1960 the two Chambers sitting together elected as head of state Joseph Kasabuvu, leader of Abako. On 30 June the Congo set sail on the difficult waters of independence. The 'radicals' were in command but in the differences between the two radical traditions, as set out here, as well as in the strong regionalism of the Congo lay the seeds of future trouble.

Notes

1. Crawford Young *Politics in the Congo—Decolonisation and Independence* Princeton University Press 1965 p. 282
2. Young p. 252
3. Paul Raymaekers in *Zaire* Vol. XIII No. 7 1959 p. 688
4. Raymaekers p. 689
5. Raymaekers pp. 737 and 738
6. Raymaekers p. 680
7. Raymaekers p. 728
8. Raymaekers p. 692
9. René Lemarchand *Political Awakening in the Belgian Congo* University of California Press 1964 p. 171. Quotations for the rest of section B. unless otherwise credited come from pp. 171–4
10. Young p. 253
11. Lemarchand p. 181. Quotations for the rest of section D. come from pp. 175–80
12. Young p. 295

13. Lemarchand p. 183
14. Alan P. Merriam *Congo—Background of Conflict* Northwestern University Press 1961 p. 84. Quotations for the rest of section D. unless otherwise credited come from pp. 85-9
15. Crawford Young p. 290
16. Lemarchand p. 159
17. Young p. 280
18. Lemarchand p. 159
19. ABAKO 1950-60 C.R.I.S.P. Publication p. 50
20. Merriam p. 82
21. Lemarchand p. 160
22. Lemarchand p. 155
23. Merriam pp. 323-4
24. Merriam p. 333
25. Lemarchand p. 163
26. Merriam p. 81
27. Young p. 278
28. Merriam p. 83
29. Merriam p. 114
30. ABAKO p. 11
31. ABAKO p. 30
32. Merriam p. 331
33. ABAKO p. 119
34. ABAKO p. 136
35. ABAKO pp. 146-7
36. ABAKO p. 197
37. ABAKO p. 205
38. ABAKO pp. 208-9
39. ABAKO pp. 229-30
40. ABAKO p. 245
41. ABAKO p. 256
42. Congo 1959 C.R.I.S.P p. 26
43. Congo 1959 pp. 30-1
44. Merriam pp. 144-5
45. Merriam pp. 152-3
46. Lemarchand p. 283

Recommended Reading

Crawford Young *Politics in the Congo—Decolonisation and Independence* Princeton University Press 1965

Rene Lemarchand *Political Awakening in the Belgian Congo* University of California Press 1964

Alan P. Merriain *Congo—Background to Conflict* Northwestern University Press 1961

R. M. Slade *King Leopold's Congo* Institute of Race Relations London 1962

Catherine Hoskyns *The Congo Since Independence* Royal Institute of International Affairs London 1965

Roger Anstey *King Leopold's Legacy* Institute of Race Relations London 1966

George Martelli *Leopold to Lumumba: History of the Belgian Congo 1877-1960* London 1962

M. N. Hennessy *Congo* London 1961

Edouard Bustin The Congo in *Five African States* ed. G. Carter Cornell University Press 1963

Georges Brausch *Belgian Administration in the Congo* Institute of Race Relations London 1961

R. M. Slade *The Belgian Congo* Institute of Race Relations London 1961

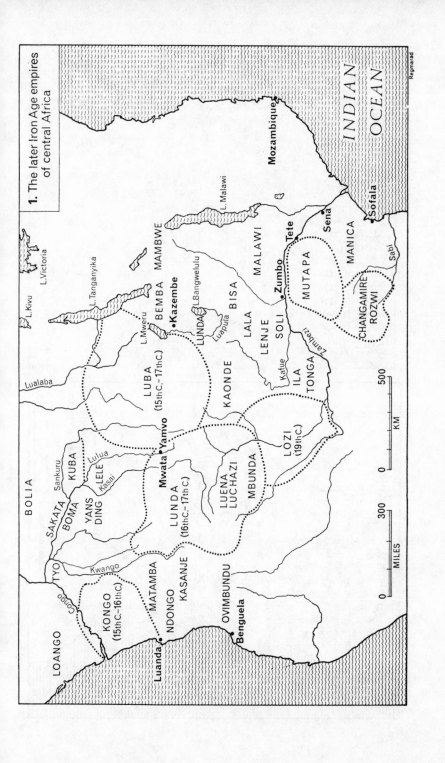

1. The later Iron Age empires of central Africa

INDIAN OCEAN

Mozambique

Sofala

Sena

Tete

Zumbo

MANICA

MUTAPA

CHANGAMIRE ROZWI

Sabi

L. Malawi

L. Victoria

L. Kivu

L. Tanganyika

L. Mweru

MAMBWE

BEMBA

Kazembe

LUNDA

L. Bangwelulu

Luapula

BISA

LALA

LENJE

SOLI

MALAWI

Zambezi

ILA

TONGA

Kafue

KAONDE

LUBA
(15th C.–17th C.)

Lualaba

LOZI
(19th C.)

MBUNDA

LUENA
LUCHAZI

BOLIA

SAKATA

Sankuru

BOMA

KUBA

Lulua

LELE

Kasai

YANS
DING

TYO

Mwata Yamvo

LUNDA
(16th C.–17th C.)

Kwango

MATAMBA

KASANJE

NDONGO

OVIMBUNDU

Benguela

KONGO
(15th C.–16th C.)

Congo

LOANGO

Luanda

500

KM

0

300

MILES

0

Regmarad

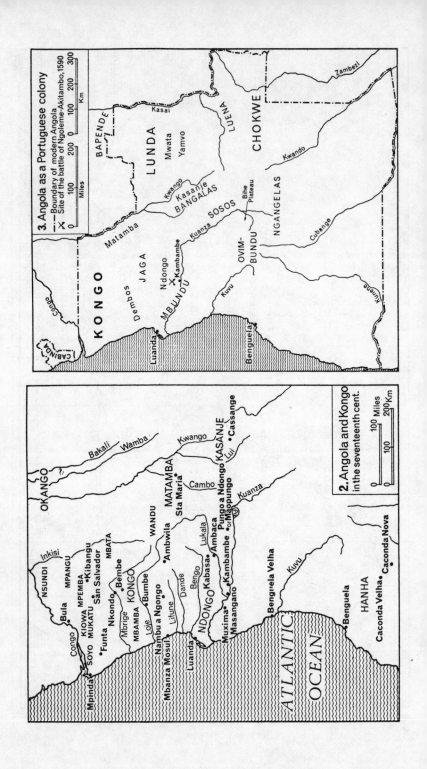

3. Angola as a Portuguese colony

---·---·--- Boundary of modern Angola
✕ Site of the battle of Ngoleme-Akitambo, 1590

Km 0 100 200 300

Miles 0 100 200

Zambezi

Kasai

BAPENDE

LUNDA

Mwata Yamvo

LUENA

CHOKWE

Kwango

Kasanje

BANGALAS

SOSOS

Kuanza

Matamba

Bihe Plateau

Kwando

NGANGELAS

Cubango

KONGO

Congo

(CABINDA)

Dembos

JAGA

Ndongo

✕ Kambambe

MBUNDU

Kuvu

OVIM-BUNDU

Kunene

Luanda

Benguela

2. Angola and Kongo in the seventeenth cent.

0 100 Miles 200
0 100 200 Km

OKANGO

Bakali

Wamba

Kwango

KASANJE

Lui ● Cassange

MATAMBA

Sta Maria ●

Cambo

NSUNDI

Inkisi

MPANGU

Bula ●

KIOWA MPEMBA

Kibangu ●

SOYO MUKATU

San Salvador ●

Funta ●

Nkondo ●

Bembe ●

MBATA

WANDU

Ambwila ●

Pungo a Ndongo
or Maopungo

Kuanza

Mpinda ●

Congo

Mbrige

KONGO

MBAMBA

Loje

Bumbe ●

Nambu a Ngongo

Lukala

Ambaca ●

Mbanza Mosul ●

Litune

Dande

Bengo

Kabasa ●

Kambambe ●

NDONGO

Luanda

Muxima ●

Masangano ●

Benguela Velha ●

Kuvu

HANHA

● Benguela

Caconda Velha ● ● Caconda Nova

ATLANTIC OCEAN

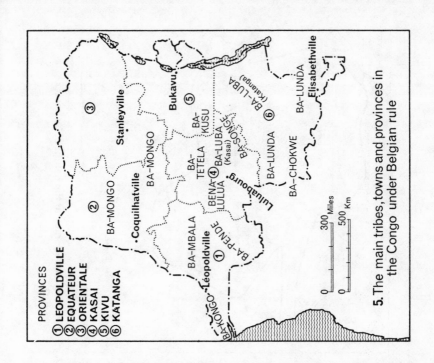

5. The main tribes, towns and provinces in the Congo under Belgian rule

PROVINCES
① LEOPOLDVILLE
② EQUATEUR
③ ORIENTALE
④ KASAI
⑤ KIVU
⑥ KATANGA

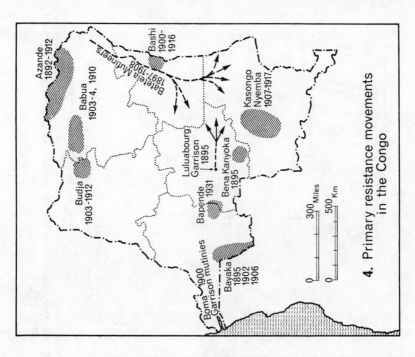

4. Primary resistance movements in the Congo

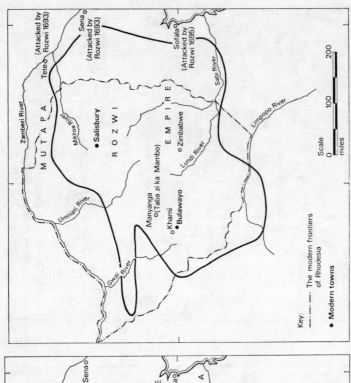

Key:

7. **The Rozwi Confederacy at the height of its power, c.1700 A.D.**

Key:

6. **The Provinces of the Mwene Mutapa Confederacy at its height c.1500 A.D.**

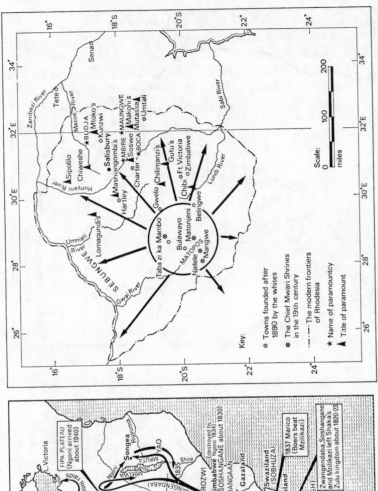

9. **Approximate areas of Ndebele settlement and of regular raiding and tribute collections c. 1830–c. 1890.**

Key:
- ⊙ Towns founded after 1890 by the whites
- ⊗ The Chief Mwari Shrines in the 19th century
- —·—·— The modern frontiers of Rhodesia
- ★ Name of paramountcy
- ▲ Title of paramount

Scale:
miles
0   100   200

8. **Sotho and Nguni migrations into central Africa**

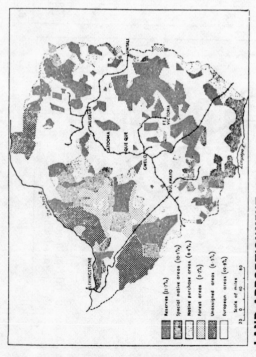

LAND APPORTIONMENT
RAILWAYS AND MAJOR
TOWNS IN RHODESIA 1955

Note that the key areas of the Ndebele and Shona risings of 1896-7 were what is now 'white' land along the line of rail and the main road systems linking Bulawayo with Salisbury and Salisbury with Umtali.

The Africans resident in these areas until 1896 were pushed away from the lines of communication by white military operations against the rebels. Note also that the core area of Ndebele settlement shown on map 9 is now 'white' land under Land Apportionment.

Reserves (21.7%)
Special native areas (10.1%)
Native purchase areas (8.4%)
Forest areas (3.7%)
Unassigned areas (6.5%)
European areas (50.8%)

Scale of miles
20 0 20 40 60 80

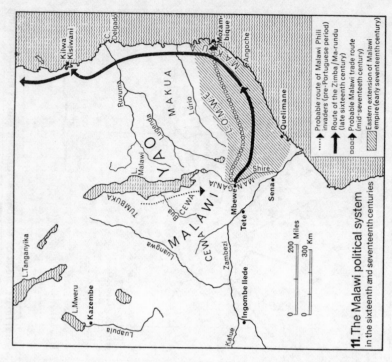

Probable route of Malawi Phiri invaders (pre-Portuguese period)
Route of the Zimba/Ma-rundu (late sixteenth century)
Probable Malawi trade route (mid-seventeenth century)
Eastern extension of Malawi empire (early seventeenth century)

11. The Malawi political system in the sixteenth and seventeenth centuries

0 200 Miles
0 300 Km

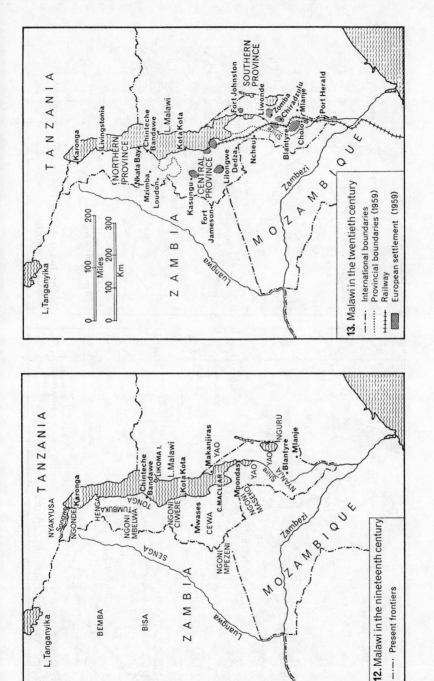

13. Malawi in the twentieth century

International boundaries
Provincial boundaries (1959)
Railway
European settlement (1959)

12. Malawi in the nineteenth century

Present frontiers

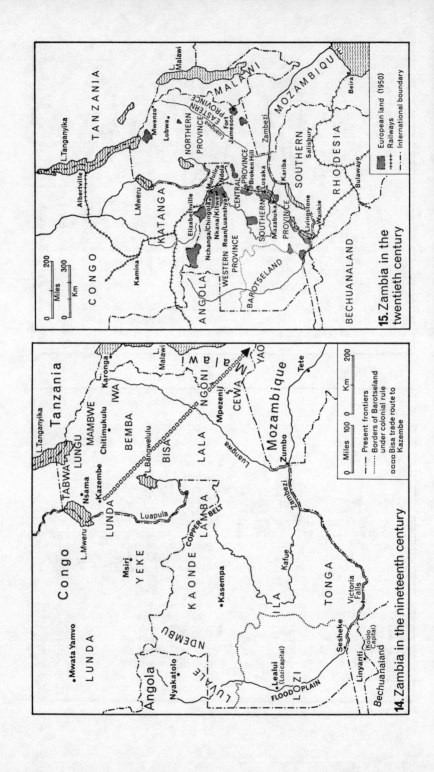

14. Zambia in the nineteenth century

15. Zambia in the twentieth century

Index of Themes

AGRICULTURE: African (see LAND)
Pre-colonial agriculture: Bemba agricultural environment, 74; Lunda introduce cassava, the economy of the Luapula valley, 75; the economy of the Lozi flood-plain, 75–6; failure of the Kololo to manage it, 79; introduction of new food crops into Zambia, 83; agriculture in nineteenth-century Malawi, 97–8; agricultural societies in Malawi as collaborators with the whites, 108; Ngoni raids for food, 101; nineteenth-century Shona agriculture in Rhodesia, 113–14.
Impact of colonial economic system on African agriculture: disturbance of Angolan rural economy, 64, 66; effects of migrant labour on Zambian rural economies, 163, 164; resistance to enforced agricultural rules in Zambia, 177; resistance to agricultural rules in Malawi, 204, 205, 206; Shona opposition to agricultural rules, 224, 232, 233; the Land Husbandry Act of 1961 and African opposition in Rhodesia, 235, 236, 238, 240; abandonment of implementation of the Act since U.D.I., 244.
African agriculture since Independence: problems of developing Zambia's rural economy, 180, 181; Cewa agricultural prosperity since independence, 208.

ARAB activity in central Africa, see ISLAM

BRITISH activity in central Africa
British South Africa Company, 87–9, 90–2, 93–4, 127, 129, 132–8, 142–52. African Lakes Company, 106, 109. British administration in Malawi, 89–90, chapter 8.

British administration in Zambia, chapter 7.
British administration in Southern Rhodesia, chapter 9.

EDUCATION: European education and African response
Before the Nineteenth Century: the Mani-Kongo and Portuguese education, 31, 32, 34.
African response to missionary education in the nineteenth century: Lewanika's desire for education in Barotseland, 87, 139; Yao repudiation of mission education in Barotseland, 87, 139; Yao repudiation of mission education, 105; Tonga eagerness for education, 106; different responses of Ngoni groups to education, 106–7; Ndebele indifference to education, 139.
European provision of education and African pressures in the twentieth century;
In Zambia: Lozi educational advantage, 158–9; Government provision of education in 1950's, 183; entry of educated young men into nationalist politics, 184; emphasis on education after independence, 187.
In Malawi: Tonga and other Northern peoples gain educational advantage, 190–1; African demands for more education and the organization of independent schools, 195, 197; declining Government and mission expenditure on education in 1920's and '30's, 198; protests of African elite, 198–9; second wave of independent schools, 200–1, 202; tensions between educated elite and Government after independence, 207, 208; Yao lack of education and support for opposition, 208.

Index

Mwata Kazembe, 26
Mwata Yamwo, kingdom, 59, 60
Mwene Mutapa, 8, 10
Mwenzo, welfare association 166–7
Mwibele, built, 38
Mwine Kadilo, 39
Mwine Mpanda, 43
Mzila, 129
Mzilikazi, 17, 120, 121
Mzingeli, Charles, 230, 232, 236, 237, 238

Naweej II, 42
Nchanga, copper deposit, 161
Ndai, 39
Ndau people, 118
Ndebele state, 78, 120, 121, 125; rising 210
Ndlovu, Masoja, 230, 240
Ndola, welfare association, 167
Ndongo kingdom, 52
NeMbire, 7
Nehanda, senior medium, 115
Nemapare, E. T. J., 233
Nganda Bilonda, 43
Ngano, Martha, 224–5
Ngoleme Akitambo, battle, 53, 57
Ngonde, 97, 104
Ngonde culture, 98
Ngoni, 78, 92, 100, 129, 158; raids by 102
N'gonomo, 106
Nimi a Lukeni, *see* Wene
Nkamanga, 98
Nkana, strike at, 171
Nkomo, Joshua, 231, 237, 239
Nkond, 40
Nkumbula, Harry, 178
Novais, 33
Nsama, 82
Nsingu, 93
Ntandu, 37
Ntemi chieftainship, 98
Nyahuma, 11
Nyakambira (usurper), 16
Nyakatolo, 94
Nyamanda, 211, 219–22
Nyamwanga tribe, 72
Nyamwezi traders, 81
Nyandoro, George, 232, 238
Nyanja 96, 97, 103; language, 18
Nyasas, in Copperbelt, 166
Nyatsimba, Mutota, 10
Nyirenda, Tomo, 168
Nxaba, defeat of, 118
Nzeza, Simon, 258

Nzinga Kuwu, king, 31
Nzinga Nbandi, 56

Ovimbundu, 35, 53, 55, 59

Pandamatenka, 87
Pashu, 127
Pemba, 99
Petillon, M., 260
Petro II, 36
Phiri, Hanock, 200
Piri-Chirongo clan, 19
Porto, Silva, 80
Pyaang, attack by, 47

Quelimane, 12

Rhodes, Cecil, 87, 108, 134, 214
Roan Antelope mine, 161, 170; strike at, 171
Rozwi empire, 7, 8, 112, 120
Ruanda-Urundi, 260
Russell, Charles Taze, 252
Rweej (matrilineal succession), 40

Sambo, Robert, 228
Samkange, (Rev) Douglas Thompson, 230
Samkange, Sketchley, 240
Samkange, Stanlake, 136, 237
Sampa, 90
Sangala, James Frederick, 203
Sao Thomé, traders of, 33, 34
Sebitwane, 79, 80
Selous, F. C., 117, 129, 139, 142
Sena, 2, 12
Sepopa, 79
Shaka, 17, 118
Shamuyarira, Nathan, 235
Sharpe, Alfred, 89
Shona, area, 112; rising in, 210
Shona culture, 4, 5, 6
Shona people, 130
Shyaam, king, 47
Simao de Silva, 32
Sithole, Ndabaningi, 233
Sofala, Portuguese at, 2
Solongo, 37
Somubalana, oration, 137, 151
Songea, 120
Soshangane, 118, 129
Soso, 37
Sosos, 55
Sousa, Ana de, *see* Nzinza
Sousa, Manuel Antonia de, *see* Gouveia
Stanleyville, riots, 258